Essays on Sean O'Casey's Autobiographies

Essays on Sean O'Casey's Autobiographies

Edited by
ROBERT G. LOWERY

BARNES & NOBLE BOOKS
TOTOWA, NEW JERSEY

First published in the U.S.A. 1981 by
BARNES & NOBLE BOOKS
81, Adams Drive, Totowa,
New Jersey, 075 12

ISBN 0-389-20180-4

Printed in Hong Kong

Contents

Acknowledgements

I wish to thank the contributors whose articles make up this collection of essays: thanks for their patience, for their guidance, and for the comradeship we have shared over the years. In the field of O'Casey studies I am especially grateful to a trio of scholars: David Krause, Bernard Benstock, and Ronald Ayling — all of whom helped in more ways than they could possibly know. I am deeply grateful to Maureen Murphy for her enthusiasm for me and for her unsuccessful attempts to teach this *balbhan* the Irish language. Equal appreciation to Alf MacLochlainn, Ireland's national librarian; Eileen O'Casey, Ireland's national treasure; Tom Buggy, a *mensch*; T. M. Farmiloe of Macmillan for his unflappable efficiency; and to my dear wife, Patricia, whose patience would have made Job nervous.

The editor and publishers wish to thank the following who have kindly given permission for the use of copyright material: Raymond J. Porter, for the material from his essay, 'O'Casey and Pearse', *Sean O'Casey Review* (1976); the Macmillan Publishing Co. Inc., for the extracts from four books by Sean O'Casey — *Drums under the Windows* (Copyright © 1945, renewed 1973 by Eileen O'Casey, Breon O'Casey and Shivaun O'Casey), *I Knock at the Door* (Copyright © 1939, renewed 1967 by Eileen O'Casey, Breon O'Casey and Shivaun Kenig), *Pictures in the Hallway* (Copyright © 1942, renewed 1970 by Eileen O'Casey, Breon O'Casey and Shivaun O'Casey) and *Rose and Crown* (Copyright © 1952, renewed 1980 by Eileen O'Casey); the Society of Authors, on behalf of the Bernard Shaw Estate, for the letters to Sean O'Casey from Bernard Shaw; and the Trustees of the Will of the late Mrs Bernard Shaw for two letters written by her.

Notes on the Contributors

DEIRDRE HENCHY is an honours graduate in history and French of University College, Dublin. She has a diploma in librarianship, and was the winner of the gold medal of the Old Dublin Society Essay Competition in 1972 for her essay 'Dublin Eighty Years Ago', published in the *Dublin Historical Record*.

WILLIAM J. MAROLDO at present teaches, researches and writes at the English Faculty of Texas Lutheran College. He has taught English and comparative literatures and philosophy, as well as, at an earlier period, government and political science at New York University, Maryland, Colorado, and the US Air Force Academy. He holds advance degrees from the University of Colorado, New York University and Columbia, where his doctoral dissertation offered a definition of autobiography as an aesthetic mode and literary genre, proceeding thence to test this definition in an analysis of form and content in the 'Irish Books' of Sean O'Casey's autobiographical sequence. This work is being reworked and reshaped for publication in the not too distant future.

E. H. MIKHAIL is Professor of English at the University of Lethbridge, Canada. His works include *Sean O'Casey: A Bibliography of Criticism; A Bibliography of Modern Irish Drama 1899–1970; Dissertations on Anglo-Irish Drama: A Bibliography of Studies 1870–1970; The Sting and the Twinkle: Conversations with Sean O'Casey* (co-edited with John O'Riordan); *J. M. Synge: A Bibliography of Criticism; W. B. Yeats: Interviews and Recollections;* and *Lady Gregory: Interviews and Recollections*. He is an associate editor of the *Sean O'Casey Review*, and is currently completing a book on Brendan Behan.

BERNARD BENSTOCK is Professor of English and Comparative Literature at the University of Illinois. His books include *James Joyce: The Undiscover'd Country; Paycocks and Others: Sean O'Casey's World;* and *Sean O'Casey.* He is co-editor of *Approaches to James Joyce's 'A Portrait': Ten Essays,* with Thomas F. Staley; and of the recently completed *Who's He When He's at Home: A James Joyce Directory,* with Shari Benstock. He has written many articles for the scholarly journals, has served as president of the James Joyce Foundation, and is an editorial consultant for the *Sean O'Casey Review* .

RONALD F. AYLING is an Associate Professor of English at the University of Alberta in Canada. Dr Ayling acted as literary executor to the O'Casey Estate and catalogued the extensive O'Casey papers in the Berg Collection at New York Public Library. His books include *Blasts and Benedictions,* a posthumous selection of O'Casey's writings; *Sean O'Casey,* an anthology of O'Casey criticism for the Modern Judgements series; and *Continuity and Innovation in Sean O'Casey's Drama.* With Michael Durkan, he is the author of *Sean O'Casey: A Bibliography,* recently published by Macmillan, London.

RAYMOND J. PORTER is Professor of English at Iona College, New Rochelle, New York. His books include *P. H. Pearse; Brendan Behan*; and, with James D. Brophy, *Modern Irish Literature: Essays in Honor of William York Tindall.* He has published widely in literary journals, and is currently working on a study of Brian Moore.

ROBERT G. LOWERY is editor and publisher of the *Sean O'Casey Review,* and will be editing *An O'Casey Annual* (Macmillan, forthcoming).

MAUREEN MURPHY is an Assistant Professor of English at Hofstra University, Hempstead, New York. A fluent Gaelic speaker she has also held courses in Anglo-Irish literature and the Irish language. She is an associate editor of the *Sean O'Casey Review.*

CARMELA MOYA is a lecturer on English and Anglo-Irish litera-
ture at the British Institute, the Sorbonne and Lille Univer-
sity in France. She has published several critical studies on
O'Casey in French journals and is currently writing a book on
O'Casey's autobiographies. She is an associate editor of the *Sean
O'Casey Review*.

DAVID KRAUSE is the editor of *The Letters of Sean O'Casey* and
The Dolman Boucicault, and the author of *Sean O'Casey: The
Man and His Work, Sean O'Casey and His World* and *A Self-
Portrait of the Artist as a Man*. With Patrick Funge, he dramatised three volumes of O'Casey's autobiography for performance
at the Lantern Theatre in Dublin. He is the author of the
chapter on O'Casey in the MLA Review of Research publication
Anglo-Irish Literature and has written articles on Yeats, Synge,
O'Casey and Irish comedy for various scholarly journals. At
present he teaches Restoration drama, and also Irish and modern
drama, at Brown University, and is an editorial consultant for
the *Sean O'Casey Review*.

Introduction

The merit of originality is not novelty;
it is sincerity. The believing man is the
original man.

Thomas Carlyle, Heroes and Hero-Worship

Every great and original writer, in
proportion as he is great or original, must
himself create the taste by which he is to
be relished.

William Wordsworth, 'Letter to Lady Beaumont'

When Sean O'Casey died in 1964 the *New York Times* called him one of those who could not come to terms with the evil in the world, and said that 'injustice and human misery summoned up in him a savage indignation'. The tribute called attention to his exalted language and his essential humanity, but mentioned his drama only once in three paragraphs. Instead, the piece ended by saying: 'His multi-volumed autobiography, certainly one of the most enduring works of this century, is more than a lyrical evocation of a lifetime. It is witness of an indestructable spirit that blazed joyously independent to the end.' It is quite remarkable that the autobiography should be called 'one of the most enduring works of this century,' for O'Casey was primarily a playwright, and the autobiographies were written initially to supplement his always meagre income, and perhaps later to serve as another outlet for his creative energies. What the editorial emphasises, though, is that O'Casey's autobiographies should be treated as more than merely tangential to the preferred main body of his work — his plays — and that they deserve serious study by O'Casey students and scholars. The autobiographies are in fact the other side of a singularly remarkable work and, if one accepts the emphasis of *The Times*, it seems that O'Casey not merely persevered in two genres but that he excelled in them.

This conclusion sets O'Casey apart from nearly all modern Anglo-Irish writers of first rank and from most other twentieth-century writers of merit. Certainly W. B. Yeats's plays and prose are never judged in the same qualitative light as his poetry, and James Joyce's play and poetry are of historical rather than literary interest. By definition the great writers of this century excelled in at least one genre – poetry, fiction, drama, etc. – but in only a few is this duality of genius present. John Millington Synge and Oscar Wilde come to mind. When we speak of O'Casey's versatility, then, and specifically of the autobiographies, it is clear that we are dealing not only with an extraordinary work of art, but also with an extraordinary man.

Despite this, criticism and scholarship have been overwhelmingly proportioned towards O'Casey's drama, for several reasons. First, there was the timing. There is little question that O'Casey's plays saved the Abbey Theatre from financial and artistic ruin. Because of the military conflicts and other reasons, the Abbey was floundering badly in both areas. But O'Casey's initial success became the first play ever to last for two weeks at the Abbey and only the second to permit a 'house full' sign to be displayed. Equally, his contemporary themes found enthusiastically receptive audiences who, war-weary from the years of insurrection, were perhaps psychologically ready to view themselves on the stage. Evidence for this is that even after fifty years O'Casey's first three plays rank one-two-three in the number of times performed at the Abbey. On this point alone the opportunity for drama criticism has been considerable, for whenever and wherever there was a revival – and there have obviously been many – O'Casey's drama came under critical scrutiny, now two-and-a-half generations of critical scrutiny.

Another reason for the disproportionate amount of drama criticism stems from the controversies surrounding his plays: the riots over *The Plough and the Stars*, the rejection of *The Silver Tassie*, the banning of *Within the Gates* in Boston, the hysterical reception accorded *The Bishop's Bonfire*, and the semi-

banning of *The Drums of Father Ned*. Each of these incidents
overshadowed the play in question, but they also spotlighted
O'Casey as dramatist, and these plays can never again be performed without the controversies being reviewed and debated.

Finally, O'Casey's drama is overemphasised because of – in
the eyes of many – the failure of his later plays. The question
of how a man could be so enormously successful in his early
years and, seemingly, a failure in his later years has yet to be re-
solved.

By contrast, the autobiographies have received scant attention. Perhaps this is the nature of the beast. The books are reviewed as they appear, but after that few take notice of a reprint
or a new edition. In this genre there is no counterpart to constant dramatic revivals.

This is not to say they have been totally ignored. Many English
and American critics have found them to be glorious pieces of
writing. Irish critics have not been so generous, though Ireland
did pay O'Casey the supreme compliment – by banning the
first two volumes. Brooks Atkinson, the only critic to review
all six volumes, suggested that O'Casey might be remembered
more for his prose that for his drama. Richard Watts found in
Drums under the Windows 'the exuberance of a brave and un-
bridled imagination . . . which . . . makes his book so monumen-
tal a work'. To J. C. Trewin, O'Casey's prose was 'supple, varied,
bold, excitingly pictorial'. George Jean Nathan found *I Knock
at the Door* 'a grandly beautiful job'. In Ireland, Austin Clarke
wrote of its 'savage satire' and its lyrical spontaneity 'that recalls
the masterful blarney and gab of Joyce'. The editors of *Irish
Writing* commented that the first four books 'contain some of
his most memorable writing' and makes 'most other contemporary
autobiographies seem dingy in comparison'.

But others were equally emphatic in their condemnation of
the books. Sean O'Faolain found them 'wearisome belly-aching,
a corrosion of self-pity', and complained of 'the poor quality of
the narrative', the 'embarrassing jocularity', the 'heavy-handed
satire' and the 'bad English'. Oliver St John Gogarty wrote that
O'Casey had a 'grudge against life' and that 'some parts of [*I
Knock at the Door*] should have been buried full fathoms five

or more'. Padraic Colum, though generally supportive, denigrated O'Casey's originality by writing several times that the books were written by a writer 'who had read his James Joyce'. And George Orwell echoed this, calling O'Casey's writings 'basic Joyce'.

The controversy surrounding the autobiographies centred on one main point: were the books to be judged on their artistic merits or as autobiography. If the former, was there too much 'basic Joyce' to mar O'Casey's lyrical style, or were they creative portraits of a *Zeitgast*? If they were indeed autobiography, the overriding question was their accuracy and whether O'Casey, by using a mixture of several experimental styles, blurred the distinctive features of the traditional autobiographical genre. To call the books art opened up a whole range of questions. Now, it is not difficult to understand the ongoing debates over artistic questions, though it is not clear whether great art stirs debates or whether great debates make great art. But it is clear that the artistic merits of O'Casey's autobiographies will continue to be thrashed out by all who read them.

The accuracy of the autobiographies has been questioned almost as vehemently as their literary worth. For instance, after O'Casey's death a book of essays appeared that claimed that its essayists had 'probed deeper into the story of O'Casey and have backed up their theories with telling facts'. Some told, some didn't, and what most of the essays revealed was that O'Casey had not been forgiven for being, as Tony Gray wrote, 'not so much the One Who Got Away, as the one who wouldn't shut up'. All the old charges against O'Casey were dragged before the public in these essays, and the result was a collection that, with a few exceptions, contained more half-truths and errors than could have possible been found in the autobiographies.

For instance, about O'Casey's well-documented slum upbringing, Anthony Butler, who had difficulty distinguishing a tenement from a slum, claimed that the slums 'were no major influence in his life and he never lived in them'. Further, said Butler, O'Casey's father (who died when the dramatist was six) came from 'a good strata of society' and belonged to 'a small, powerful and wealthy Establishment'. Another writer, also armed with 'telling facts,' charged that O'Casey only worked for the

Great Northern Railway of Ireland for fifteen months, when in fact he was employed there for nine years, from 1902 to 1911. Still another found O'Casey's earlier political years (when the dramatist was involved in nationalist and socialist organising) a 'dubious' record, when in fact, as Sean Cronin commented, O'Casey was learning and speaking Gaelic at a time when De Valera was still playing the imperial game of rugby football, and was a member of the Irish Republican Brotherhood when the revolutionary activists amounted to only a handful.

These essays point up one fact about O'Casey's autobiographies: it has always been difficult to separate them from the man who wrote them. It has been difficult to see the books as literary craftsmanship without focusing on the objects of O'Casey's wrath or adoration. The degree to which one agreed or disagreed with O'Casey on life, people and subjects has not been unimportant in deciding the literary qualities of the books. For instance, Ulick O'Connor found the autobiographies 'on the whole second-rate', pointing to 'the barrage of bad puns, his over-use of adjectives, [and] his immature attempts at fantasy'. As the essay revealed, though, O'Connor was primarily incensed by O'Casey's handling of several of the critic's favourites: Arthur Griffith, George Russell, Douglas Hyde and others. Other criticism over the years has been in the same vein, and few have been able to judge the merits of the autobiographies without judging the personal merits of O'Casey and those he attacked or defended.

O'Casey's comments on his autobiographies are revealing. It is safe to say that he considered them to be both accurate and artistic, albeit experimental to be sure. In a letter to Frank Hugh O'Donnell in 1952, O'Casey commented on the alleged inaccuracies in the books: 'Bar the obvious fantasy, they are an accurate portrayal of men and things, there with you and here with me.' When their accuracy was challenged O'Casey was quite willing to cite chapter and verse for verification. For instance, in ridiculing Arthur Griffith in *Drums under the Windows*, O'Casey included one of Griffith's silly nationalist songs. In a review, Padraic Colum, a close friend of Griffith, disputed the song's authorship. O'Casey responded with book, author and page number where the song had first been published – over

Griffith's name. (Colum evidently accepted this, for in later reviews — really nothing more than rewrites of the first review —
no mention was made of this point.) Other questionable incidents
are as easily verified. In fact, as I've indicated, it is O'Casey's
preciseness about less attractive features of Irish personalities
that has riled many critics.

O'Casey also defended his manner of writing, even though it
was clearly very different from that in his most successful plays.
In an April 1939 letter to Brooks Atkinson, O'Casey wrote that
while it may be true that his prose was foreign to his *best* style
it was not necessarily foreign to his only style. He had, he said,
written satiric fantasy many years earlier in various articles for
Irish newspapers. Even an early play (now lost) had been in this
vein. Therefore, he was writing fantasy many years before hearing of Joyce. As to the charge of imitating Joyce, O'Casey wrote
in 1962:

> I wasn't influenced by James Joyce any more than all who
> read him were. I was too old to be influenced by him . . . The
> glimpses of influence given in the biography were more a de-
> sire to show my admiration for this great writer; as a symbol
> of standing by one who was being attacked on all sides; ban-
> ned by nation and publisher, yet unshaken and supreme in
> his glorious and God-given integrity . . . Joyce's influence was
> like a bugle-call, loud and clear at first, fading away as it was
> being heard . . . very soon forgotten.

These are of course O'Casey's considered comments, written
many years later. But it is clear that even in 1939 he was searching, almost frustratingly, for another genre in which to express
his vision. Taking note of the reviews by Clarke and O'Faolain,
he continued to Atkinson:

> Where does the truth lie? I must say, I don't know. I can do
> naught, but feel my way forward — or backward, as the case
> may be. But this I know: I do get tremendous joy out of the
> writing of fantasy, more than out of anything else . . . I loved
> writing it [*I Knock at the Door*]. I really think there is some

Elizabethan gusto in it. And of another thing . . . I am as positive as a human can be: there is no posing in the book from one end to the other — that is 'art' posing. For I can honestly say I don't care a tinker's damn about art, simply because I know nothing about it. But I love the way I imagine the Greeks wrote . . . & I love the way I know the Elizabethans wrote; & I am anxious & eager to try to make use of both in the things I try to write. Ambitious? Damnably so; but, even so, what is success (if I succeed)? What is failure? (if I fail). Who can tell?

There is yet another question to be considered: are O'Casey's autobiographies equal to his plays? At first, this might appear as a comparison between apples and oranges, except that they were both written by the same man using the same fertile imagination, the same exalted language, the same 'savage satire', and the same technical genius. They were in a sense two fruits from the same tree. Perhaps the autobiographies were O'Casey's *alter ego*, or perhaps they were only two parallel rays of light emanating from the same source. Eric Bentley, writing in the *New Republic*, commented that the best parts of the autobiographies were dramatic scenes O'Casey never got around to writing. They were, it seems, natural drama, and one of the clearest vindications of this view can be found in the dramatisation of the autobiographies, first by Paul Shyre then by David Krause and Patrick Funge. In fact, when O'Casey died New York's tribute to him was the Shyre adaptation.

Moreover, in both genres there is a similar vision of life. In both works are found O'Casey's passionate concern for the dispossessed and their condition, whether in a decaying tenement house in Dublin or on the bloodstained battlefields of Europe. In both works we encounter the hero and the heroines, the clowns and the buffoons, and the poor and the downtrodden. These conditions of life are rooted not in man's ignorance or in man's inhumanity, but in man's social class; a class in which he finds himself trapped through an organisation of society in which he played no part and had no voice. At the same time, this environment can only be changed by man himself; by man who must read and learn and understand the beauties of the past and the potential of the future. O'Casey called this Communism, but other generations called it Christianity, democracy and independence. In both his plays and autobiographies, O'Casey's vision of life is that it is ongoing, and while the politicians, the Church and the gunmen continuously botch up the scene, we must find and cherish those moments of merriment: a lament in one ear perhaps, he once said, but always a song in the other.

This spirit, this evocation of a good life, free from disease, from ignorance and from poverty, is fundamental to everything O'Casey wrote, and it is abundantly present in the autobiographies. Without the autobiographies, O'Casey would still live; but with them O'Casey's living brings to us what *The Times* called 'his indestructable spirit that blazed joyously independent to the end'.

These essays reflect a growing interest in a multi-faceted O'Casey: dramatist, essayist, letter writer, and a uniquely provocative man. The appearance of the first two volumes of the playwright's letters and the activities of the O'Casey centenary (1980) have augmented a rise in O'Casey scholarship. Increasingly, the autobiographies are being studied, analysed and judged without the rancour of the past. This collection presents a balance of literary and biographical approaches to the autobiographies. All add to a scholarly study of a great and insufficiently explored work.

Editor   ROBERT G. LOWERY
Sean O'Casey Review

1 The Origin and Evolution of a Dublin Epic

RONALD F. AYLING

There is no description so hard, nor so profitable as is the description of a man's own life.

Montaigne

I

Sean O'Casey's autobiography was written over a period of more that a quarter of a century. The first volume, *I Knock at the Door*, was published early in 1939; it was followed by five further instalments: *Pictures in the Hallway* (1942), *Drums under the Windows* (1945), *Inishfallen, Fare Thee Well* (1949), *Rose and Crown* (1952) and, finally, *Sunset and Evening Star* late in 1954. In these books considerable liberties are taken with form and subject matter. O'Casey writes in the third person, exhibiting both originality and virtuosity in style and formal presentation in order to realise a wide range of public and private experience and many different states of mind and feeling. As one might expect, a skilful dramatic sense is observed in the evocation of mood and atmosphere, the juxtaposition of scenes, and the large-scale creation of character. An even more impressive quality, however, emerges from the cumulative power of the narrative as a whole: a sense of historical occasion and continuity, which, aided by considerable powers of observation and psychological insight, gives a series of individual events the compass of an epic.

Critical reaction has been fiercely divided not only regarding the relative merits of individual volumes, but about the literary and even historical qualities of the narrative as a whole. Several prominent critics – including Brooks Atkinson and the distinguished Irish playwright, Denis Johnston – think that O'Casey's reputation may ultimately rest more on the autobiographies than on the plays. Many others, among them George Orwell, Sean O'Faolain and Ulick O'Connor, have been extremely scathing about the work as literature and personal revelation. While the dramatist's most loyal defenders have never denied the unevenness of the narrative and its occasional glaring faults – hardly surprising in a work comprising more than half a million words – it is abundantly clear that the majority of its detractors, though they condemn it on literary grounds, are not in fact primarily concerned with literary values.

Two unprofitable critical approaches are common. The first is to regard the autobiographies primarily as background source material. The second is to consider the narrative sequence purely and simply in terms of it being a personal memoir. This approach entails ignoring the aesthetic reasons for writing in the third person and for introducing a variety of styles and formal devices, including fantasy, in order to mould the material in the manner of a novelist. It is as though *A Portrait of the Artist as a Young Man* was to be assessed only in terms of how well it reflected Joyce's early life. Naturally, personal elements are important in any autobiography, but O'Casey's intentions are clearly not limited to projecting his own personality or the circumstances of his life. Of course, one may not lightly dismiss the many critics and reviewers who have been baffled by the novel-like form of the work, even though one of the most brilliant examples of autobiographical art operates along somewhat similar lines; I am thinking of George Moore's trilogy, *Hail and Farewell*, which might well repay study in conjunction with O'Casey's autobiography. Clearly, there are problems in approaching works that might be called novelised autobiography (one critic has called Moore's trilogy 'a new form of the autobiographical novel'),[1] for, as Professor Roy Pascal has pointed out, the technique involves what seems to be an inherent 'contradiction between form and viewpoint'?[2] At the same time, such a contradiction can itself contribute a meaningful structural tension within the work of art.

Having attempted elsewhere to assess the published criticism of O'Casey's autobiographies,[3] I do not propose to discuss the subject here; instead, it seems that, in the present critical context, my most useful contribution might well be to provide a bibliographical introduction to O'Casey's sequence (seen mostly through his eyes and, as much as possible, in his own words).[4] However, one must take cognizance of certain criticisms of style and genre as well as of the authenticity of the experience O'Casey describes. Indeed, the attacks on form and theme are often linked. Anthony Butler's criticisms are typical of this approach in resorting to journalist psychiatry, claiming that the autobiographies and O'Casey's aggressive defence of his writings against critics and reviewers reveal 'an almost text-book paranoid attitude'[5] The style as well as the content of the autobiographies apparently supplies evidence of psychosis. The element of fantasy, for instance, suggests that O'Casey 'could withdraw into a dream world', which (to Butler) is 'yet another symptom' of paranoia. In literary or even psychological terms the charge is completely untenable. Significantly, no attempt is made by any of these critics to analyse the purposes to which fantasy is put in the course of the narrative — if they did, it would be found that the uses include serious as well as light-hearted satire, together with visionary flights of fancy. Several 'dream' episodes may legitimately be criticised as clumsy examples of parody or overdone burlesque, but they are at no point escapist or paranoid writings; and many other examples of fantasy in the autobiographies, as in the plays, are both hilariously funny and sharply satiric. Professor Roy Pascal rightly includes fantasy among the elements used by the author to assert positive social attitudes, referring to 'the extravagance of fantasy with which the simplest of people [in the autobiographies] react against the weight of poverty and humiliation'.[6] By such means, in style as well as subject matter O'Casey realises his own spiritual resilience in the face of adversity and hardship, and his creative use of fantasy and dream processes may be compared with Charles Dickens's practice.

Butler further declares that O'Casey's stress on poverty in the autobiographies 'is another expression of his persecution complex',[7] but this view completely ignores the artistic as well as humane uses to which the writer puts the sufferings of his family and himself. Through them he projects on to a universal plane the frustrations and torments of a whole class, an entire subject nation at a cataclysmic period in its history. Critically, it is necessary to recognise that the narrative serves a wider purpose than the discovery of the self or the evolution of a writer. Like Gorki's autobiographical trilogy, O'Casey's work is seriously misrepresented if evaluated only in terms of one man's or even a family's life story, though such experience did appear to be the sole motive for the sequence at its commencement, as we shall see in tracing the work's origins and development.

II

Though *I Knock at the Door* appeared in print as late as 1939 the boyhood experiences that it recreated had for more than a decade been in O'Casey's mind and imagination as material for a book. The earliest hint that I have been able to trace is found in a letter to Macmillan & Co. dated 14 August 1926 (some two years after the publisher had first corresponded with him and one year after the company had printed his first book of plays), where he wrote: 'I have thought of writing a book reminiscent of my experiences'. The idea was slow to germinate and the work was, at first, almost certainly envisaged as a series of short episodes or self-contained short stories, swift glances back at his earliest years ('sketches' and 'pictures' were words often used by the author to describe what he was aiming to do and, indeed, still accurately portray what he did initially create). In an essay written in 1956, 'Sidelighting on Some Pictures', O'Casey revealed that the autobiography was begun without any definite set plan or overall scenario. Between writing plays, while his family slept, he sat down and wrote 'of past experiences – the moulds in which myself was made'.[8] Beginning in the late 1920s with a few sketches of his early childhood, and writing in the first as well as the third person, the playwright clearly had no thought of the sequence assuming its eventual epic proportions. In October 1930, in an entry in one of his notebooks, O'Casey outlined a plan for a volume of seventeen short stories, the ideas for some of them being clearly autobiographical. On and off, from about 1929 onwards, he was engaged in writing what he called 'biographical sketches'; or, in the words in which he described the first book of autobiography, writing 'stories' about 'what I saw and heard and felt during the first eleven or twelve years of my life'. These stories or events appear in one continuous narrative in several exercise books, undivided by chapter or title. Sometimes there is no break at what is, in the published version, the end of a volume. In one exercise book, for instance, the unbroken narrative sequence contains the final chapters of *I Knock at the Door* and the opening ones of *Pictures in the Hallway*; another contains a long draft which eventually became nine chapters in *Rose and Crown* and ten chapters in the following book, *Sunset and Evening Star*.

The first public acknowledgement that the dramatist was writing the story of his life appeared in a newspaper interview[9] in 1930; the voluntary offer of this information might seem to indicate that O'Casey was by then confident that the work was already assuming an acceptable artistic shape, yet this was in fact far from the truth. Instead, I think, it shows that his mind was at this time so full of ideas for the project and, indeed, so busily engaged in writing many of the early episodes that he could not help but discuss in an interview that which was already taking up a good deal of his time and creative energy. In the period 1929 to 1930, while writing *Within the Gates* (notes for lyrics in the play appear in the earliest handwritten draft of sketches for *I Knock*), he wrote in an exercise book a continuous series of personal adventures experienced in the first eight years or so of his life. Some of these incidents took place before his father's death and some afterwards; several have never appeared in print in any form, while others were published in *I Knock* in substantially revised texts. Several are written in the first person and, indeed, some of these episodes were subsequently taken a stage further by being typed by O'Casey still using the first-person narrator.

The earliest holograph exercise book contains an unpublished story of a fight between the young protagonist ('Jimmy' at this stage) and his sister 'Bella'. The scene, which takes place before the death of their father, shows Jimmy learning to read and, in the process, deliberately disturbing Bella's studies; she retaliates by snatching his book and he, in turn, roughly attacks her in order to get it back. The story is written in the third person. The narrative then continues, without a break, with a description of the father's funeral and several other incidents that subsequently appeared (in expanded and revised versions) as chapters in *I Knock at the Door*. One is the chapter – though there are no such formal divisions in this draft – in which the narrator (now named 'Jack') strikes his teacher during a school lesson after he has been unfairly punished by him. Subsequently, the boy's mother is visited by the clergyman and teacher in an episode that is, as we shall see, radically different from the published account. Other self-contained episodes in the exercise book include a reluctant trip by the boy to the seaside at Bray, accompanying the newly married Bella and her husband, Nick Benson, together with an interview between the Rector and Jack's mother about the boy's possible admission into a charity Blue-coat school.

To give something of the flavour of the earliest fragmentary draft of autobiography and allow readers to make their own comparisons with the text as it was published in the chapter 'The Lord Loveth Judgement' in *I Knock*, I have chosen to reproduce the scene in which the narrator's mother is visited by the school manager, the Reverend Mr Hunter, and by the teacher, Mr Hogan. The textual comparison here is particularly interesting because, whereas in most other episodes the published text contains much additional material that is, often, the most noticeable feature of the revisions (especially the increased emphasis on stylised linguistic patterning and on the accumulation of realisitic details that afford a denser surface texture to the various settings), the early draft in this case is in significant respects a fuller text than is the printed one. O'Casey's revisions here reveal a disciplined restraint in the paring down of characters, dialogue and of comic business for the sake of thematic concentration. This earlier draft is almost certainly nearer in circumstantial details (including the teacher's name, which was Hogan and not Slogan) to what actually happened to the young O'Casey. In the revised text the teacher is omitted from this scene altogether and so, for practical purposes, is the boy himself, who is supposed to be asleep in the bedroom during Hunter's visit. In the early draft there is some amusing comedy (overdone in places, admittedly) at the expense of the two men, which is primarily dependent upon them both being present; however, such incidental matters — including the dialogue concerning Hunter's son — detract the reader's attention from the main confrontation between Hunter and the here unnamed mother. Moreover, the stress on the vicar's economic blackmail and on the fearful presence of the son throughout the scene (both elements eliminated altogether from the published version) gives to it too pervasive a note of special pleading; the revised text is still heavily weighted against the educational establishment but it is less wholly black and white a picture. Moreover, when the early draft is compared with 'The Lord Loveth Judgement', we see that in the later text the mother's courageous if troubled independence of spirit is celebrated in a more disciplined and stylised manner, though certain repetitious details like 'the butter-box covered with the old red cloth' are overdone. The following extract from the manuscript occurs immediately after Jack's return from school, badly bruised from a beating and fearful of further punishment:

And if they bring up a policeman, sure you won't let [them] take [me] to prison [?]

Bring up a policeman — you didnt steal anything, did you [?]

No, no, oh no. Only watched while they played cards, an' Hogan caught us an' bet me till he was tired.

Now, said my mother, very seriously. You've done something you shouldnt have done, so what is it?

No, nothing, really nothing, only watched for them, that was all.

Why then did you say anthing about a policeman [?] What else did you do besides watching [?]

I hesitated and then said slowly: Nothing really. After Hogan — Only after Hogan bet me I gave him ever such a little tap on the top of the head with an ebony ruler.

Then came the sound of voices outside that gave an uneasy

flutter to the beating of my heart, followed by a knock at the door, and a voice saying, There's the Protestant Minister (looking) waiting to see you, Mrs . . . . Little Jack has done something wrong — given a terrible skelp on the head to Hogan. Are you in?

You beat me, mother, I said, and dont let Hogan get me again.

He'll kill me.

Ssh, lie down, son, said my mother sternly, and we'll see what they want me for, and going to the door, she opened it to admit Mr. Hunter and Hogan, who had a large lump of sticking plaster on the top of his head.

I'm very sorry to say, Mrs . . . , commenced Hunter, that I have a very serious matter to talk to you concerning your boy Jack. I'm very much afraid, if his tendencies arent immediately and effectively nipped in the bud, that he will turn out to be a rascal — yes, a rascal, Mrs . . .

Sit down, sir, please, said my mother, deferentially and humbly, to oul Hunter, and you, Mr. Hogan, please, and she gave another chair to the schoolmaster.

Has your boy told you what he did to his schoolmaster, asked Hunter.

Yes, sir, answered mother, he told me that after getting a heavy beating from Mr. Hogan for nothing, he gave him a little tap on the head with an ebony ruler.

What does she say, sir, asked the half-deaf Hogan, looking at Hunter and cocking his ear in the direction of my mother's voice.

Says her boy gave you a little tap on the head with an ebony ruler, said Hunter loudly into Hogan's ear.

Little tap, he bellowed in [illegible word] contradiction. It was a blow, a heavy, cruel, bitter, vicious, vengeful, blaguardly blow.

Hunter raised his slim white paw for silence, and said to my mother, Mr. Hogan is still feeling noises in his head. Your boy might even have killed him for he is an old man, well-stricken in years.

Well able to manage boys yet, though, grinned Hogan intrusively, with his ear now cocked in the direction of Hunter's voice.

Mind's natural strength still undiminished, undiminished sir, afraid that even a hint of his age might hasten his retirement.

Again Hunter raised his delicate looking paw for silence, and went on, Mr. Hogan was helpless for more than half an hour after the impact, went on Hunter, and that fact does not suggest to me that the blow was only a little tap on the top of the head. But the question of whether your boy struck Mr. Hogan with an ebony ruler or with a feather (goosequill) is not the point, but the fact, moral fact, immoral fact that he struck, raised his hand with violence against his schoolmaster. He raised his hand with violence, Mrs. C., against one whom we believe has been appointed by God for the instruction and correction of our children. Now I dont want to say anything about the probability of his misdemeanour making him liable to detention for a period in a Reformatory, that would be a too (possibly, let us hope) strict and merciless punishment for the boy, but I dont remember who was it said that we must be cruel to be kind —

Hamlet, sir, said Hogan intrusively, to his mother in the celebrated bedroom scene.

Hunter held up his paw for silence, and went on, (To put him there would unfailingly attach to him a criminal attribute, and if at all possible, we must avoid that) but he must be made immediately to realize the singular and full enormity of his misconduct.

He does realize it, sir, said my mother, for he is quite sick with fear.

One moment, Mrs. C., said H[unter], lifting the paw a little, I havent quite finished yet. The boy, as I have said, must receive an adequate punishment for his unexpected and flagrant misbehaviour. And that punishment will be the immediate return of the boy with me and Mr. Hogan, where he will plead that he is sorry before everybody, and where he will be again caned for what he's freshly done.

He's had enough, sir, said my mother, for his poor legs are in a terrible state.

They deserve to be in a terrible state, Mrs. C., said Hunter severely, and you really mustnt allow yourself to be, to be a means of stretching evil tendencies in the child.

'Tisnt fair, sir, that he should be made a show of before the whole school, and besides there [were] others worse than him, who werent touched, and fair is fair, even with my Jack. His legs were in a terrible state, and besides, when I brought him to the school I warned Mr. Hogan that he wasnt to be beaten because of his poor eyes, and there were others in the game that werent touched.

He didnt say as much as boo to them, I added.

You see how your excuses are lifting him into the error of lessening his outrage on the decencies of discipline, said Hunter. Come, Mrs. C., look at the matter calmly and sternly and help us to save your son.

I imagine that the other boys should have been punished, too, muttered my mother, stubbornly.

I am your pastor, said Hunter firmly, and Manager of the School, and I must say emphatically that I repose the fullest trust and confidence in the stewardship of Mr. Hogan, so that I cannot take any notice whatever of your observations.

Hogan grimaced gratefully at his Manager.

I have three tickets here for coal, Mrs. C., but since you persist in participating in your boy's shocking (by condonement) conduct, perhaps I ought to devote them to others that will prove any claim by a humbleness of heart which appreciating [sic] fully the efforts we make for the temporal and spiritual welfare of our people.

My mother's lip quivered, and she sat stiff and silent, uneasy at the thought of losing what would mean warmth and additional security of life to her and to me.

I'll admit, sir, Jack has been a very bad boy, and that it was a terrible thing for him to raise his hand to his schoolmaster, but further punishment, while making things no better for Mr. Hogan, will make things much worse for the poor boy.

Poor boy, poor boy, ejaculated Hunter, irritably. Really, Mrs. C., you push me beyond patience. We do all we can to help you. We give you your share of coal; we have through the kindness of our Chemist Churchwarden, procured C[od] Liver Oil and Parrishes' Syrup for your boy at cost price. Can you not realize, woman, that what Mr. Hogan and I are trying to do is done through conscientious affection for the boy's future? Can you [not] realize that if what this boy has done goes un-regarded in the way of punishment, he will be encouraged to do again and again things that will finally unfit him to take his place in a decent and soberly disciplined world. Now we have had quite enough of this obstinate nonsense. Hunter was get-ting angry and his voice was now loud and threatening, so that I gripped more tightly the sleeve of my mother's dress. The boy has richly earned a severe caning, and he is going to get it, till he goes down on his knees to Mr. Hogan before the whole school, and begs his pardon for what he has done, and that lesson may save him from the deepening of the ruffianly young rascal in his nature.

(He is very sorry for it, and he can say so here. And turning to me she said, Arent you very sorry, Jack, for striking poor Mr. Hogan on the head with a ruler [?]

But I looked at her, and said nothing. There was a pause before she said again, Come, Jack, you neednt be afraid here. You are sorry, arent you [?]

Answer your mother, you young rascal, said Hogan.

Then stiffening my body up, I said, No, I'm not sorry. He bet me till I was black and blue.

Now you see, said Hunter angrily, the kind of a boy Mr. Hogan has to deal with.

(Why didnt he slam the others as well as me?). Already see how deeply wickedness has dipped into his nature. With such a boy gentleness is lost leniency. No use to persuade or to coax such away from harm. One has to punish such a nature away and the best way to do this is to show him through the smart of a generous caning that it no longer pays to sin.

Mother's face flushed up, and she got on to her feet, and I saw in her black eyes little points of fire that fixed themselves on Hunter's face. I saw her hands shake and (He must be made to say that he is sorry. Yes, she answered. He must be made to tell a lie. He cannot feel sorry, but you want to take him

away to beat him till he tells a lie. You beat him [at] times
to make him tell the truth, then you beat him again that his
tongue may blossom into a lie. Well, you will go without him,
for he is my child, and I will have the last word as to whether
or no he will be caned. And he is no more a rascal or a ruffian,
Mr. Hunter, than your own son, Master Herbert.

Mrs. C., said old Hunter, seriously, you mustnt for one
moment couple the name of my son with yours. That is an
impudent familiarity that I certainly will not allow.

Perhaps you dont know, sir, why your [sic] teacher of his
class always sees that your son sits in a desk between two boys.

How dare you count your rag and tatter rascal with my boy.

Mother had burned up all her caution in a flash of anger. My
rag and tatter rascal, she cried loudly, hasnt been made by his
[teacher to] sit in his Sunday School class between boys, to
save when he used to sit between two girls he never stopped
trying to finger their legs.

Hunter stood silent and astonished for some moments before
he said, bitterly, What you have just said, Mrs. C., is an excep-
tionally vile slander on my child, and we'll see if such things
can be spread about with impunity.

A blasted slander, sir, said Hogan, and you will pardon the
expression, but the circumstances made the profanity inevitable.

Every woman that has a girl in the class, went on my mother
rapidly, can tell you it's true.

Hold your tongue, woman, for shame, shouted Hogan.

You old hypocrite, said my mother, turning savagely on
Hogan, how you can wheel round when you think it suits you,
for you yourself first told me about it, and patting me on the
back, with a jeering laugh, when you were going away, said
that it was rather a red look-out for the future of a parson's
son.

Hunter pulled his soft round Minister's hat on furiously,
gathered up his gloves and umbrella, and swiftly left the room.

You're simply flinging pearls before swine, sir, said Hogan.
It is a vile lie, an extraordinary lie, a spiteful lie, a lie that no

apology can swallow back! A detestable lie, a lie that hasnt a word to say for itself —

What did she say, sir, asked Hogan, angrily cocking his ear in the direction of Hunter's voice.

I could not, would not repeat what she has dared to say, said the now purple-faced Hunter.

That his son had to be stopped at Sunday School, said Mrs. C. loudly, near to Hogan's ear, from sitting between little girls because he was always trying to finger their legs.

Trying to finger what? asked H.

Legs, legs, shouted my mother.

Who did? he asked again.

Gilbert, shouted Hunter into his ear, Gilbert!

Shameful thing to say, said Hogan, Master Gilbert wouldnt think of doing such a thing.

He's a pure boy and a pious boy, said Hunter. Such a statement about Gilbert is a growth in the gutter minds of the lowest of our people. If I hear any further reference to this gutter bred statement about my son, Mrs. C., I shall have to associate the lie with you, and, believe me, I will act in such a way that you will swiftly repent you of brooding out these corrupt inventions about the character of those who are above you.

Call the other women here, and they'll substantiate it.

Whose legs?

Smart too with his Latin. Tried to trip him up in his roots but it was no go. Just answered pit, pat, pit, like a beating heart: rodeo, I rode; sodeo, I sowed; flodeo, I flowed; nodeo, I knowed. Answered everything pit pat. Gratifying. You should be proud of him.

My mother sat in silence for a long time after the two had gone.

Sat long, looking into the fire and thinking.

You have gone and made things nice and crooked for us now, she said suddenly to me . . . What will we do in the cold weather when we [have] no coal . . . and no money to buy any?

And I put my head under the bedclothes and silently cried myself to sleep.[10]

III

The manuscript 'stories' are often crude, even rudimentary in form, and the first-person narration seems to be, if anything, an inhibiting device. Gradually, however, the work took on a more expansive life of its own, demanding expression on a scale much larger than the one volume of childhood reminiscence originally envisaged; moreover, to distance himself from the experiences related and to give the narrative something of a novel-like texture, O'Casey eventually decided to write solely in the third person.[11] Perhaps, if the writer's avowedly experimental dramas from *The Silver Tassie* (1928) onward had been welcomed by the commercial theatre, or even if he had been encouraged by the availability of good theatre workshop facilities such as have been proviced in London since the mid-1950s by the Royal Court and Stratford East Theatres and, more recently, by the National Theatre and Royal Shakespeare Company he would have devoted most of his time and energy to writing plays. In that case his autobiography might not have progressed beyond taking a few 'swift glances back' at things that had made him — to paraphrase his own subtitle to the first volume. But conjecture of this kind is fruitless. The fact is that the general lack of interest by theatre managements in O'Casey's dramas after *Within the Gates* (1933), and the onset of the Second World War, which further hampered opportunities for stage presentation of serious new plays, meant that the dramatist was forced at this time to earn a living by writing works other than plays. Thus circumstances conspired to stimulate the growth of the autobiographical writings. It should be made clear from the outset, however, that the autobiography was written for its own sake and engendered its own aesthetic momentum from a fairly early stage in its composition. It was never conceived as a pot-boiler intended to subsidise the dramatic experimentation (which was proceeding at the same time, of course), though in fact it did largely help to maintain O'Casey and his family during the lean years of the war and its aftermath. Nor was it the random recollections of a dramatist put down in leisure moments. Critically, it should be approached as a work designed and executed in accordance with the demands and the pressures of imaginative literature, the product of a creative artist in prose.

It was some considerable time, however, before the author himself fully realised the true magnitude of the sequence he was creating, let alone the lengthy time-span and wide-ranging social panorama to be encompassed in the completed narrative. In a letter to William J. Maroldo of 10 August 1962 the author declared: 'As for my own "Auto-biography", it was not first conceived as such, but just as incidents I had experienced. Indeed, three of them appeared in print before the idea of a biography came into my head.' The first episode was published in the *American Spectator*. When George Jean Nathan asked for a contribution for the journal, O'Casey sent him 'A Protestant Kid Thinks of the Reformation'. It was printed in the issue for July 1934 and met with such success that, as the author wrote in the *New York Times* on 16 September 1956, 'The biography started in earnest'. The story was considerably expanded for its appearance in *I Knock at the Door*. 'His Father's Dublin Funeral' appeared in the journal *English* in 1936 and was subsequently enlarged to become the chapter 'His Father's Funeral'. 'The Dream School' chapter is a slightly expanded version of 'The Dream School: A Story', which appeared in the issue of *Yale Review* for June 1937. Here the young boy is still 'Jackie' and, though there are but slight differences from the same account published in *I Knock*, the changes in the later version are more subtle and effective: for instance, the teacher shows the class his cane before Jackie's daydreaming during the lesson and this presumably leads to the women 'guardians' harmlessly waving canes in the boy's fantasy, a pleasant escapist interlude harshly broken by the application of a real cane to his hand.

Round about 1937 O'Casey seems to have really settled down to writing these sketches of his early life, though he wrote casually to Peter Newmark on 19 February 1937: 'I am doing a little with my "Autobiography". Have just finished a chapter on

"Sunday-school & church", ending – not beginning – with the text, "And God said let there be light & there was light".' This was probably the chapter which was published under the title 'A Child of God'. In an undated letter (written in January 1938) he wrote to Harold Macmillan, 'I have a few things in hand (doing something with a play, and a few fantastic pages of biography), but they haven't reached the stage yet that would interest a publisher.'

Once the author got down in earnest to the work, however, the writing went smoothly. Many years later, in a letter of 10 August 1962 to William J. Maroldo, O'Casey explained that when 'the idea came to me' it soon

> grew expansively out and down deep, so that a letter I have before me, from Macmillan's dated July 1938, tells me the material sent in [came to] 60,000 words. They thought that amount would make a book, but would prefer 75,000 words. I evidently sent word saying material was plentiful (the ideas were growing), and that I would send in additional chapters; for a following letter from them says they are 'glad to hear that you will find no difficulty in sending further material'.

By 21 June 1938 he was completing the manuscript, as he wrote to Harold Macmillan: 'I'll do my best to add the 15,000 words wanted. I've already done two sketches – "The Tired Cow" and "The Street Sings", with another – "Vandhering Vindy Vendhor" – well on the way. A few more should make a volume.' He was, however, having trouble with the title, as he explained in the same letter:

> I'm not satisfied with the title 'The Green Blade'; and I am trying to think of another – 'Father of the Man,' or 'Of Such is the Kingdom of Heaven' – too long? 'Studies' in Autobiography seems to have too much of a scholastic touch about it for me. I'll have to try to make the sub-title simpler.

A fuller explanation for his change of mind was made in the letter to William J. Maroldo that has already been quoted from earlier:

I first intended to take titles for the work from 'First the Green Blade, then the Corn, then the Full Corn in the Ear'; but the rapid development of what I was conceiving in my mind, additional ideas crowding in after the conception of previous ideas, made me alter the titles to the present ones which top the various volumes.

In a letter of 7 October 1938 to Harold Macmillan the author said much more about the first book and indicated his plans for future volumes:

The Book — the 23 chapters or sections is an organic whole — at least I hope it is — ; and the whole book is autobiographical, from Alpha to Omega, of the first twelve years of my life [1880–92]. I have thought of two more volumes: 'Come On In', and the third 'The Lighted Room'. The second to consist of what happened till I joined the Irish Movement, & the last to deal with all or most of what happened afterwards.

Subsequently, in a letter of 21 December 1938 to the publicity department of Macmillan, he asked 'If you can, don't use the word "Biography" — what a detestable word it is —, for the Saxon "Lifestory" is far better and much more musical.' Further comments by the author may also be found on the dust jacket of the 1939 English edition of *I Knock at the Door*:

This is the story of the first twelve years of the author's life, full of sound, sometimes full of fury, and always signifying a lot . . . . The book discloses the life of a boy in the Dublin Streets, a Dublin School, a Dublin Church; in scene and conversation the squalor and glamour of a mean and splendid city is presented wearing again in drab and sparkling colours the strange patterns that went to make the man.

Later volumes in O'Casey's autobiographical sequence were criticised for their alleged excessive wordplay in the manner of James Joyce, but the author argued that this element was a consistent feature of the work from the very beginning. In a letter to Ralph Thompson dated 8 December 1948 he wrote:

The piece called 'A Protestant Kid Thinks of the Reformation' . . . was first welcomed by the Editor of *The American Spectator*, George Jean Nathan, and his Associate Editors – who, I think, were E. O'Neill, T. Dreiser, E. Boyd and Sherwood Anderson, years before I began work definitely on the biographical venture. The piece in question is, I think, a Joycean effort, or would be called one, or is pricked with a Joycean influence, though it was written in a full flood of spontaneity. So, it would appear, it was from eminent minds in your Country that I got a first encouraging clap for a 'Joycean' indiscretion.

The generally favourable critical reception which greeted *I Knock at the Door* and, most probably, the knowledge that wartime conditions were unfavourable for the production of serious new plays, spurred O'Casey into continuing his life story. In any case, whatever the reason, he wrote as early as 28 November 1939 to tell George Jean Nathan that he was hard at work on the new volume and that the probable title would be 'Rough House'. In a letter to Peter Newmark dated 30 March 1940 he said, 'I am busy on my autobiography, (now isn't lifestory a better word than that?) & hope to have most of another volume done by the end of the year.' The following day he informed Nathan, 'I am still working on the second book of my life. I have ten chapters done; and I think some of them are very good.' The work proceeded steadily but the author was worried by the worsening war situation, with increasing air raids on Britain and heavy ship losses. In a letter of 24 April 1941 to Jack Carney he noted that

For the last few months I've typed more than ever in my life. Had to. I wanted to make sure of the MS. for second volume of 'I Knock at the Door'; so I typed copies of twenty chapters, threefold: one for the U.S.A., one for Macmillans of London, and one for meself. So they'll hardly be bombed in three places at once. Three or four more chapters should do the trick. And I've never learned to dictate. Couldn't do it even to a letter.

Pictures in the Hallway was completed in the first half of 1941.

Writing to Peter Newmark on 9 July 1941 the author said:

I have just finished the second biograph vol. to be called 'Pictures in the Hallway.' I've over-shot the mark in amount of material, writing over 100,000 words; & have now, I fear, to think of what can come out to make it sell for less than a quid.

A week earlier, on 1 July, he had told Daniel Macmillan:

I have been surprised that the stuff I sent in was so full of words. I have since looked over and looked over the list of chapters, and find it undesirable to evict any of them from their holding. They, one by one, follow the years, and any of them would be out of place in any succeeding volume. I had thought of four [books] altogether, with the last one to be called, 'The Clock Strikes Twelve'. What the intervening one may be called, God only knows; if indeed any other thing can be written. If there be, it will be per ardua ad astra with a vengeance. However, I can drop out the last chapter — 'He Paints His First Picture,' and end the volume with the part that gives the title to the book: 'Pictures in the Hallway'.

The latter arrangement was followed and 'He Paints His First Picture' was omitted; it remains unpublished and no trace of it was to be found among the playwright's papers at his death.

The time sequence covered by *Pictures in the Hallway* is roughly 1892–1905, during which time the author progressed from twelve to twenty-five years of age. The dust jacket of the English edition, written by the playwright himself, described the book in these terms:

We are shown how O'Casside first touched the hand of Shakespeare, and how he first came close to the living theatre in a playhouse that is now the main part of the Abbey Theatre. We find him thrusting himself into the presence of Milton and other fine minds, seeking, in face of obstacles, and even perils, the rich and daring company of great men . . . The visit to Kilmainham Jail, the lordly fight in the Cat 'n Cage, ending in a flight from the police, the glow of the demonstration in Dublin streets voicing its sympathies with the Boers mingle with the Te Deum and the steady roll of the Orange drums . . . We find him too, working for Harmsworth and heaven, hand in hand; and we are shown how colour and line and form swept into his life through the pictures of Constable and Fra Angelico. Dublin in her deep shade and glittering sun strikes up her drum again as Sean O'Casside sails down her stream of life in a gold canoe.

On 18 February 1942, on seeing the pre-publication copy, O'Casey wrote to Daniel Macmillan of *Pictures in the Hallway*: 'I am downright glad that the book appealed to you so much. I think it better, on the whole, than 'I Knock at the Door'; though that thought may be due to the illusion that the more you write, the better you get.' Later, in a letter dated 17 May 1942, the playwright told George Jean Nathan,

> I am so glad that you liked my new book, Pictures in the Hallway, and how much rest your fine opinion of it gave to me . . . To keep my head from flying too high, I see James Stern, in the New Republic, has said some stern things . . . He's kind enough to say that the chapter 'I Strike a Blow' has grand writing, but 'the road leading there is monotonous and mighty long in which O'Casey dismally recalls the years.' There's me for you! thinking the years recorded grand effort and the will to live . . . Some [critics] think that the talk of St. Patrick to the Irish and the Protestant Kid's Idea of the Reformation was got from Finnegans Wake; but I have a recollection of writing the latter fourteen years ago, and of being encouraged to go on by a fellow named G. J. Nathan publishing it eight or nine years ago in THE AMERICAN SPECTATOR [actually, in July 1934]; and saying it was good.

The following volume, *Drums under the Windows*, was written between 1942 and mid-1944. On 10 March 1942 O'Casey confessed to George Jean Nathan, 'I dread looking forward to writing the next volume.' Two months later, on 17 May, he told the same correspondent, 'I am so glad that you liked my new book, Pictures in the Hallway . . . I have started notes for a further volume; but I am so much occupied with many things that only God knows when it'll be well on the way.' On 26 June 1942 the dramatist writes to him again: 'In the midst of many interruptions, I'm trying to get together a few chapters of the 3rd volume of biography, which I think I'll call Drums Under the Window.' The following year, in a letter to Jack Carney dated 26 August, he was able to say: 'I am doing a little with a new volume of "biography". I've got about nine chapters done, which leaves me about fourteen more to do.' The writing proceeded steadily so that by 8 February 1944 the playwright could express the hope that the book would be completed that year. On 9 June in a letter to Daniel Macmillan he says,

> I have almost chosen the title DRUMS UNDER THE WINDOWS for this number. I will send on the other chapter as soon as it is done. I was thinking of writing a short FLASH FORWARD to describe my thoughts at the present time (some of them anyway), and so give an unusual end to it. I think I shall finish it off with a fourth volume to be called THE CLOCK STRIKES TWELVE.

On 1 February 1944 he had sent seven chapters to Macmillan of New York for safekeeping; on 29 May 1944 a further five chapters were sent; finally, on 12 July he was able to inform Jack Carney that he had submitted a complete typescript of the book to Macmillan.

This third volume covers the period from approximately 1905 to 1916, during which he moved from the age of twenty-five to thirty-six; it thus includes the most crucial and intellectually formative years of his life. The book's title (the author used both *Window* and *Windows* in comments both before and after its publication) was most probably suggested by a phrase from W. B. Yeats's 1928 letter rejecting *The Silver Tassie*. Of O'Casey's early work the poet had said,

> You were interested in the Irish Civil war, and at every moment of those plays wrote out of your own amusement with life or

your sense of its tragedy; you were excited, and we all caught your excitement; you were exasperated almost beyond endurance by what you had seen or heard as a man is by what happens *under his window*, and you moved us as Swift moved his contemporaries.[12]

A letter of 8 July 1945 from O'Casey to Lovat Dickson of Macmillan asserts confidently (once again the reference is to the same letter by Yeats):

> Prefatorily, let me say that in DRUMS UNDER THE WINDOWS, I primarily aim at doing something that Yeats might call 'unique'; that the whole work will be a curious biography, entirely, or almost so, different from anything else of its kind; and, in its way, a kaleidoscopic picture of the poorer masses as they surged around one who was bone of their bone and flesh of their flesh.

Here, and in the blurb he wrote for the book's dust-jacket, we can see a new awareness that the life story has now, substantially, a more ambitious focus than it had had in the first two volumes. Originally, the autobiography had been an intimate personal story of a half-blind child, shown primarily in everyday domestic surroundings with but occasional glimpses of the larger social and economic realities beyond his home or street environment. It is true that, for the observant reader, there *is* always a sense (however shadowy it may be for much of the time) of greater forces moving beyond the immediate surface action. Even in the very first chapter of the first book the private drama of a mother fighting to save a child from disease and then subsequently grieving over his death is unobtrusively placed within a social framework that shows preferential medical attention being given to socially superior people; moreover, this domestic tragedy is juxtaposed with the mass movement of a Parnellite march for Home Rule. None the less, here as elsewhere in the first two books, the public drama is generally kept firmly in the background. By the third book, however, O'Casey consciously seeks to create a Gorki-like saga of a wide world in revolutionary ferment (whether or not he knew Gorki's three-volume autobiography at this time — he certainly did so at the end of his life — is irrelevant to my argument), as he shows in his dust-jacket commentary on the work:

Here, in *Drums Under the Windows*, we get the third part of the author's experiences in the life of Dublin, itself fiercely and humorously dodging, charging, and dancing in and out through the revolving life of the world. Here he is, flitting about Dublin streets, under black and amber skies, to be changed soon to a rosy red when they are lit up by the frantic fires of Easter Week. The old green banners are superseded by the gayer ones of the Gaelic League and Republicans, and high among these flies the flag of the Plough and the Stars carried by the Irish Citizen Army. Drums beat outside every door and under every window, so that old men again see visions and young men dream dreams. Here is Jim Larkin, roaring out his evangel in the curving space around the Customs House. Away, further on, to a few followers and a tiny group of listeners, James Connolly, standing on a box, in the falling sleety rain, expounds the Socialist policy of economics alongside the deaf and stony ramparts of the Bank of Ireland. And yonder, through cheering and more respectable streets, lit by a thousand torches, Douglas Hyde rides in a carriage and pair, on his way to gather funds in America for the Gaelic League. We catch a glimpse of Yeats framed in the doorway of the Abbey Theatre, or battling with a screaming crowd, mad with righteous shame at hearing the word 'shift' said from the stage in Synge's tantalising play. We gain a fleeting sight of AE, crouching in mauve or purple twilight corners, letting off theosophical fireworks to create a new firmament over Dublin city. In all this ferment, stir, light, and darkness, the author found time to close the eyes of his favourite brother, Tom, and hurry his dead sister into the grave. We see all this excellent, fanciful, and drab life move inexorably to one focus, to merge finally into the smoke and flame of revolt [in the Easter 1916 Rising]. A further volume, to be called *The Clock Strikes Twelve*, is to end the story.

(The 'further volume' was called *Inishfallen, Fare Thee Well* but O'Casey went on to write not one but three further volumes of his life story.)

Writing to Daniel Macmillan on 6 November 1945, after publication of the third volume, he said: 'I do [like the book] very much; though the design on the jacket (mine own) isn't I'm afraid, quite so good as the previous two. The book itself is near as good as a book can be.' The following month, on 17 December, he wrote to Jack Carney, 'I have been told by Macmillans that *Drums Under the Windows* is sold out. Curious that, for neither of the previous two [volumes] had such a quick sale.' O'Casey's apparent surprise here is a little disingenuous. The new-found popularity was hardly surprising, as the author's dust-jacket description intimates: national affairs and the political and literary topics in the foreground as well as the background inevitably made *Drums* a more immediately striking book than its two forerunners. Nationalists and labour men alike were eager to read O'Casey's views on politicians and public personalities he had known and, in some cases, worked with in various organisations and clubs. The public nature of the drama thus led to extensive critical coverage and increased sales, hampered though these were by wartime paper restrictions (the book was soon sold out and could not be reprinted for several years). The author's personal involvement in these momentous events, which would no doubt have heightened the writing in any case, was increased by the new social conflict in which he felt embroiled even while he wrote the book. The Second World War was raging about him in England while he was describing the influx of wounded soldiers returning to Dublin in the early years of the Great War; the juxtaposition of the two conflicts, both felt deeply by the dramatist, gave an added edge and bite to his narrative. There's no doubt that the subsequent world cataclysm was often in his mind's eye while he wrote about the Great War and the Easter Rising of 1916.

The fourth volume, which the author thought when he began it would be the concluding one, was written between 1945 and 1947. As late as 26 November 1946 a letter to Jack Daly speaks of the author working 'at the "last" vol. of Biography. It will end at the time when I leave Ireland for England. "The last glimpse of Eireann".' The following year, in a letter dated 14 March, the playwright informed George Jean Nathan:

> I have just finished another vol. of biography, which ends this work for awhile. I end it when I leave Ireland, and am calling it (I had a trying time thinking of a title; Clock Strikes Twelve was used as a title a few months ago here) 'Goodbye at the Door'.

Neither 'The Clock Strikes Twelve' nor 'Goodbye at the Door' was used as a title. On 15 April 1947 the playwright gave his final choice in a letter to Daniel Macmillan, which is especially interesting in its revelation that the author at that time considered the sequence to be concluded by the fourth book:

> I have completed the MS for another biographical vol. to be called, I think, INISHFALLEN FARE THEE WELL ; and I shall be glad if you would let me know whether or no I may send it on to you. This vol. ends the series with the author's departure for England.

The title is taken from one of Thomas Moore's Irish Melodies (ninth number) entitled 'Sweet Innishfallen, Fare Thee Well', an ironic title when the sweetness in the book is seen to encompass the appalling years covering the guerrilla warfare against the British and the subsequent Civil War that followed the British withdrawal; on the personal level, too, it embraces the increasing isolation O'Casey experienced within the trade union movement following Larkin's departure from Ireland, his feelings of anger and frustration when, on its début, *The Plough and the Stars* was the subject of sustained hostility from critics and audiences, and, above and beyond these humiliations, the intense sense of estrangement that for some years followed the death of his mother.

The book covers approximately the years 1918–26, beginning with his mother's death and ending with his decision to leave Ireland. The dust jacket of the English edition, almost certainly written by the author himself, speaks of the book recreating, with 'grim realism and poetic imagery', the Ireland of the days when death lounged by the corner of every Dublin street, or waited in the primrose-spangled country lanes. It depicts the turbulence of the Black and Tans, the uneasy truce, the dispute over the treaty, and the bitter feud that raged between its supporters and the Republicans while 'Eire was deafened and dumbfounded and nearly destroyed by gun-peal and slogancry.' In other pages the author writes of more peaceful things, of visits to Lady Gregory's home, Coole Park in Galway, where she reads aloud by the fire from Hardy, Hudson and Melville, or saunters in the garden talking of her Abbey Theatre among the birds, butterflies and bees. Others in her circle are met as the author enters into the life of the Abbey Theatre, finding that it is not the cave of harmony he had expected it to be. We catch a glimpse of Yeats, 'a banner without an army,' but always trailing a silvery shadow behind him.[13] We see, too, the clergy helping to change the terrible beauty born out of revolution into the top-hat and the black broadcloth of Irish respectability. The book shows O'Casey bidding a long farewell to his mother, as she leaves her life of toil for an everlasting holiday; to his brother Michael; to a girl for whom he had a deep admiration; and at last to Ireland herself, and, though this was not foreseen, to the Abbey Theatre.

The dust jacket of the first US edition includes the comment that,

> Like Mr. O'Casey's other biographical volumes, *Inishfallen, Fare Thee Well* is written in the third person, recording the thoughts, opinions and experiences of one Sean Casside, a Dublin firebrand who became a writer . . . It includes a masterly sketch of his mother's death in a moldy tenement and of her poverty-stricken funeral, and a memorable character portrait of Lady Gregory — 'a robin with the eye of a hawk.'

During this fourth book there are the beginnings of a change of emphasis in the narrative. As I have argued elsewhere, using the autobiographies for purposes of psychoanalysis or biographical gossip is clearly a critical cul-de-sac. Yet to condemn such pre-occupations is not to ignore the fact that criticism must come to terms with certain problems of form and artistic intention. An essential point here is the fact that O'Casey realises the central character in the work with fluctuating degrees of personal involvement and artistic detachment. The shifting perspectives can be traced through the six volumes as young 'Johnny Casside' becomes, first, 'Irish Jack', the nationalist-minded labourer, then 'Sean O'Cathasaigh', the labour agitator, and, finally, 'Sean O'Casey', the playwright, 'a voluntary and settled exile from every creed, from every party, and from every literary clique'.[14] But as well as the various shifts in viewpoint and vision in the course of the six books, there is a more important change of emphasis — as has been noted by several critics, though without following up the observation. Once the central figure becomes O'Casey the writer — as happens during the fourth book, *Inishfallen, Fare Thee Well* — there is a change in perspective. As Roy Pascal says:

> the character of the autobiography involuntarily begins to change, the story loses in concrete substantiality; convictions which had the massiveness of experience now thin out into opinions and opinionativeness; and when O'Casey leaves Dublin, inconsequent reminiscences, tender or hilarious, take the place of autobiography. The four earlier books are not reminiscence, but life regained, relived passionately with all the intensity of a man still fiercely engaged.[15]

The difference lies in the fact that O'Casey wrote about two worlds of personal experience. In the first four books he created the one in which he grew up. There is a natural progression in self-awareness (national as well as individual) throughout the narrative, which is firmly rooted in a particular *locale*, with recurrent and unifying themes and characters. Writing from a considerable distance in time and circumstance, the playwright recreated his early life with the balanced detachment of a novelist, while yet communicating the enthusiasms and commitments of his protagonist with a vivid immediacy. In the final two books and partially in *Inishfallen*, however, he wrote of more recent events from a relatively static viewpoint — for, as a mature man, his outlook on life was understandably settled and constant – so that the narrative becomes more recognisably reminiscence in an orthodox sense. Of course there are experiences as accurately observed and as finely realised in *Inishfallen, Rose and Crown* and *Sunset and Evening Star* as in the earlier books; likewise, there is a considerable range of thought and feeling, with compassion, comedy and polemic in good measure. But, for all the passages of fine writing in them, there is not the progression, the concrete homogeneity of setting and subject matter that gives aesthetic unity to the first four books. The lack of a balanced critical analysis of this apparent change of emphasis in the narrative sequence and its artistic consequences is one of the big gaps still remaining in O'Casey criticism; it is my hope that the present critical anthology will help to remedy this situation.

Rose and Crown, the fifth volume, covering approximately the period 1926–35, was written between 1947 and 1951. In a letter dated 29 August 1947 O'Casey tells Daniel Macmillan of his plans for 'writing a further vol. dealing with my arrival in England, and carrying it on, maybe, to the day that now is'. On 31 October 1947 he writes again to Daniel Macmillan (his comments on the change in emphasis is most interesting, particularly in the light of Roy Pascal's criticism quoted earlier: it shows once again the author's instinctive critical sense):

> The vol. on my impressions since I came to England will take a lot of thinking about; but I may try to start it soon in a rough way. It would be, I think, a more thoughtful one, and less exciting, which may be a bad or a good thing. I'm not sure.

The work occupied much of his time during the following three years. Writing to Ralph Thompson on 3 December 1948 the playwright said: 'At the moment, I am jotting down thoughts and incidents for another vol. which will, of course, open up in England, with a pen in one hand and a spy-glass in the other – to take an odd look at Eirinn through.' On 16 January 1951 he informed Daniel Macmillan:

> I've written a lot of a 5th vol. of biography, & now fear I shan't be able to end it without another one. I'd like to send

what I've written to you so's you can see, and estimate whether another one would be necessary — provided it wouldn't be too much trouble to return [the chapters] to me for a last look-over before I finally OK them. The most of them are a year old now, & so my mind will be fresh for the last look over them. I've quite a lot to do yet — I'm now setting down remarks on my visit to America in 1933 [the visit was actually made in 1934] — say 9 or 10 additional chapters to end the work. I propose to call the next vol. 'Rose and Crow

The following month (15 February) he sent the completed manuscript to the same correspondent with the comment: 'It brings me to 1933–34 having just left the United States for home . . . What do you think of the title? "Rose and Thorn" might be more realistic, but I imagine, wouldn't suit any of the chapters as a title.' The dust jacket of the first English edition contains the following description of the book, again almost certainly written by O'Casey himself:

It brings O'Casey to England to stand among the alien corn, and like it. He marries an Irish girl, and makes a home there . . . But stormy days were still before him. There was the dispute with the Abbey Theatre about the rejection of *The Silver Tassie*; a bigger row later with the clerics and their Press; and the tumult in America about *Within the Gates,* which was banned in Boston and other cities. Pictures are given of American life in New York and Pennsylvania, where O'Casey made many friends. Well-known and famous figures pass us by . . . Sean visits Ireland, and plays his first and last game of croquet against Yeats on the poet's lawn. He visits Yeats again in his lodgings in London, where the poet is working at his anthology; his affection goes to the sick man, and, finally, saying goodbye, he doesn't know that he has given a last farewell to Ireland's great poet and great man.

As with the two preceding volumes in the series, the publisher was anxious about possible legal action in connection with incidents in the narrative. In a letter to Daniel Macmillan dated 7 March 1951 O'Casey wrote of *Rose and Crown:*

I dont think there is anything libellous in it. I certainly had no feelings of writing any thing so derogatory while I was working at it. If I be inclined to libel anyone, I am inclined to libel myself. But, as you wisely say, it is better to make as sure as assurance can be by getting a lawyer to look over it. I am sure that no one can write anything worth a damn without annoying someone: Joyce did; Yeats did; Hardy did; and so did Tennyson. And Jesus annoyed a crowd of people. However, I havent written anything just to annoy, but simply wrote down what I felt I must write down. And that was done, not to annoy any person, but to free myself from annoying God. Of course, some of my conceptions may be wrong – nay, all of them may be so – but they are all honest; though that isnt saying that they are true or proper. Let a man examine himself, says St. Paul, and I have done this often, and most often when I am writing, so as to try to prevent anything malicious creeping in to what I am setting down.

Sunset and Evening Star, the sixth and final volume in the series, covers the period from 1936 to 1953. Completed early in 1953, it was delivered to the publisher in April of that year. As late as 7 May 1951 – in a letter to George Jean Nathan – the author still referred to this last volume as 'Goodbye at the Door', the title he had initially given to *Inishfallen, Fare Thee Well* when that book was planned as the final one in the autobiographical sequence. 'Goodbye at the Door' was presumably intended to round off, appropriately, the series that began with O'Casey knocking at the door of life. This idea, eventually dropped from the title, is picked up visually on the dust jacket of *Sunset and Evening Star* which itself echoes the design on the dust jacket of *I Knock at the Door*. Both jackets were sketched by the writer. In the earlier design a young boy is showing rapping at a door superimposed on a large Celtic Cross; in the later one, an old man drinks a farewell toast to life (as he does in the text at the very end of the book) outside a half-open door with the same Cross in the background. Pictorially, therefore, the writer attempts to show the unity within the sequence from first to last.

Sunset is described on the dust jacket of the English edition in the following terms (some of the phrases — such as 'under the mute compassion of the evening star' — may well have been written by O'Casey himself):

> The concluding volume of Sean O'Casey's remarkable auto-biographical series is written, as it were, under the mute compassion of the evening star. The book opens on his return from the United States, and brings us up to the present. Scene after scene springs to life as he writes: the London refugee children flooding the Devon lanes and fields, spending most of their time trying to tear their loneliness to pieces; American soldiers in O'Casey's Devon home; a cold night in a cold room in a Cambridge college, and the thoughts it stimulates. There is a long passage on Bernard Shaw. Life, as seen through O'Casey's eyes, and perhaps more markedly in this last volume, wears all its masks, gay, sad, ridiculous and terrible; but life, we are reminded, is young, and has plenty of time to make good. The note that is left with the reader is one of courage and of wonder. No writer of our time has produced so searching an examination of himself and combined it with so vivid and memorable a picture of this strange, difficult and remarkable world in which we are living.

The American dust jacket reads,

> *Sunset and Evening Star* is the sixth and presumably the last volume of Sean O'Casey's autobiography — one of the great creative works of our time. In it he looks back lovingly and without regrets on the past fifteen years, beginning with his return from America and his settling in Battersea . . . these were the years in which his great talents, lying in obscurity in plays which were never produced, burst forth in the glorious prose of his autobiography . . . As Sean O'Casey was writing this unforgettable story of his life, England was blanketed in the darkness of war. The light of his descriptive genius has never shone more brilliantly than in these black years when, from his home in Totnes, he watched Plymouth being pounded to fiery bits . . . The book ends fittingly with a glorious tribute

to his native Ireland, and with a salute to Life, to the past, the present and the future.

Thus the long sequence — begun in a relatively modest way as a series of 'sketches' of childhood experience, as 'a few fantastic pages of biography', according to a letter of January 1938 addressed to Harold Macmillan — is here completed after attaining an epic compass unimagined by the author at its commencement. Looking back at the first four volumes, after *Inishfallen* appeared in 1949, O'Casey commented:

> The biographical books were begun more than twenty years ago. Often through reveries of the past, I have watched myself going about among movements and people, one with them in most of what they did, but sometimes colliding with an opinion or a cause. I watched myself dodging through the dark pains and coloured joys of life; weeping now, singing then; dancing on state occasions; working and striking with discontented men; seeing how men and women and little children lived and died; separate from each, yet one with them all. It was all a rich tapestry of life, and I wove therein a design peculiar to, and imagined by, myself. I decided that the pattern was worth recording, so I set it down in books.[16]

As he told William J. Maroldo in a letter dated 10 August 1962, the sequence 'grew as it was written, changing to the long and varied work that grew out of the first fragile green blade'. However, in a significant regard the final volume, like its predecessors, realises the strange and diverse elements that O'Casey claimed for the work from the very beginning. In a letter of 4 May 1937 to George Jean Nathan he wrote that the Dream School episode (subsequently included in the first volume) was 'autobiographical and unconventional', adding the prophecy, 'My autobiography'll be a curious thing, if I ever get to the end of it'. It is difficult to dispute that in this respect, if no other, each book in the narrative sequence lives up to the author's expectation. As for its end, it could be argued that *Sunset and Evening Star* was not his final piece of autobiographical writing. Three contributions to *Under a Coloured Cap*, published in 1961 – 'Under a Coloured Cap, Part One' ('An Army with Banners'), 'Under a Coloured Cap, Part Two', and 'Under a Greenwood Tree He Died' – depict events at both the beginning and the end of O'Casey's long and fascinatingly recreated life.

NOTES

1. Meredith Cary, 'George Moore's Roman Expérimental', *Eire-Ireland*, IX, 4 (Winter 1974) p. 150.
2. *Design and Truth in Autobiography* (London: Routledge & Kegan Paul, 1960) p. 165
3. See my introduction to *Sean O'Casey: Modern Judgements* (London: Macmillan, 1969), pp. 33–41 and 'The Autobiographies of Sean O'Casey', *Research Studies*, XXXVII, 2 (June 1969) pp. 122–9.
4. Readers of *Sean O'Casey: A Bibliography* (London: Macmillan, 1978) will be well aware of my indebtedness in the present essay to the splendid bibliographical work of Michael J. Durkan.
5. S. McCann (ed.), *The World of Sean O'Casey* (London: Foursquare Books, 1966) p. 28.
6. *Design and Truth in Autobiography*, p. 153.
7. *The World of Sean O'Casey*, p. 29.
8. 'Sidelighting on Some Pictures' (not O'Casey's title), *New York Times*, 16 September 1956. The article was written as an introduction to the 1956 New York production of an adaptation of one of the early autobiographical volumes.
9. G. W. Bishop, 'Sean O'Casey, Poet-Playwright,' *Theatre Guild Magazine* (February 1930) p. 55. Information kindly supplied by Robert Lowery.
10. Extract from the MS exercise book now in the New York Public Library (Berg Collection), quoted by kind permission of Eileen O'Casey and of the Berg's curator, Mrs L. Szladits.
11. Although O'Casey seems to have abandoned the use of a first-person narrator early in the 1930s, he did write a long autobiographical essay in the first person, 'I Come to Coole', in 1942. It was published in this format as 'The Lady of Coole' in *The Saturday Book* 1943 (London: Hutchinson, 1942). Much of it, changed into a third-person narrative, was reprinted in *Inishfallen, Fare Thee Well* in 1949.
12. Letter from W. B. Yeats to Sean O'Casey dated 20 April 1928: my italics.
13. If one had no further evidence for O'Casey's authorship of this blurb for the book's dust jacket one would claim it from the phrase describing W. B. Yeats – the poet 'always trailing a silvery shadow behind him'; a similar description was used by O'Casey for the poet in a radio

tribute he broadcast in 1946 (first published under his title, 'Ireland's Silvery Shadow', in *Blasts and Benedictions* in 1967).
14. *Inishfallen* (London: Macmillan, 1949) p. 287.
15. *Design and Truth in Autobiography*, p. 151.
16. 'The Rich Tapestry of Life', *Book Find News*, no. 79 (1949) p. 4.

2 Dublin in the Age of O'Casey: 1880–1910

DEIRDRE HENCHY

Dublin, in O'Casey's early years, was a city of many contrasts: 'Partly of a colony, partly of a nation',[1] it was a city of conflicting traditions. Outwardly it looked east – politically to Westminister and socially to Buckingham Palace. This was the Dublin of the Anglo-Irish gentry, of the Castle Catholics and a rising and ambitious class. At the heart of imperial Dublin lay Dublin Castle, its administrative centre, while Trinity College and the Kildare Street Club formed its educational and social pillars. Leadership lay in the hands of the Protestant gentry, who were determined it should stay there. According to L. A. G. Strong, this influence was maintained by

> a class numerically and spiritually narrow, a tiny blackcoated incubus, a ruling caste: the Protestant well-to-do, in whose hands was vested all influence, all authority, all patronage: a class so deeply, so instinctively prejudiced that Grandpapa, the most charitable of men, who would pick up a worm from the path for fear it should be trodden, cried out indignantly if a strange Catholic approached his door. Yet his cook, his gardener, all his servants were Catholics. He treated them with the utmost consideration and kindness, and they bore him no ill-will for his opinions, which they found as much a fact as the facts of wealth and poverty, birth and humble living.[2]

There was also the hidden Dublin, not immediately visible to the visitor: the sordid slum conditions of Dublin's back streets and ghetto ateas, where almost one-third of its population lived in conditions of grinding poverty, far removed from the prosperity of the distant suburbs of Rathmines or Ballsbridge. Dublin's slum problem stemmed not from the worst effects of the Industrial Revolution as in comparable English cities, but primarily from Dublin's lack of industrialisation. For despite its traditional status as second city of the Empire, Dublin had, since the Union in 1800, declined in manufacturing and productive power. Chiefly an administrative and commercial city, its main source of employment lay in the restricted spheres of clerical work and unskilled labour. The ranks of the unemployed were continuously enlarged by the illiterate poor, the unskilled, those in seasonal or casual labour, and by the influx of rural migrants. Rural migration was a marked feature of this period and, while largely composed of those who, if not of the middle class, had middle-class aspirations, served to aggravate the already serious conditions in the city's working-class areas. By the turn of the century, a militant working-class movement had developed in Dublin, forged under the influence of outstanding leaders like James Connolly and James Larkin. The anger of the 'risen people' was to heighten the underlying policital tensions and shatter the complacency of Victorian and Edwardian Dublin.

Politically, the years after the death of Parnell form a vacuum between the passing of one Home Rule Bill (1893) and the next (1914). The disruption of the Irish Parliamentary Party, coupled with the failure of the Bill of 1893, had a depressing effect on American supporters of Home Rule, and there was a considerable falling off in their subscriptions to party funds. The Irish at home, disillusioned by the divisions and squabbles of the Irish Members at Westminster, lost interest in politics, and the excitement and enthusiasm of Parnell's time was succeeded by apathy and even cynicism.

The greatest achievement of the period was a cultural renaissance and a revival of intellectual activity. In many respects, Dublin assumed the role of capital of the emerging Irish nation and became its chief intellectual centre. The hitherto rural bias of nationalist politics during the lifetime of Parnell had isolated Dublin from the mainstream of popular politics. With the decline of the Land League, and as Home Rule appeared to approach its realisation around the early 1890s, Dublin regained its national importance. The intellectual fervour provided by Sinn Féin, the cultural nationalism promoted by the Gaelic League, the local patriotism inculcated by the Gaelic Athletic Association, the subversive spirit of the secret Irish Republican Brotherhood, together with the discontent of the working class, combined to make these years formative not only for the emerging Irish nation, but also for the young O'Casey.

O'Casey's view of his native city as it emerges from the autobiographies is, of necessity, subjective and, while it is of undoubted historical value, it is important to understand O'Casey's early years and subsequent political development, which colour his perspective. The picture of Dublin O'Casey paints is a complex one and not easily categorised. Born in 1880 into a lower-middle-class family on Dorset Street, O'Casey, as a child, knew deprivation, but not, as he infers, or as later historians have assumed, utter poverty. He had, by the standards of the time, known relative comfort. The house on Dorset Street contained that hallmark of respectability 'the little parlour, kept perpetually swept and garnished for visitors that demanded some ceremony, and were entitled to see all the best that the family had'.[3] His sister Bella was a qualified primary school teacher and his brothers Mick and Tom held much-coveted positions in the Post Office as clerk and as sorter, proudly wearing 'their trim little bowler hats, the badge of all their tribe; [and] nicely-cut ready-to-wear suits'.[4] In retrospect, O'Casey overemphasises his working-class roots, for, in reality, the family ethic, despite vicissitudes after the death of the father, was firmly middle class. Mr Casey died at the age of forty-nine, leaving little savings. His children, however, were of working age, with the exception of Sean, who was the last born. In the years that followed, the family's fortunes waxed and waned as Sean's brothers and sister left home, either to marry or enter the army. The Caseys occupied a series of rented accommodations, of varying standards but all adequate and well kept.[5] Mrs Casey was ambitious for her children. It was particularly feared that Sean, lacking formal education due to poor eyesight, might become 'a common labourer . . . when the time comes for him to take his place in life'.[6] Ironically, in 1903, Sean chose to work as an unskilled labourer on the railway instead of as a shop clerk and made the first important break with his family background.

While O'Casey's social background cannot be said to readily suggest the slums of working-class Dublin, still less does it reflect Protestant Unionist Dublin. O'Casey's attitude was, from his earliest years, one of confusion in the face of the traditional allegiance of most of the members of his religion to the British connection. Within his own family, he had the example of his brother Archie, who worked on the Unionist *Daily Express* and was unequivocally anti-Parnell, while Tom and Mick joined the British Army. The British soldiers were traditionally the most colourful target of abuse to the nationalists of Dublin and stood as the hated figures of the English presence in Ireland. According to O'Casey, the soldiers were even confined to barracks during Parnell's appearances, for fear of provocation to his followers in Dublin.[7] O'Casey's uncle, in addition, had proudly fought in the Crimean war and was a member of the Dublin Orange Order.[8] Yet O'Casey was to find that he had more in common politically with his Catholic counterparts than with the aspirations of the gentry. The first two volumes of the autobiographies trace the rejection of his inherited loyalties in favour of Gaelic nationalism and, in turn, of socialism. To fully understand these developments one must examine the wider background of the Dublin beyond Dorset Street.

Dublin's population, expanding rapidly during this period, intensified the existing social problems of poverty, unemployment, poor housing conditions and a high mortality rate. Despite a rise in real wages from the 1880s to the early twentieth century, the living standards of the unskilled labourer remained at a consistently low level. By as late as 1914, 34 per cent of the population of Dublin was living below the poverty level.[9] A survey conducted in 1910[10] found that food and rent alone accounted for 78 per cent of the average working-class family's income, leaving little for clothing, fuel or other necessities of life, and only a fraction for savings. The more immediate causes of hardship were the unexpected unemployment of the head of the family (witness the effect on the family's fortunes of Mr Casey's injury); the death of the chief wage earner (as in the case of Ella's husband); and the irregularity of unemployment, (which for the young O'Casey meant eggs and meat in days of employment and bread and tea otherwise.) A third of the city was living in only 5000 tenement houses, 78 per cent of which were one-roomed dwellings, some declared unfit for human habitation. One observer noted:

> These conditions have existed for a century and a half. Generation after generation were born under these, grew up under these; they were governed and controlled by them mentally; the masses never conquered these conditions, nor rose above them, and the one fact borne in upon them is that they are largely impervious to their surroundings, and when pinched or hurt their trust in God for a better tomorrow is supreme. Nowhere did I find a revolt against the housing conditions; on the contrary, I found expressions of fear that anything was going to be done which would limit the tenements by the destruction of houses, and that they would be rendered houseless.[11]

James Connolly indicated that 'the number of deaths in Dublin is highest in the first three months — January, February and March — the winter months when the severity of the season makes its worst ravages amongst the poor, too enfeebled by hunger and cold to withstand its shocks'.[12] By 1914, the city's death rate was the fifth highest in the world.[13] The chief causes of mortality were listed as follows by the Chief Medical Officer, Charles Cameron: the unfavourable conditions of the poorer classes; the tenement house system and overcrowding; the prevalence of tuberculosis; the want of nourishment and excess of drink; the neglect of personal cleanliness and pure air (a particularly Victorian fetish); the exposure of ill-clad and very young children to bad weather; and the improper and insufficient feeding of infants. It is characteristic of the period that Cameron's voice, as CMO, should be the loudest and most consistent in expressing concern for the poor of the city. The tenement conditions, mortality rate and wider social problems were examined purely as sanitary and housing problems with little reference to their underlying economic causes. Indeed, to the popular English mind, as typified in *Punch* for example, the poverty of the Irish sprang from their innate laziness, addiction to drink and low expectations. The necessary long-term and widespread solutions called for progressive social and economic measures, most notably in the form of guaranteed wage levels, greater taxation, and government subsidies on housing. Such a degree of government interference was, however, anathema to the Victorian ethos of *laissez-faire*, and the slums of Dublin were casualties of both the age and the particular circumstances of the city.

By contrast, Belfast's export, textile and ship-building industries were expanding rapidly to meet the near-by English market to become, by the end of the nineteenth century, the major port and industrial capital of Ireland. Competitive rates of pay, supplemented by the womens' earnings in the mills, resulted in a better standard of living for the Belfast worker. Speculative builders were attracted to erect solid working-class dwellings at competitive rates. In Dublin, though, housing standards, given the existing wage level, were particularly bad. The landlord, often a butcher, greengrocer, or money-lending gombeen man, existed in many cases at a level not far above that of his tenants.

In true Victorian fashion, however, charitable bodies attempted to redress the evils of the system. Most successful among the house-building charities was the Artisan Dwelling Corporation, founded in 1876 by some members of the Dublin Sanitary Association. Almost twenty sites had been cleared and reconstructed by the turn of the century, three in co-operation with Dublin Corporation. Unfortunately, the Dwelling Corporation failed to help the lowest levels of the poor. Building cottages in the 1880s for a rent of 4s. 6d. per week when the average labourer's wage was 12s. per week, the schemes could only help the more skilled tradesmen. At the same time, the housing crisis was further aggravated by the necessary displacement of the lower working class from the cleared areas to the already overcrowded tenements. Significant developments were made in 1890, however, with the foundation of the Iveagh Trust, which not only supplied accommodation for the very poor, but also provided hot water without cost in the Iveagh Baths in order to improve sanitary conditions.

Dublin Corporation was unable to subsidise housing by levy until the twentieth century. It could only borrow from the Exchequer at a reduced rate of interest and was therefore forced to make a profit on its housebuilding operations. In the auto-biographies O'Casey is highly critical of the Corporation. He presents it as a politically corrupt body, socially unrepresentative of the city's interests, and its members as the willing perpetrators of a ruthless economic system. Dominated largely by nationalists who used it as a political platform, the Corporation concerned itself, at the expense of local services, with the disestablishment of the Church of Ireland, the Land Question, Home Rule and the Parnellite split and other problems beyond its scope. Such mis-guided enthusiasm may, perhaps, be forgiven in the cause of patri-otism. Self-interest by the nationalists, who dominated the Corp-oration, revealed itself increasingly, however, in political jobbery, gerrymandering and political bribery. On local issues, corruption was most evident. Criticism, coming initially from the more spurious Unionist organs, such as the *Irish Times,* or from Con-servative politicians, gained ground and, by the turn of the cen-tury, the nationalistic weekly newspaper, *The Leader,* was one of the Corporation's most vociferous attackers. In 1910, for example, one-third of Dublin Corporation was composed of pub-licans. 'Is it any wonder that the question of housing of the working classes is not tackled vigorously,' proclaimed the edi-torial of 28 September 1901, 'when so many of the members of the Corporation are interested in the drinking of the working classes?' Equally disquieting was the fact that, by 1914, one-fifth of the Corporation members were tenement owners, three of them substantial landowners. Not surprisingly perhaps, the Corp-oration turned a blind eye to infringements of the housing and sanitation acts and showed remarkable lack of reforming zeal in bringing about much-needed reforms.

While the statistics yield a depressing picture of life for the Dublin poor, O'Casey's autobiographies show the courage and community spirit of Dubliners in coping with their harsh environ-

ment. Neighbours depended on one another during bouts of unemployment, times of financial hardship and the ever-recurring
periods of illness or death. Unfortunately, this virtue could be
counter-productive. One contemporaty noted:

> What makes it easier to live at a low level, and harder to climb
> to a higher one, is the tenement house system with the com-
> munistic way of life . . . It would be very inhuman not to
> admire the virtues these poor people display; but every virtue
> has its seamy side. The patient and cheerful endurance of
> poverty merges into apathy and even laziness; the easy and
> generous man who helps a friend in need is equally ready to
> rely on him in turn; to improve one's position and become
> really independent would be a kind of treachery to the small
> community.[14]

While life in the slums was stagnant, the pace of social change
in the world outside was accelerating. The main thoroughfares
and chief suburbs were among the first areas in Dublin to be lit
by electricity at the turn of the century. The first municipal
supply came in 1892 from a station in Fleet Street, which supplied a large part of the near-by city centre, and was replaced
by the larger Pigeon House station in 1903.[15] Yet O'Casey
continued to read by simple oil lamp into the new century[16] and
watch the gaslighter illuminating the street outside his window.
While the growing number of theatres and lecture halls provided
for the leisure hours of the middle class, the ballad singer and
organ grinder still flourished in the back streets of Dublin. The
ballads were usually local and topical, lamenting the death of a
hero or satirising the arrival of a new Viceroy in Dublin. O'Casey,
a keen songwriter, reproduces typical ballads of the period in
the autobiographies. The comment of his mother 'since we
haven't anything to give him [the ballad singer], it isn't fair to
listen'[17] indicates the high entertainment value put on balladeering
during the period. The well-known ballad singer Zozimus
(Michael Moran) acquired such a widespread reputation that a
comic Dublin weekly adopted his name as its title.[18]
    With the development of the transport system and an improve-

ment in working conditions, the horizons of the more prosperous citizens of Dublin expanded. During O'Casey's boyhood the main means of transport had been the railways, hackney carriages and cabriolets, costing sixpence per mile, the simple horse, bicycles and, within Dublin, the horse-drawn tram. The trams were converted to electricity from the 1890s, but the first car did not reach Dublin until 1897 and the cost remained prohibitively high at £200–£800 until after the First World War. The penny-farthing was introduced into Ireland in 1872, and was developed into the three-wheel version a decade later. Costing between £10 to £12 in the 1890s, the bicycle did not, however, enter the mass market until the 1920s. For O'Casey's class, the factory, public house and church still remained the fixed points of a grim existence. Hours of work were long, for example. At the age of fourteen, O'Casey began his first job at 'Hymdim, Leadem & Co.' (Hampton-Leadem & Co. in Henry Street), working over twelve hours per day, six days a week, with no half days and no annual holidays. O'Casey was not to know the scenic beauty of Connemara, the health-giving spa of Lisdoonvarna nor the seaside resort of Bray, which were fast becoming the most popular holiday resorts of the period.

By the turn of the century, Dublin had become more commercially sophisticated. An examination of Thom's *Directory* reveals the range of trades and variety of shops in the city. The growing number of engravers, coopers, nailers, shoemakers and the increase in chemists' shops (or Medical Halls), confectioners, tobacconists and stationery shops indicates a modest boom in economic activity. In the poorer districts, however, trading was erratic and the living standards and purchasing power as low as that of a generation before. The pawn shop still determined the pace of trading generally by providing credit during lean periods. 'The number of articles pawned in the City of Dublin is very large from enquiries which I made some years ago,' wrote Charles Cameron. 'I ascertained that in a single year 2,866,084 tickets were issued, and the loans to which they referred amount to £547,453 or at the rate of £2.4s per head of the population. By far the larger proportion of the borrowers belonged to the working classes.'[19] When O'Casey obtained a job on the railways 'his first fortnight's pay opened the heart of the dirty little grocer, purveyor of the workers' district, so that for the first time for a year and more he and his mother fed well.'[20]

The street vendor of Dublin's back streets was a colourful feature of the day, with cries of 'Twenty a panny ripe plums, twenty a panny!' or 'Fresh cockles! Hey – missus – fresh cockles!' O'Casey faithfully describes the travelling glazier, who often carried a window-sash strapped to his back, stocked with panes of glass of various sizes. At the bottom of the sash there was a box, resembling a small window-sill, and in it he would carry his putty and knives.[21] Other tradesmen included locksmiths, with their cries of 'locks to mend!' umbrella menders, and newspaper sellers. Competition was strong among the street traders and the anti-Jewish feeling expressed in O'Casey's neighbourhood[22] stemmed from the number of Jews who became pedlars on the streets of Dublin as a result of the purges in Russia in the 1880s and again in the 1890s.[23] It was short-lived and had no political overtones.

Middle-class Dublin was not totally unaware of the backwardness of one-third of its fellow citizens. Some improvements did take place through philanthropic individuals, charitable bodies or state aid. Between 1906 and 1915 Lady Aberdeen, wife of the Viceroy, initiated some useful social work. Aware of the great neglect of the city, she founded the Women's National Health Association, which opened playgrounds in the Dublin slums, established a depot to supply milk to the city's sick children, and ran an intensive campaign against tuberculosis. The patronising and often sectarian spirit of most Victorian alms-giving can be gleaned from the notices of the charitable societies in the city. 'None are admitted but the most deserving,' proclaimed one institution, while help was offered only to 'the genuine poor', the 'deserving poor', those of 'unblemished character', or 'those who have known better days'. As a Protestant, O'Casey was in an advantageous position compared to his Catholic neighbour. It was hardly surprising that, in a city where its prominent businessmen were Protestants, the Protestant bodies were among the best endowed. The Protestant Orphan Society, for example, had been founded 'to provide education and support for the destitute orphans of mixed marriage . . . who, having had only one Protestant parent, are ineligible for the Protestant Orphan Society'. The Association for the Relief of Distressed Protestants, stressing the value of self-help, offered a no-interest loan which would save the Protestant poor 'from the contamination of the workhouse'. On a lighter note, the innocuous-sounding Dublin Country Air Association furthered sectarianism in its aim to 'provide fresh air for ailing members of the Dublin Protestant poor'. The boy O'Casey soon discovered that his religion was a passport to a better job than that offered to his Catholic counterpart: 'A letter from the new minister had got Johnny a job as van-boy in the great wholesale firm of Jason & Son'[24] and 'every worker in the front shop and every clerk, or the possible makings of a clerk, in the dispatch department, was a Protestant of one kind or another. The Catholics drove the vans, took charge of the crates, muled in the stores, did the packing and acted as messengers.'[25] Through the influence of his religion, O'Casey's brother gained admittance to the Protestant Adelaide Hospital in preference to the workhouse.[26] This Protestant sectarianism, though, had its counterpart. Catholic charitable bodies, less numerous and more often operating at a parish level, banded themselves into a strident sectarian group during the 1913 Lockout, campaigning to prevent the hungry children of Dublin being sent for safe-keeping to Protestant England.

State aid to the poor was equally patronising. The workhouses, last refuge of the destitute, were largely inhabitated by the aged, the sick and their dependants, all herded together in degrading conditions. The stigma which the workhouse carried is well conveyed by the dogged persistence of O'Casey's mother in paying 6d. each month for her son's treatment. The sum was not obligatory. St Mark's Opthalmic hospital was 'open to the poor without distinction, creed or locality . . . Each out-patient, with the exception of paupers, is expected to pay 6d. per month for medicine and attendance.' The difficulty his mother had in finding the cost of O'Casey's treatment stems not from the indifference or inflexibility of the institution, as O'Casey conveys in the autobiographies, but rather from her own understandable desire not to be classed as a pauper.

While welfare legislation developed to keep pace with the social problems of industrialisation in England, Ireland fell behind in many respects. For instance, the Royal Commission on the Poor Law of 1910 recommended the establishment of state labour exchanges, a system of insurance against unemployment, the reduction of juvenile labour by an extension of the period of education and the phasing out of the workhouse. However, noting the discrepancy between the 70 per cent urbanised area of England and Wales and the 30 per cent of Ireland, the Commission advised postponement of these measures to Ireland, at least until they had been tried in Great Britain. The Old Age Pensioners Act, though, was put into operation in Ireland from 1 January 1907 and, as in Britain, applied to those over seventy years of age, the maximum allowance being 5s. per week, which Mrs Casey received. In many cases, doubts were raised as to the exact age of the applicants, since compulsory registration of births had not been introduced in Ireland until 1864, and the necessary documentation was often lacking. The customary verification of the applicant's age by the clergy proved less reliable in Ireland, where clergymen of nationalist sympathies were often over-generous in estimating their parishioners' ages. To combat such 'clerical errors' a special sub-committee was later set up to examine the applicants' claims.

In the area of education, developments were more systematic. The National School system, progressive by contemporary English standards, was introduced in 1831. Partly as a result of demographic factors, and also as a result of the failure by the Commissioners of National School Education to resist the pressures of the religious bodies for separate schooling, this educational system became denominational as the century progressed. O'Casey attended briefly the local Model School in Marlborough Street. These schools had been established in 1834 to train teachers for National Schools, but, controlled by the Commissioners and not the local patron (usually the parish priest) as in the National Schools, were chiefly supported by Anglicans and Dissenters. While advances were undoubtably made in the provision of free primary education, nevertheless the level of illiteracy remained consistently high.[27] Overcrowding and absenteeism were among the chief causes. From the brief picture we get of O'Casey's formal education, we can gather that teaching methods were unimaginative, the syllabus restrictive and teachers often authoritarian. O'Casey's informal education came from the books he had inherited from his father or bought later for himself. He could have borrowed books from the public library, the first having opened in Dublin in 1884 at Capel Street and Thomas Street.[28] In the previous year, a general meeting of the citizens of Dublin had recommended the establishment of a special committee to report on library facilities in the city. It reported that, while Dublin possessed some valuable library collections, the facilities for reading by the general public were insufficient. The spread of public libraries was not of any advantage to O'Casey, however, for, as he points out,[29] his bad eyesight made it difficult for him to find his reading material.

Having identified O'Casey's social environment, we must now examine the various cultural and political influences of his early formative years. Though a Protestant, O'Casey did not identify with the Ascendancy and became increasingly alienated from it. Religion had long been in the popular mind the immediate distinguishing mark of political allegiance. Outside Ulster, Unionism was numerically strongest in Dublin. The close connection between religion and politics is tellingly displayed by O'Casey in the incident where the Orange group of his parish exerted pressure to secure the dismissal of their ecumenistically minded minister.[30] By the turn of the century, however, there was growing co-operation between Nationalists and Unionists in the areas of land reform, local government and the co-operative farming movement of Horace Plunkett. As the shift in power was accomplished from Ascendancy class to Catholic middle class, the Protestant groupings awakened to a new cultural identity, more in common with the native tradition. However, the Protestant and literary-minded O'Casey was not attracted to this Anglo-Irish cultural renaissance. The salons of Merrion Square, where Yeats, Lady Gregory and others celebrated the glorious past of Celtic Ireland, had little appeal for the pragmatic O'Casey. 'Rotten Dublin; lousy Dublin, what had it for anyone? What had it for him? Poverty and pain and penance. They were its three castles'[31], cried out O'Casey in dismay. Alienated from his traditional environment, O'Casey, a young man of vitality in search of a cause, was, for the next decade, to become gradually absorbed into the vigorous nationalistic movements which flourished from the 1890s.[32] Between 1896 and 1910, he was to progress from the non political Gaelic League to the militant Irish Republican Brotherhood, ultimately rejecting both in favour of the labour movement.

The first important incident which was to bring about a new awareness of Gaelic nationalism for the young O'Casey was the celebration in Dublin 'of something to do with the Majesty of Victoria, Queen of Great Britain and Ireland and Empress of India.'[33] The event resembles the later Jubilee Day celebrations of 1897 and the counter-demonstrations organised by Connolly's Irish Socialist Republican Party and by Maud Gonne, and may perhaps have been confused or merged by O'Casey to suit the chronology of the autobiographies. Maud Gonne describes in detail how, in defiance of the loyal displays mounted in Grafton Street, lantern slides were shown in a near-by window depicting eviction scenes and other features of the 'Famine Queen's' reign.[34] With the help of sympathetic corporation workmen, it was further arranged to cut the electricty supply to the Unionist shops. A procession through Dame Street featured a symbolic coffin of the British Empire led by W. B. Yeats, Maud Gonne and many of the already formed 1798 Centenary Committee to the strains of the 'Dead March'. Inevitably, under provocation from Nationalist and Unionist sides in an emotionally charged atmosphere, the rival crowds came to blows. A police charge ensued and reinforcements of mounted police from near-by Dublin Castle were called. The image of a loyal Dublin had been shattered, not least for the young O'Casey, who had first attended as a loyal spectator with his mother:

'the tram moved slowly back the way it had come . . . out of the pomp on the walls and the bloodshed in the street; out of sight of the gleaming crowns and beaming blessings, back to the dimness of Dorset Street and home.'[35]

In 1898 the long-planned commemoration of the 1798 Rising

was formally inaugurated and provided an ideal opportunity to spread the Wolfe Tone doctrine of Republican separatism throughout the country. The aim of the celebration was primarily propagandistic and not provocative. 'The preparations for it had been the really important part', noted Maud Gonne, who had otherwise been disappointed. 'It had given,' she said, 'an opportunity to bring the hope of complete independence and the means of its attainment — Wolfe Tone's means — , slumbering in the hearts of the whole Irish race, to the surface consciousness of the people.'[36] The events were orderly and aroused little loyalist reaction. The main features were a march to the Phoenix Park attended by an estimated 10–12,000 people, which included a sizeable IRB presence, and, in August, the laying of the foundation stone on the Wolfe Tone Memorial at the top of Grafton Street. Although a public organisation, the Wolfe Tone Memorial Fund Committee had been dominated by the IRB.[37] Indeed, the celebrations were carried over into 1899 with the help of IRB participation. It was at this stage that O'Casey began to take an active interest in the Republican interpretation of history.[38]

In 1899, the widespread opposition within Ireland to England's war with the Boers resulted in a greater enstrangement from his family political background by O'Casey. His brother Tom, a former member of the Dublin Fusiliers and on its reserve list, was recalled to fight in the Boer War, where he served for one year. 'Johnny and Tom had a real affection for each other', we are told, and Johnny had marched by his brother's side, taking the rifle in his hand, as Tom set off with the Fusiliers. Yet Johnny 'thought bitterly' of the 'thousands of Irishmen out there on the veldt, risking all for England; for her honour, and . . . for the gold and diamond mines of Johannesburg.'[39] Torn between loyalty to his brother and anti-British feeling, 'Johnny's whole world was divided against itself.'[40] 'Ireland had', O'Casey wrote, 'become a place of stormy argument, with Dublin as its centre. Every man, woman, and child fought battles hour by hour, either for the British or the Boers.'[41] The British government made several attempts to quell disloyalty, including the visit to Ireland of the aged Victoria in 1900.

The pro-Boer meeting which O'Casey attended as a spec-tator[42] was one of many organised by the Irish Transvaal Committee. The committee comprised a loose coalition of various national and labour bodies, organised to provide re-cruits and medical supplies to the Boers. These were the years of Griffith and Connolly. But O'Casey in the early 1900s had little in common with the labour cause.[43] Neither was he inspired by the leadership of Griffith. Speaking of Connolly and Griffith, he held that 'both were a wide way from the real Ireland, and it was not in either of them to come closer.[44] To O'Casey at this time, the true Ireland was the Irish-Ireland of the Gaelic League and, until his late twenties, he was an unequivocal Gaelic League supporter.

O'Casey was initially attracted by the emphasis on cultural nationalism by the Gaelic League. Particularly strong in the Dublin area,[45] the League had a broad appeal: 'The earliest lists of members of the League show that bishops, priests, Protestant clergymen, members of parliament, lawyers, journalists, teachers, students, civil servants, post-office workers, soldiers, policemen, tradesmen and labourers had joined.'[46] At this stage, Johnny Casey gaelicised his name and developed an interest in Gaelic literature. During his work at Eason's newsagents he came to wince at the 'sordid names of *Ally Sloper, Answers, Titbits, Pearson's Weekly, Sunday Companion, Scraps, Weekly Budget* and *Forget-me-not*.'[47] Such English journals were quite indicative of reading tastes at the time and were a product of the anglicis-ation of the Irish mind so stongly criticised by Hyde in his re-nowned lecture of 1892, 'The necessity for de-Anglicising Ire-land', in which he stated:

> It had always been very curious to me how Irish sentiment sticks in this half-way house — how it continues to apparently hate the English and at the same time to imitate them; how it continues to clamour for recognition as a distinct nation-ality, and at the same time throws away with both hands what would make it so.

The remedy, he had insisted, was to recover as much as possible from the native past of the country – its language, its manners and customs, its games, its place-names[48] and surnames. But Hyde's prinicipal point was that Irishmen should abandon English books and periodicals as their staple reading. It was suggested that instead they should be reading the works of Thomas Davis or Peadar O'Laoghaire, whose works were bestsellers of the period. The nationalistic *Leader* is notable for the campaign it launched to encourage readership of Irish illustrated journals and dailies. 'One cannot help being struck, on looking into the stationers' shops in Dublin, by the extraordinary amount of Xmas magazines in the window and on the counters which help in completing our subjection to West Britonism,' wrote its editor, D. P. Moran, in the issue of December, 1900.

But O'Casey soon became disillusioned with the work of the Gaelic League, a development also found in other young idealists in Dublin at this time. The factors for this are well tabulated in *Drums under the Windows,* which details the vacillations of the Gaelic League during the Michael O'Hickey affair, the increasingly sectarian tone of its nationalism, its shortsighted avoidance of political issues and its conservative, middle-class outlook.

This third volume of O'Casey's autobiography is dedicated to Dr O'Hickey, Professor of Irish at Maynooth College from 1898 to 1909, because of the important role he played in the Irish revival movement and for his stand against the Catholic hierarchy on the issue of Irish as a compulsory subject for matriculation in the college. O'Hickey was not sparing in his criticism of those who opposed compulsory Irish, denouncing them for their 'dastard policy' and 'squalid and foolish apostasy'. Dismissed without opportunity to defend his actions, he was further denied the right to take the matter to the civil courts on the grounds that his dismissal was an act of ecclesiastical jurisdiction and therefore subject only to canon law – a dubious claim since the Maynooth trustees were a civil corporation established by Act of Parliament. The Gaelic League was reluctant to involve itself on O'Hickey's behalf in a battle with the Catholic Church and preferred to see the issue instead as one of ecclesiastical rather than national significance, and consequently beyond its scope. O'Casey, who had supported O'Hickey to the extent of contrib-

uting a substantial sum of his meagre wages to the cause of his
defence, found the Gaelic League's cowardice unforgivable.

Though the Gaelic League was led by Hyde, the son of a Protestant rector and educated at Trinity College, its predominantly
Catholic outlook became increasingly evident. O'Casey tells of
his failed efforts to open up the Irish-Ireland movement to all
Protestants:

> The damned nonsense of the League Executive, forcing a
> group of Protestant enthusiasts, Seumas Deacon, Ernest
> Blythe, George Irvine, himself, and others, to abandon their
> special efforts to get the Protestants interested in the League's
> work, because, the fools said, it was bringing in sectarianism
> into the Movement; though all it sought to do was to bring the
> League into touch with those who opposed, or were sus-
> picious of it, by sending to Protestant parishes enthusiasts of
> their own persuasion to put the objects of the Irish Ireland
> Movement plainly before the Protestant people.[49]

O'Casey's group had initially approached the Dean of St Patrick's
Cathedral to celebrate Holy Communion in Irish on St Patrick's
Day, 1906. Without the backing of the Gaelic League, the depu-
tation, composed of Protestant men of no property (O'Casey
himself had to wait outside in the garden, not being suitably
clad to appear before a dean) carried little authority. An alter-
native St Patrick's Day service in Irish was, however, arranged in
St Kevin's Church and established itself there for a number of
years. In 1912, a Communion service in Irish was celebrated in
the Cathedral itself, where, some time later, an Irish Communion
service on the first Sunday of each month was introduced. Where
previously the Irish language had been used by the Established
Church as a means of proselytism, the language had now become
an end in itself in the Protestant Church. But for O'Casey the
change had come too slowly and too reluctantly due to the
intransigence of the Gaelic League.

As the Gaelic movement became a serious threat to the parliamentary campaign for Home Rule, it inevitably became polit-
icised. It commanded the most successful public meetings, gained

widespread publicity, and Hyde's trip to the United States[50] to collect money for the Gaelic League meant in effect the loss of funds sorely needed by Redmond for the Irish Parliamentary Party fund. 'The Gaelic League', reports Sean's friend the hurler, 'is a strictly non-political organisation, and so it is the strongest political party in Ireland!'[51] The eventual division of the League into the moderate Sinn Féin wing and the extremist IRB group was consistently denied by Hyde. It was not until 1915 that a resolution was adopted adding to the stated objectives of the League a clause that it was working for a free Ireland. Only then did Hyde feel obliged to resign. His anxiety to placate all parties — typified in the St Patrick's Day banquet incident[52] — was an affront to the principles of the young idealists such as O'Casey to whom the whole tenor of the Gaelic League — hesitating, compromising, ambiguous — was temperamentally unsuitable.

The prevailing middle-class composition of the Gaelic League made O'Casey question the possibility of internal reform. Though the League was predominantly a city organisation, the values of rural Ireland were represented by the significant numbers who had migrated to Dublin. 'Who are the Gaelic Leaguers of Dublin — not Dublinmen. Who are the Sinn Feiners of Dublin — not Dublinmen. Who hurl in the Park — not Dublinmen. To answer these questions affirmatively is to answer Provincials!,' proclaimed the *Leader* of 27 July, 1907. O'Casey's muffler[53] stood as a symbol of defiance against these middle-class values throughout his membership of the Gaelic League. To O'Casey, the League was 'for the people, maybe; with the people, maybe; but not of the people.'[54]

The cultural insularity of the Gaelic League, itself an extension of its middle-class values, completed O'Casey's enstrangement process. By their protest at the image of themselves portrayed in J. M. Synge's *Playboy of the Western World*, O'Casey saw that Dublin theatre-goers smugly rejected a living national culture. He was disheartened to see the Gaelic League pass a resolution of censure on Synge, W. B. Yeats and the Abbey Theatre and join with

bawling clergy, professors and students of Cork, Dublin and

Galway colleges, thousands of sacred confraternities, wide-minded boyos of the Catholic Young Men's Association, the boys of Kilkenny and the boys of Wexford, side-car drivers and cabmen of the Anti-Taxi Association, brimming with zeal for Ireland's holy reputation.[55]

O'Casey veered to the more extreme section of the Gaelic League, favouring separatist Republicanism as opposed to Griffith's Dual Monarchy concept. There was already a significant development in this direction when, in 1900, O'Casey had noted as ineffective the public demonstrations organised by the predominantly Sinn Fein Transvaal Committee against Queen Victoria's visit to Dublin. By contrast, the underground IRB was considering planting a bomb for the occasion. But, while sympathetic already in outlook to the IRB, and a member of the Gaelic Athletic Association, which had long-standing connections with the IRB,[56] the shift stemmed chiefly from his disillusionment with Gaelic League policy. While he still remained a member of the League, he was, from 1908, when he became a member of the IRB, content to allow it to be used as a recruiting ground for the Brotherhood.[57]

O'Casey became an active member of the Teeling Circle of the IRB, and this was his chief interest until 1910. Dublin was the centre of the growing IRB network, and the *Irish Independent* offices in Middle Abbey Street its chief meeting place. Since the death of Parnell, a notable working-class element was making its impact on the IRB. This element was described by Superintendent John Mallon of the Dublin Metropolitan Police G Division (which watched possible subversive societies in the Dublin area) as 'the ragged and unwashed' inhabitants of Dublin's back streets who rallied to the rescue of every drunk the police attempted to arrest!'[58] A more balanced picture of the IRB, however, was one of a strongly middle-class organisation, almost entirely composed of practising Catholics. The condemnations of secret societies by the Hierarchy, reiterated at intervals in the Lenten pastorals or Cardinal Logue's public condemnations, seriously threatened to weaken the organisation. O'Casey describes how it was even necessary to arrange a talk by a Catholic priest on the justice of the IRB cause.[59]

The IRB did not hold O'Casey's allegiance for long, the reasons for which he enumerates in detail. First, O'Casey was unwilling to accept the hierarchical structure of the Circles and the limited channels which were offered for criticism. Second, the sectarian outlook of the IRB, and in particular of its older members, disturbed him as a Protestant and as a Republican. But the philistine approach of the organisation towards the new Ireland was, to him, the most disheartening of all: 'Apart from Pearse, Seumas Deakin and Tom Clarke, few of the others showed any liking for book, play, poem, or picture.[60] On the other hand, O'Casey praised James Larkin, the energetic and uncompromising labour leader who was making an impact on Dublin from 1908. 'He could put a loaf on a plate and a vase on the table,' said O'Casey. The combination of materialism and idealism offered by Larkinisim, in contrast to the pragmatism of the IRB, was one of the chief attractions of the labour cause for O'Casey. And, just as he had retained his links with the Gaelic League in order to recruit for the IRB, O'Casey similarly attempted, though unsuccessfully, to forge a link between the IRB and the militant labour movement for several years, until his resignation from the IRB in 1913. Such overlapping between Gaelic, Republican, and labour movements is characteristic of the period and reflects the earnest heart-searching for new values after the death of Parnell. In this O'Casey is very much a product of his age; but that he had to consciously reject his inherited social, cultural, and political background, makes O'Casey a rebel of great courage.

Larkinism to O'Casey was not only an agitation for better wages and economic change, it was also a force for social development, cultural growth and educational expansion. Centred in Dublin, the labour movement was gaining impetus by the first decade of the twentieth century and offered strong leadership. Larkin, sporadically involved in Dublin affairs from 1907, had, by December, 1908, established the Irish Transport Workers' Union for Dublin's hitherto largely unorganised unskilled workers. During 1908 alone, he successfully called strikes by the carters, canalmen and maltmen, despite the hostility of the traditional trade unionists, the background of high unemployment and threats of black-legging. By 1911, the Dublin Employers' Federation was formed. Offering to 'afford mutual protection to, and indemnity of, all employers', and, more significantly to 'promote freedom of contact between employers and employees', it was indicative of the immediate impact of Larkin's efforts, and also foreshadowed the battle between Larkin's union and the employers in the Lockout of 1913. James Connolly had returned from America in July, 1910 and, though working in Belfast, kept contact in person and through his writings with his base in Dublin. Connolly was important not only as a leader and organiser of the Dublin labour movement, but also for the significant contribution to the intellectual life of the period made by his attempted synthesis of traditional Irish nationalism and the modern creed of socialism. Connolly's maxim 'the cause of labour is the cause of Ireland: the cause of Ireland is the cause of labour. They cannot be dissevered' closely reflected O'Casey's own views, though he was later to reject the Romantic nationalism of 1916 — the 'Blood Sacrifice' of Pearse — for the personal vision of Dublin slum life and the ideal of material satisfaction and human dignity. The year 1911, therefore, saw O'Casey as a member of the IRB and of Larkin's union.

The labour movement was a principled movement, fearless of the opposition of the Church, the nationalists and the extreme conservatives. The Church's hostility was to be expected; the tone of its attacks, was, however, unusually strident. It warned the flock against the 'Satanic Socialism' of Larkin and his followers. In fact, Connolly had been baptised and married in the Catholic Church; had sent his children to Catholic schools; was to accept a Catholic priest at his execution; and refused to regard religion and socialism as incompatible systems.

The rise in Larkin's following was noted with dismay by local and national politicians. The first municipal elections held under the extended franchise of 1898 demonstrated popular support for Labour in the towns. Griffith saw his movement being threatened at this time by the loss of working-class membership to the labour cause:

The richer folk have long been un-Irish in their sympathies and outlook, but the poorer people and middle-class, until quite recently, were distinctively Irish in most things. The middle

classes are still not too far gone on the road to denationalis-
ation, at least Gaelic Leaguers, Sinn Feiners and Irish Ireland-
ers generally leaven the mass, but the people who were the
backbone of all national movements in the past, from '98 to
Parnell's day, have steadily kept out of ours, and are devoting
any energies which are left in them to improving their own
status.[61]

Griffith accepted the new trade unionism for its particularly
Irish framework, since previous unions had been affiliated with
the parent body in Great Britain, but he criticised its disruptive
effects, which threatened to compete with his own plans for
industrial revival in the new Ireland. Neither did Larkinism suit
'the middle class, the agriculturists, the house jobbers, slum landlords, and drink sellers,'[62] who advocated that no reforms should
be made until the establishment of a national legislature. The
labour movement as a result was continuously one of action and
strongly appealed to a person of O'Casey's personality.

By 1910, therefore, O'Casey had found his cause. He was
formed by the intellectually stimulating background of Dublin
in the transition years between the death of Parnell and the revival of the Home Rule movement. The era for Dublin was one
of intellectual self-questioning, cultural renaissance, and social
discontent, the culmination of which was the Easter Rising.
What happened after 1916 was a national movement, but 1916
itself was peculiarly Dublin. Its leaders were poets and thinkers,
men like Pearse and Connolly – men whom O'Casey had grown
up with in the élitist and underground movements of the city.
The later ugly realities of war and civil war between 1916 and
1922 ousted the idealists and intellectuals and inaugurated the
'republic of grocers'. The politics of survival had no room for
dreamers and romantics. Cut off from his lifeline, the intellectual atmosphere of the Dublin of his youth, O'Casey found
that there was nothing more left in Ireland for him and sought
the way of the emigrant writer in 1926.

NOTES

Throughout the notes that follow, the pagination in O'Caseys autobiographies refers to the Pan paperback edition, published London, in six volumes, 1971–3.

1. Robert Lynd, *Home Life in Ireland*, (London: 1909) p. 185. William Bulfin makes a similar observation in his *Rambles in Erinn*, (Dublin: 1917) pp. 125–7:

   > Belfast is called by its admirers the capital of Ireland, but it is far from having any solid claim to that distinction. It may be very select and call itself progressive, but it is not an Irish city . . . In Dublin you meet Ireland at every step . . . The stamp of the alien is upon much of its architecture, but undoubtedly its street statuary has something to tell of a national past. . . Dublin, not Belfast, is the capital of Ireland.

2. L. A. G. Strong, *The Garden* (London: 1931) p. 161.
3. Sean O'Casey, *I Knock at the Door,* p. 39.
4. Ibid. p. 66.
5. It is important to remember that the term tenement during O'Casey's youth carried its full legal meaning of rented accommodation and only later did it become synonymous with a slum dwelling. The Public Health Act (Ireland) of 1878, for example, defined a tenement as 'any house . . . occupied by members of more than one family, and in which the average rent charged to the occupier shall be less than 7s. per week and the lowest rent charged to anyone shall be not more than 5s. per week'. Such sums would have been largely beyond the reach of unskilled and casually employed workers of Dublin.
6. O'Casey, *I Knock at the Door,* p. 186.

7.   The soldiers are confined to barracks, went on the cab-driver; an' its just as well, for we're in no humour to be lookin' calmly on at the red coats on their backs and the crowns an' roses in their caps, noddin' misrule and persecution to the whole of us. [ibid., p. 16.]

8. Sean O'Casey, *Pictures in the Hallway,* p. 27.
9. Mary Crowley, 'A Social and Economic Survey of Dublin, 1860–1914', abstract of MA thesis in *Irish Economic and Social History*, vol. 1 (Belfast: 1974). This is illustrated in the case of an average family quoted by Charles Cameron, Chief Medical Officer, as one of the 'many thousands of families who have weekly incomes not exceeding 15s.':

   > The family resides in Dame Court. His occupation is that of tailor, but he can only earn 10s. a week. His rent is 2s.6d., which leaves

7s.6d. for food, fuel, light, clothes, bedding etc. Their breakfast consists of dry bread and tea. They have only another meal, dinner and supper combined: it consists of dry bread and tea and herrings, occasionally porridge" [Sir Charles Alexander Cameron, *Reminiscences of Sir Charles A. Cameron, C.B.,* London and Dublin: 1913, p. 168].

10. *Royal Commission on the Poor Laws and Relief of Distress, Parliamentary Papers* (London: HMSO, 1910) L,Cmnd 5070.
11. Testimony of Mr John Cooke, honorary treasurer of the National Society for the Prevention of Cruelty to Children, 24 November, 1913, before the Departmental Committee to Enquire into the Housing Conditions of the Working Classes of Dublin.
12. Proinsias MacAonghusa and Liam Ó Réagáin, *The Best of Connolly* (Cork: 1967) p. 128.
13. Crowley, op. cit., p. 65.
14. Philip Hanson, 'Unemployment, III. Ireland: Belfast and Dublin', *New Ireland Review,* vol. 33 (March–August 1910) pp. 4-5.
15. The emphasis on street lighting was to continue until the First World War. In 1904, there were only 650 private consumers. For these and other social features see Deirdre Henchy, 'Dublin Eighty Years Ago', *Dublin Historical Record,* vol. 26, no. 1 (December, 1972) p. 20.
16. O'Casey, *Pictures in the Hallway,* p. 184.
17. O'Casey, *I Knock at the Door,* p. 171.
18. *Zozimus* was first published in 1870, and a new series reappeared in 1871-2. No copies were published after that.
19. Cameron, op. cit., p. 166. Cameron explains:

> The ordinary money-lender may charge any amount of interest on his loans — sixty per cent is not uncommon; but the interest charged by the pawnbroker is limited by law to 5d. per pound per month for sums under £10. A month's interest may be charged, though the article may be redeemed within a shorter period [p. 167].

20. Sean O'Casey, *Drums under the Windows,* p. 11.
21. A similar contemporary account is given in *Dublin Historical Record,* vol. 9, no. 3, pp. 73-83, in Edgar F. Keatinge's 'Colourful, Tuneful Dublin'.
22. O'Casey, *I Knock at the Door,* London, pp. 135-40.
23. Louis Hyman, *The Jews of Ireland: From Earliest Times to the Year 1910* (Shannon: 1972) pp. 160-6.
24. O'Casey, *Pictures in the Hallway,* p. 158.
25. Ibid. p. 78.
26. Ibid. p. 149.
27. The censuses of 1881 and 1891 revealed the following facts on the

educational status of the inhabitants of the county and city of Dublin:

	1881 %	1891 %
Read and write	66.9	71.7
Read only	9.4	6.5
Illiterate	23.7	21.8

28. Maura Neylon and Monica Henchy, *Public Libraries in Ireland* (Dublin:, 1966) p. 12.
29. O'Casey, *Drums under the Windows,* p. 81.
30. O'Casey, *Pictures in the Hallway,* pp. 193–5.
31. Ibid. p. 215.
32. The Gaelic Athletic Association and the Irish Republican Brotherhood had, of course, existed before this date, but the mounting disillusionment with Westminister-based politics after the death of Parnell gave them a new spurt of life, much-needed in the case of the ageing IRB.
33. O'Casey, *I Knock at the Door,* p. 172.
34. Maud Gonne MacBride, *A Servant of the Queen: Reminiscences* (London: 1938) Chapter XX, pp. 272–9.
35. O'Casey, *I Knock at the Door,* p. 185.
36. Gonne MacBride, op. cit., p. 280.
37. A survey of the approximate strength of secret societies prepared for the government at the end of 1898 showed that there were over 500 IRB Circles in existence, with a total membership of 25,000 plus. The possibly exaggerated count by the informants is indicative of the impact that the IRB was making at this time. For further information, see Leon O Broin, *Revolutionary Underground: The Story of the Irish Republican Brotherhood,* 1858–1924 (Dublin: 1976) p. 92.
38. O'Casey, *Pictures in the Hallway,* p. 212.
39. Ibid. p. 197.
40. Idem.
41. Ibid. p. 198.
42. Ibid. pp. 198–204.
43. O'Casey, *Drums under the Windows,* p. 16.
44. Ibid. p. 22. O'Casey, however, did not reject the cause of Sinn Féin, even though he criticised its leadership. He subscribed to the *Sinn Féin* newspaper (*Drums under the Windows,* p.34) and canvassed for Sinn Féin in the municipal elections (*Drums under the Windows,* p. 28).
45. T. F. O'Rahilly, *Irish dialects past and present* (Dublin and London: 1932) p. 14, was of the opinion that this one of the weaknesses of the League from the beginning: 'it was essentially a townsmen's organis-

ation, centralised in Dublin, and never took real root in the Irish speaking or semi-Irish-speaking districts.'

46. Brian Ó Cuív, 'The Gaelic Cultural Movements and the New Nationalism', in Kevin B. Nowlan (ed.), *The Making of 1916: Studies in the History of the Rising,* (Dublin: 1969) p. 13.
47. O'Casey, *Pictures in the Hallway,* p. 175.
48. It is during this period that street names more commonly appear in both Irish and English.
49. O'Casey, *Drums under the Windows,* p. 147.
50. The excitement of this journey is conveyed by O'Casey in *Drums under the Windows,* pp. 101–15, and this chapter appropriately gives the third volume of the autobiographies its title.
51. O'Casey, *Drums under the Windows,* p. 114.
52. Ibid., pp. 156-7. O'Casey's account can be corroborated by Myles Dillon's 'Douglas Hyde', in Conor Cruise O'Brien (ed.), *The Shaping of Modern Ireland* (London: 1960) p. 56.
53. Ibid. p. 66. O'Casey also describes himself as 'mixing his tatters with the elegant array of tweed suits, high white collars, and poplin ties of civil servants, doctors, chemists, revenue officers and teachers' [*Drums under the Windows,* p. 12].
54. Ibid. p. 114.
55. Ibid. p. 118.
56. A bodyguard of GAA members had received Parnell's remains on its arrival from England on 17 October, 1891 at Westland Row station, and the procession to Glasnevin Cemetry was headed by 2000 GAA members in military formation, each man carrying a camán draped in black. The hurling and football finals of 1890 and 1891 had already been postponed due to the political preoccupations of the Association. The camán was to become an emblem not only of political but also of social significance in an age when the pastimes of hunting, cricket, golf, croquet and tennis carried undoubted upper-middle-class and Anglo-Irish connotations.
57. One notable recruit brought into the IRB from the Gaelic League by O'Casey was the seventeen-year-old Ernest Blythe, later Minister for Finance in the Irish Free State and Director of the Abbey Theatre.
58. O Broin, op. cit., p. 50.
59. O'Casey, *Drums under the Windows,* p. 146. This priest had returned from the American missions and was a member of Clann na Gael, the IRB sister organisation in America.
60. O'Casey, *Drums under the Windows,* p. 235.
61. J. Dunsmore Clarkson, *Labour and Nationalism in Ireland,* (New York: p. 277).
62. MacAonghusa and O'Reagain, op. cit., p. 16.

3 The Development of Sean O'Casey's *Weltanschauung*

ROBERT G. LOWERY

Th' whole worl's in a terrible state of chassis.
Captain Boyle in *Juno and the Paycock*

It is not the consciousness of men that determines their existence, but on the contrary their existence determines their consciousness.
Karl Marx, *Critique of Political Economy*, Preface

Work — work — work
Till the brain begins to swim!
Work — work — work
Till the eyes are heavy and dim!
Thomas Hood, *The Song of the Shirt*

To evaluate the world view of Sean O'Casey assumes at least two things: (1) that he had a world view, and (2) that it is worth evaluating. That he had such a view is given: we all have one. We all try to make sense of the world around us and ourselves in it. We probably don't call it a *Weltanschauung* (certainly O'Casey didn't), but there are few words that say and mean so much. Moreover, the word *Weltanschauung* is preferable to philosophy. A philosophy implies at least a worked-out system of dos, don'ts, laws and axioms, and O'Casey did not systemise his world in that way. To presume that O'Casey's world view is worth studying is undoubtedly subjective. At the same time few can deny his importance to Irish drama, his impact on Irish and world literature, and his international stature as a world figure.

In this essay I will examine O'Casey's world view from the perspective of the influence of labour on three areas of his thought: nationalism, religion and socialism. I will show that the development of his mature class outlook on life stemmed from a combination of influence by others and practical experiences. These influences encompassed the labour leaders of Ireland and a number of English and Irish writers. His practical experience comprised his employement as well as his acute observations of the surrounding conditions in early twentieth-century Dublin.

This essay will emphasise the 1900–12 period. I have purposefully chosen not to include the events of 1913 and 1916 for several reasons. First, that period of O'Casey's life is reasonably well-known. Few doubt that the 1913 Lockout was one of the greatest experiences in O'Casey's life, or that the Easter Rising was one of the momentous events in Irish history, *pace* O'Casey. His championing of the first event and his criticisms of the second are readily available to any interested reader.[1] Second, it is the purpose of this essay to examine the influences that led O'Casey to champion and criticise the two events rather than their influence on him. Finally, because the events were so momentous it is unfair to judge O'Casey outside their context. The political climate from 1913 to 1916 was radically different from that of the 1900–12 period, not only in Ireland but in Europe and the world.

For the purposes of this essay I will use the first three volumes of O'Casey's autobiographies, with an emphasis on *Drums under the Windows (DUTW)*,[2] and his early and later essays.

Although the years 1900–12 were far from being O'Casey's most fruitful literary period, they were his most important formative years. It was a period that saw the dramatist's initial efforts at political journalism; his first experience with the Anglo-Irish renaissance; his deepening involvement — and disillusionment — with the Irish nationalist, religious and cultural forces; and the start of his lifelong devotion to James Larkin, to George Bernard Shaw, and to socialism. From a dramatic point of view this period is extraordinarily important. In the majority of his plays there are several consistent themes that hark back to those early days: the reactionary forces of sectarian nationalism and clericalism betraying the aspirations of the people; the personal tragedies

and helplessness of the poor against the bureaucratic machinery
of the state; the demise and failure of the trade union movement
to go beyond simple economic reforms; and the touchstones of
Larkin, Shaw, Darwin, Keats, Shelley and Ruskin. Moreover,
parts of this period and immediately after are subjects for three
of O'Casey's greatest plays: *The Plough and the Stars, The Silver
Tassie* and *Red Roses for Me*, and another play, *The Star Turns
Red*, is dedicated to 'The Men and Women who fought through
the Great Dublin Lockout in Nineteen Hundred and Thirteen'.
Therefore, from a biographical and artistic perspective this period
of O'Casey's life was highly influential in the development and
maturation of his world view, and deserves more than a passing
look.

   It is instructive to review the chronological developments in
O'Casey's life during this period.[3] Despite family problems it was
a time of personal fulfilment and stability, a stability that was
to elude him for another fifteen to twenty years. O'Casey began
the decade at twenty years of age at 18 Abercorn Road, a small
house in North Dublin where he lived with his mother. O'Casey's
father, Michael, had died in 1886, leaving behind a family of six
whose fortunes markedly deteriorated after his death. O'Casey's
brothers, Tom, Michael and Archie, and his sister Ella were on
their ówn, either in the British army, or married, or working.
Sometime in 1902 or 1903 O'Casey began to work as a labourer
on the Great Northern Railway of Ireland (GNRI) and he remained there until December 1911. Somewhere around 1903
or 1904 he joined a number of organisations, mostly nationalist
and cultural: the Gaelic League, the St Laurence O'Toole Club,
the Irish Republican Brotherhood (IRB), the Irish Transport
and General Workers' Union (ITGWU) in 1911 or 1912, and the
Irish Citizen Army (ICA) in 1913. In all these organisations he
contributed to the ferments and debates of revolutionary Ireland,
and in the process became a revolutionary himself. He learned
the Irish language and gaelicised his name to Ó Cathasaigh. He
began to write stories and articles, first for the O'Toole Club
and W. P. Ryan's *The Peasant and Irish Ireland*, then later for the
Irish Worker, organ of the ITGWU. Blessed with a flair for
writing and an unaccountable talent for orderliness, he was appointed or elected to the position of secretary for no less than four

organisations: the Drumcondra branch of the Gaelic League, the St Laurence O'Toole Pipers' Band, the Wolfe Tone Memorial Committee and the Citizen Army. This position gave him access to all the organisational intricacies of a representative cross-section of Irish national, cultural and socialist politics, an advantage that contributed to his insightful criticisms of these organisations in later years. In 1911, just after a widespread railway strike, O'Casey was dismissed from his job on the GNRI for refusing to sign a form agreeing not to join Larkin's union. From this point onwards O'Casey became virtually unemployable, securing only the odd job for the next ten or twelve years.

O'Casey's attitude towards work, the creation of wealth and capital, was ambiguous. On one hand he took great pride in being able to pull his own at the hardest jobs. As a railway labourer he frequently could be found laying ties, repairing bridges, or clearing the land for new passages. He often worked six days a week 'with hack, shovel, sledgehammer, or hod'[4] and twelve hours a day. (*DUTW*, pp. 92–3, 124). He rarely missed a days work, even when injured, for there was little compensation even for job-related injuries (*DUTW*, pp. 126, 130). One is left with the impression that he prided himself on developing a rock-hard body, muscles made firm by years of sweat and toil.[5] This would have been a psychological boost for the weak-eyed O'Casey who was written off as a child by nearly everyone.

On the other hand O'Casey realised that the work process had a debilitating effect on the working class. Long hours and low pay, even when regular, barely fed families. Though O'Casey lived only with his mother (who was collecting an old age pension for part of the time) his meagre wages hardly covered the bread for the table, never mind the lily. Moreover, O'Casey and other members of his class were forced to participate in various deeds of graft and corruption inherent in the system, sometimes using inferior building materials with scant attention to safety standards (*DUTW*, p. 243). In addition, the industrial abuses of using women and children was fairly widespread, especially in the linen and textile mills in the north of Ireland; victims who

were fined for laughing, or stopping to smoothe down their hair; and the little children fined when sick, twice as much as they could earn in the same time, using the quickest speed their little hands could know [*DUTW*, p. 248].

O'Casey could relate quite easily to this, having had similar humiliations in his early teens at Easons's, 'Harmsworth's', and Hampton-Leedom.[6] To O'Casey it was simple: 'Work? Ay, work's all right; but is this work? No; it's the ripe robbery of life from the very young and the little older' (*DUTW*, p. 249).

There was, then, an alienation from the work process for O'Casey. Work was a necessary evil, a means to an end, and not a fulfilling and rewarding part of life. O'Casey was not a craftsman; he was a labourer who rarely saw the finished product of his labours. His work was not creative; it required only the intelligence to stay alive, to survive, to remain uninjured and to return the next day for more of the same. He could not identify with the aims and goals of the railway because their interests were in contradiction; he could barely afford the price of a ticket to ride over the rails and bridges he helped repair and build; and he had to find his fulfilment in life away from the place in which he spent the majority of his waking hours. His labour was a commodity, bought and sold, used and discarded like the tools of his unskilled trade, the hack, shovel, sledgehammer and hod. And because labourers were plentiful, because there was always a reserve army of industrial unemployed, the value of labour was little. They created much but reaped little.

This alienation from the work process forms an integral part of O'Casey's *Weltanschauung*. The railway work was to be his last full-time job for the rest of his life, and it left an indelible mark upon his psyche. He would use the exprerience in his plays long after the fact,[7] and would never find satisfaction at any job where he worked for others, even his own comrades.[8] It was only when he turned to writing that he realised the fruit of his labours. As a writer he became a craftsman – conceiving, creating and completing – something that eluded him as a labourer.

Some workers escaped the long dull hours of work and no play by joining the political and cultural movements in Dublin. To say they had a wide choice is an understatement, for in the

period 1880–1923 Ireland was alive with its own special excitement. In rapid succession a series of organisations, events, and
great men and women matured and coalesed to thrust Ireland's
star into the galaxy of cultural greatness, political rebellion and
a war of independence before it crashed back to earth with a
devastating civil war. One looks in vain for any comparable
period in any national life that matched those forty-odd years
for excitement, boldness and audacity. The ballad for Americans
in 1776 choked in a few years on the sour notes of slavery and
women's rights; the glory of the French Revolution was drowned
in less than a decade by the Parisian bloody streets; and the birth
of a new age of proletarian internationalism was stopped in little
more than a decade by the dirge of socialism in one country. In
Ireland, though, nearly every issue sustained itself in varying
degrees for forty years; agrarian reform, political and cultural
nationalism, socialism, feminism, trade unionism, syndicalism,
armed rebellion, and even dual monarchy to give the years an
Alice in Never-Never-Land flavour. It was of such times that
Wordsworth found that 'to be young was very heaven.'

It probably was heaven to be young at that time if one was
reasonably well-educated and had a secure, paying job with hope
for advancement. The cultural and political movements were
thriving, and it was an exciting diversion to learn the language
and literature of the ancients or plan a country's future. By and
large, though, it does not appear that the working class supported
any of these movements except the drive for trade union recognition, beginning in 1907 with the arrival of Larkin. Instead, as
O'Casey relates,

Not one of these brawny boys had ever heard of Griffith or
of Yeats. They lived their hard and boisterous life without a
wish to hear their names. A good many of them had done
seven years service in the British Army, and now served on the
Reserve, for sixpence a day wasn't to be sneezed at. What to
them were the three Gaelic candles that light up every darkness: truth, nature, and knowledge. Three pints of porter, one
after the other, would light up the world for them. If he
preached the Gaelic League to any one of them, the reply

would probably be, Aw, Irish Ireland me arse, Jack, not makin'
you an ill answer, oul' son. What would the nicely-suited,
white-collared respectable members of the refined Gaelic
League branches of Dublin do if they found themselves in the
company of these men? [*DUTW*, p. 27.]

Nevertheless, O'Casey joined the Gaelic League and the IRB.
For a few years nationalism dominated his life, but it was a
nationalism that had a deep personal meaning, for at least two
reasons. First, it was an educational experience. O'Casey seems
always to have been obsessed with consuming knowledge and
pushing his mind to the fullest, possibly as compensation for his
weak eyes and because of his family's fears that he would end
up a dunce. Second, O'Casey, like others born into that social
group called Anglo-Irish, probably had an identity crisis as a child,
and his resolution of that crisis almost determined that he
would follow nationalism's way.[9]

O'Casey's world view was more than just nationalism. To be
labelled a nationalist in early twentieth-century Dublin sometimes meant a great deal and sometimes it meant nothing. Gen-
erically an Irish nationalist was one who believed in the rights of
Irish men (and sometimes but not usually Irish women). A
nationalist could believe in Home Rule or in complete independence. There were nationalist businessmen who wanted commercial freedom from England, and there were nationalist
clergymen who wanted their own independent churches. Joe
Devlin, Arthur Griffith, John Redmond and Tim Healy were
nationalists; so were Thomas MacDonagh, Tom Clarke, Sean
MacDiarmid and Patrick Pearse.[10] The Irish Parliamentary Party
and Sinn Fein were nationalist, and so were the Irish Republican Brotherhood and the Irish Volunteers.

O'Casey's nationalism can be characterised as having two
dominant strains: republicanism and class-consciousness. Irish
republicanism is that body of political thought epitomised in the
life and works of Theobald Wolfe Tone, leader of the United
Irishmen and the 1798 Rebellion.[11] Tone's republicanism was
egalitarian, democratic and internationalist. He summarised his
creed in a succint manner:

To subvert the tyranny of our execrable Government,
To break the connection with England,
The never failing source of all our political evils,
And to assert the independence of my country –
    These were my objects.

To unite the whole people of Ireland,
To abolish the memory of all past dissensions,
And to substitute the common name of Irishman
In place of the denominations of Protestants, Catholic, and
    Dissenter –
    These were my means.[12]

Tone's view was greatly influenced by the democratic ideals of the French Revolution, and almost immediately he established fraternal and military links between his forces and the new republic. He had the vision that Ireland's rebellion would be in the tradition of the 'age of democratic revolutions', and he avoided many of the sectarian pitfalls suffered by subsequent Irish attempts at revolution.

What best distinguished Tone's nationalism from the rest, though, was his internationalism. The manifesto of June 1791 of the United Irishmen, written by Tone and others, foreshadowed the spectre that would haunt Europe decades later, calling for an international effort to shatter the last vestiges of monarchy: 'Let the nations go abreast! Let the interchange of sentiments among mankind concerning the Rights of Man be as immediate as possible!'[13] James Connolly, Ireland's foremost socialist thinker, wrote of this document: 'It would be hard to find in modern Socialist literature anything more broadly International in its scope and aims, more definitely of a class character in its methods, or more avowedly democratic in its nature than this manifesto.'[14] And O'Casey echoed him:

It was odd to Sean that Tone was thought of merely as a nationalist, out for the rights of Ireland only. All seemed to be unaware that he was also out for the rights of man, that had he won, Ireland would have stood against control by monarch and prelate; that Paine's *Rights of Man* was more to him than papal bull, encyclical, or decree; that hardships on the clergy wouldn't have made him turn a hair: a democrat away in advance of his time, and well ahead still of the right, left, and step together sons of St. Patrick [*DUTW*, pp. 340-1].

In Tone, O'Casey found more than internationalism; he also found an awareness of class. Tone was acutely aware of the vested business interests of some of his coherts, and as the impact of the French Jacobins quickened the tempo of imminent revolution in Ireland the sunshine soldiers faded away. This led to one of Tone's most famous statements: 'Our independence must be had at all hazards. If the men of property will not support us they must fall. We can support ourselves by the aid of that numerous and respectable class of the community: the men of no property.'[15]

As a man of no property O'Casey was aware of the contradictions between his world and the world of the Catholic middle class represented in the organisations he belonged to. As one experience built upon another he saw things that disturbed him. For instance, in O'Casey's view, neither the Gaelic League nor the IRB seemed to care much about recruiting Protestants, and their recruiting tactics in general left something to be desired.[16] Neither organisations was interested in establishing ties with the labour movement (241), nor did they address themselves to the daily cares of the people – food, clothing and shelter. In addition, O'Casey found that some Gaelic Leaguers were more a part of the problem than of the solution. Some were merchants and others were landlords: two groups that, in O'Casey's world, fed like leeches on the poor. Moreover, neither organisation had the fortitude to stand against the Church. As Parnell, Michael O'Hickey and W. P. Ryan were nailed to the cross O'Casey's resentment grew. Finally, both organisations, as well as Sinn Fein, were found wanting in the area of literature, supposedly one of the strong points of the period. Only a few spoke out when Cardinal Michael Logue tried to ban Yeats's play *The Countess Cathleen*.[17] On the other hand few were silent during the attack on Synge's *The Playboy of the Western World*, adding their voices to condemnations of the play.[18]

It should be understood that the class-conscious component

of O'Casey's nationalism was antithetic to the aims and goals of most of the nationalist and cultural organisations of early twentieth-century Dublin. The literature and propaganda of this period was directed towards the glorification of the overwhelmingly Catholic peasant of rural Ireland, while O'Casey's world was the working class of urban Dublin. Politically, the insurrectionist and reformist movements from 1798 had, in general, been peasant-oriented. Most of the agitation, organisation and actual fighting took place in the countryside (even though most of the leadership was from the cities), probably for the simple reasons that the cities were more tightly controlled by the British administration and because the majority of the people lived on the land or in small towns. Culturally, the renaissance focused on the 'unspoiled' land — the further west the better. The literature, drama and poetry of the period was dominated by peasant themes, and one went into the countryside to learn the Irish language and to meet the 'real' Irish people. Folklorists, dramatists and poets took Horace Greeley's advice, and a steady parade of *narodniks* marched westward.[19] By contrast Dublin and other Irish cities were for most people corrupted by bureaucracy and commercialism. Industry produced a class of thousands of poorly paid wage-slaves who were at the mercy of Catholic and Protestant merchants and landlords. For every block of Georgian elegance on Merrion Square there were ten more where families were herded together in flats like cattle.

O'Casey's disillusionment with the contemporary brand of Irish nationalism came over a period of years, and coincided with his self-doubts about the values of religion. As late as 1900 O'Casey was teaching Sunday school,[20] and he apparently had some belief in God, the soul and the hereafter. He was raised in the Church of Ireland and was more than casually interested in the world of religion. But it is difficult to determine the degree to which O'Casey was influenced by religion. For one thing, religious allusion pervades his work,[21] so one is left with the conclusion that the influence was great. On the other hand, it is quite accurate to state O'Casey had no belief in religion's dogma for over fifty years of his life.

As is well-known, O'Casey was a student of the Bible. It was probably the first major book he read. He was greatly influenced by its style, rhetoric, form and imagery, and probably admired it as much for its literary merits as for the comfort it gave others in need. It contained probably his first exposure to the concepts of justice, honour, duty and the legacy of the poor and weak. Moreover, it was the story of a people seeking salvation, a beautiful story that would touch any heart. It did not require an abnormal historial interpretation for O'Casey to identify with the liberation of the slaves from Egypt in Genesis or with the intervention by God on behalf of the oppressed and needy in Amos. In fact, Amos provided a special influence, as we shall see when we examine O'Casey's view of Larkin.

O'Casey also studied the lives of the saints and found much to both admire and condemn. Those he admired had similar characteristics: they helped the poor, gave fully of themselves in service to the people, had a sense of humour and time for a song or poem. Not surprisingly, these characteristics were also present in the clergymen to whom O'Casey was able to relate and to whom he dedicated several of his works.

The world views of Protestantism and Catholicism had something to offer O'Casey. Aside from being the religion of his parents Protestantism was the religion of protest, particularly against the excesses and indulgences of the Catholic Church.[22] It was less centralised and more individualistic, less dogmatic and more personal than Catholicism. But Catholicism offered O'Casey pageantry and mystery, scholarship and learning. There were few ceremonies more beautiful than the High Mass, and Latin offered O'Casey's inquiring mind a new world of investigation. Moreover, Catholicism had an elegance of its own, enshrined and enhanced by nearly 2000 years of worship. Both religions offered salvation to the poor ... someday, but the papal encyclical, *Rerum Novarum*, probably garnered O'Casey's enthusiasm for some time.[23]

O'Casey and religion parted when theory and practice separated. He could never stomach sanctimonious dogmatists of any faith (including atheism) and their insufferable belief in their own infallibility. Both religions had long ceased to be open to new vistas of knowledge and insight, seeking only the vista of supremacy. Both religions banned or feared what they could not understand or control: a song, a laugh, or a shout in the street. Although O'Casey was repelled by the lack of morality in organised religion, this was only part of the reason for his disillusionment. However much O'Casey's heart might have accepted the romanticism of the Bible, his inquiring mind had to go further, as he illustrates with these passages:

> The bible? How he had fondly thought it had been handed down from Heaven, straight from the hand of God! A day ago, here was all knowledge, all the fear, all the hope the world wanted. Life was fashioned so that all was ordered, stately, trim, triumphant, cut out and braided as deliciously as the sacerdotal garments of the High Priest about to enter the holy of holies, down to the last little bell and pomegrante nestling among the fringes [*DUTW*, p. 120].

> Sometimes he wished Darwin had never come into the house. He had upset everything. Everything was different from what they were before he rambled in to drag him down from the thoughts of sun-tinted clouds airily sailing the blue sky, a rug under God's feet, and forced him to take an open-eyed survey of frogs and toads splashing about in the sedgy wharfage of a pond or the speary bulrushes of a marsh. *For Sean life was to begin all over again*, if he decided to think on and who wouldn't do that? [*DUTW*, p. 119; my emphasis.]

O'Casey's criticisms of organised religion and his embracing of science should not be interpreted as an abandonment of religion *per se*. On the contrary: his moral and ethical precepts were deeply rooted in the Judaeo-Christian heritage, and he continued to test and strengthen them as life went on. He would always judge churches and the actions of their representatives by these precepts; an unusually high standard, perhaps, but one by which they professed to act, and one by which he himself preferred to be judged in his lifetime. It is unlikely that O'Casey agreed with Nietzsche's judgement that there was only one Christian and He died on the cross. To O'Casey there were many Christians, even in the church among the clergy. Christians were those who were essentially honest and who cared about the physical and mental well-being of the people. All his life O'Casey would continue to champion their God, for that was also his God, as in 'The voice of the people . . . is the voice of God when it shouts against oppression; it is the voice of ignorance when it shouts against a song' (*DUTW*, p. 187). The worship of his God was the worship of the people, and it was liberating, colourful and joyful:

> When he and his young friends came to worship God, let it be by song and dance and magic story, in gaily coloured plays, flags, ribbons, and maypoles; in the music of their own bands, trumpet, cymbal, triangle, and drum; the louder and fiercer the better. Let them adore God, not in hypocritical hymn, tiresome prayer and mind-torturing catechism, but in the fullness of skipping, a hop, step, and a lep; the rage of joy in a flying coloured ball, without a care in the world, bar their own young fears and disappointments [*DUTW*, p. 324].

For over ten years O'Casey absorbed the 'songs of an Ireland astire, aware, and eager; an Ireland forging fresh thoughts out of bygone history, and present hopes to create a glowing, passionate, and permanent chapter from which a great nation would be born' (*DUTW*, p. 9). But O'Casey had also been exposed to a multitude of world views, philosophies and personalities, and there were several important events, political figures and writers that contributed to the broadening of his world view.

John Ruskin entered his life, and though O'Casey undoubtedly rejected the philosopher/critic's views on Constable, Rembrandt, Michelangelo, and others, he shared Ruskin's embracement of Turner, his truth to nature aesthetics in landscape art, and his belief that good art was a permanent repository of natural truth. Moreover, O'Casey was influenced by Ruskin's lyrical and biblical writing style, his passionate concern for the poor, his equation of art with labour, and his opposition to a *laissez-faire* economy.[24]

While O'Casey was trying to convince one of his friends of the validity of Ruskin, another friend introduced O'Casey to George Bernard Shaw.[25] Shaw influenced O'Casey all his life, beginning, it appears, with the 'Home Rule Edition' of his play *John Bull's Other Island*, published in 1912. Except for Darwin, there is no other single work mentioned by O'Casey in all his writings which is given so much credit for changing one of his fundamental beliefs. O'Casey stated quite categorically that this play persuaded him to give up 'the Romantic cult of nationalism'.[26] Considering the years O'Casey gave to nationalism and the energy he expended working night and day for it, this must have been a remarkable event for him to experience. One of the reasons it made such an impact on him was that it presented an Ireland he knew existed rather than the Ireland the Gaelic League *Kulturkampfs* imagined existed. Shaw's Ireland

> was rather grimy, almost naked, save for the green flag around her middle. She was gray with dustiness of flour mixed with the dung of pigs, and her fair hands were horny with the hard work of turning stony ground into a state of fertility. The look on her fine face was one of unholy resignation, like one once in agony, now at ease in the thick torpor of morphia [*DUTW*, p. 255].

This coincided with half of O'Casey's Ireland:

> Now there were two Cathleen ni Houlihans running round Dublin: one, like the traditional, in green dress, shamrocks in her hair, a little brian boru harp under her oxster, chanting her share of song, For the rights and liberties common to all Irishmen; they who fight for me shall be rulers in the land; they shall be settled for ever, in good jobs shall they be, for ever, for ever; the other Cathleen coarsely dressed, hair a little tousled, caught roughly together by a pin, barefooted, sometimes with a whiff of whiskey on her breath; brave and brawny; at ease in the smell of sweat and the sound of bad language, vital, and asurge with immortality [*DUTW*, p. 337].

The preface to Shaw's play was specially written for the 1912 edition. Although some of it is nothing more than Social Darwinist, imperialist nonsense about the 'civilising' mission of advanced countries (always a Fabian, even British socialist, weakness, but an argument O'Casey would have rejected not only by the experience of Ireland but also after his reading of Prescott)[27] other parts struck a sympathetic chord with O'Casey, particularly the objective international aspect of the Catholic Church and the position of Protestants in Ireland.[28] We can also be sure that O'Casey gave more than passing thought to Shaw's summary: 'In short, then, the future is not to empires, but to federations of self-governing nations, exactly as, within these nations, the future is not to Capitalist Oligarchies, but to Collectivist organisations of free and equal citizens. In short, to Commonwealths.'[29]

One of the members of Ireland's capitalist oligarchy, William Martin Murphy, provided O'Casey with the opportunity to broaden his world view. It is generally accepted that O'Casey was fired from his job on the railway in December 1911 for refusing to sign a document promising not to join the ITGWU, founded by James Larkin in 1909. More than likely, O'Casey joined the union immediately thereafter. He was probably still a member of the Gaelic League and almost certainly a member or confidant of the IRB at this time.[30] For the next eighteen months he wrote a number of articles for the *Irish Worker* and for nationalist newspapers. Using these articles, several writers have commented on O'Casey's 'instant conversion' from nationalism to socialism,[31] ignoring his gradual growth, his always-present class-consciousness, and the changing conditions that accelerated his development.

There was no apparent contradiction in belonging to the IRB, the Gaelic League and the union, though, as I've tried to show, during this time O'Casey's nationalist star was descending while his socialist star was ascending. For O'Casey, joining the union was one of the most radical steps he could have taken; more radical than belonging to the IRB, to the Socialist Party of Ireland (SPI), or to the Irish Labour Party, for the following reasons. The union openly espoused a revolutionary socialist, syndicalist and nationalist ideology, believing that a general strike by the working class would establish a commonwealth of unions that would govern the country with 'One Big Union'.[32] By the sheer magnetism of Larkin's personality and oratory the union was able to mass hundreds, sometimes thousands of workers within a short time, ready to take to the streets in mass demonstrations. Moreover, their target was not only British rule but the Irish bourgeoisie who gave lip-service to the literary renaissance but who also paid homage to the British monarch. By contrast the IRB was conspiratorial, secretive, underground and had only slogans as a plan for an independent Ireland. In addition, the Labour Party and the SPI were, in 1912, still calling for the re-conquest of Ireland by the ballot, and despite being avowedly working-class-oriented neither made any meaningful inroads into their own constituency. They had nothing to match Larkin's appeal.

In part, this explains some of O'Casey's apparent anti-socialist remarks which surfaced during his public dispute with 'Euchan', conducted in the columns of the *Irish Worker* in early 1912.[33] In this debate O'Casey's unique world view comes through. It is socialist and nationalist, and it is unique because it was perfectly suited to the objective conditions in a colonised country with industrialisation. It was nationalist because it was a colonised country, and it was socialist because it was an industrialised country. It is not national socialism or socialist nationalism. It was based on a socialist economy with national traditions predominating.

The dispute with 'Euchan' centred on the 'Labour Manifesto' of the Irish Labour Party, founded in 1912 by Connolly, William O'Brien and others. As summarised by 'Euchan' the manifesto called for the education of workers rather than the making of pikes, i.e., the road to power for the working class was through the electorial process and not through insurrection. This was in line with most of the social-democratic parties of Western Europe who, by and large, rejected nationalism and violence as an instru-ment of seizing power. In addition, the manifesto appeared to relegate Irish history to an inconsequential position which, 'Euchan' claimed, had no bearing on the present. The manifesto also presented a sterile, dry analysis of the economy and the epoch in which Ireland found herself, summarised by 'Euchan's' statement, 'the present is purely a commercial age'. Finally, the manifesto seemed to accept Home Rule as the culmination of Ireland's aspirations. This, said 'Euchan', would bring Ireland into commercial line with her neighbours, 'setting the stage for 'the battle of the future' which 'will be between Capital and Labour'.

O'Casey did not dispute that the future battle would be between Capital and Labour, though he did dispute everything else and quite systematically. For instance, he countered that votes by themselves meant nothing 'without the power to resist their nullification . . . It was the rifle on Bunker Hill, not the VOTES of the American representatives, that won American independence'. To the charge that this was strictly a commercial age, O'Casey's pointed to the plethora of democratic nationalist movements around the world that were seeking more than just bread for the table. To the statement that Ireland's past had little to do with the present, O'Casey replied that 'you cannot separate the Industrial History of Ireland from their National and Political records'. By its history, Ireland was as different from England as night was from day. Its relationship to England had always been one of oppressor and oppressed, and any statement that ignored that fundamental difference had 'a contempt for history'. Finally, Home Rule would never be enough, said O'Casey, for that was still a tie to England, and 'in language, industrialism or ultimate ideal, Ireland will never be linked with her'.

There is one important point to be made about O'Casey's remarks. It is absurd to view either 'Euchan' or the Labour Party as the epitome of Irish socialism. Like Irish nationalism, Irish socialism had its differences, some rather fundamental. For instance there was the 'gas and water socialism' of the Belfast municipal socialists. There were Irish socialists linked, in an inferior position, to the British socialists, following the lead of British socialist leader Harry Hyndman or the Fabians of Shaw and the Webbs. There were also Irish socialists in British-affiliated trade unions. Both 'Euchan' and the Labour Party were objectively closer in ideology to the British socialist movement and to the Irish Parliamentary Party than to the dynamism of the combined Irish socialist and nationalist movement. Despite

Connolly's persistance, there was no broad-based Irish trade union organisation until the arrival of Larkin. It became a mark of independence to assert the uniqueness of Irish conditions, and O'Casey was doing just that. This is the thrust of O'Casey's criticisms, and it is a mistake to label them anti-socialist.

Of course O'Casey's socialist ideas did not originate entirely within himself, any more than his ideas on nationalism were original. Socialist ideas were freely debated by trade unionists, nationalists, socialists and others in Dublin during that first decade of the twentieth century. Moreover, the socialist ideas, writings and pamphlets of Shaw, Ruskin, William Morris and Keir Hardie proliferated.

Of the Irish socialists, James Connolly, was probably the best known. Connolly formed in 1896 the first Irish socialist party, the Irish Socialist Republican Party, and consistently argued that Ireland must find her own road to socialism. Ireland's way was through her traditions, her history and her legacy, an argument with which O'Casey agreed.[34] Connolly even went so far as to suggest that Ireland's economy should be modelled on the ancient Gaelic clan system; a statement O'Casey adopted in his replies to 'Euchan', writing: 'The delivery of Ireland is not in the Labour Manifesto, good and salutary as it may be, but in the strength, beauty, nobility and imagination of the Gaelic ideal.' Connolly was also undoubtedly partially responsible for O'Casey's views on Wolfe Tone and on many facets of Irish history, which he would have found in Connolly's *Labour in Irish History* (1910).

Other figures who were influential in the development of O'Casey's socialist world vision were Karl Marx, Francis Sheehy-Skeffington, John Mitchel and Fintan Lalor, whom O'Casey called 'the Lenin of his day'. Both Mitchel's *Jail Journal* and Lalor's *The Rights of Ireland* were serialised in the *Irish Worker* in 1911. Neither were socialists, of course, but they were militant defenders of the Irish people during the revolutionary 1840s, repeatedly exhorting the peasantry to seize the land and prevent British attempts to export food during the famine. The influence of Lalor and Mitchel can be seen in the constitution of the Irish Citizen Army which O'Casey rewrote (*DUTW*, p. 335).

In Sheehy-Skeffington, O'Casey found a pacifist, an ardent

feminist and 'a purified sould of revolt against not only one nation's injustice against another, but . . . also the soul of revolt against man's inhumanity to man'.[35] It is evident that O'Casey was greatly influenced by Sheehy-Skeffington's dignity, his gentleness and his dedication to women's rights. He did not share Sheehy-Skeffington's pacifism, of course, but he undoubtedly respected it.[36] Later, O'Casey called him 'the first martyr to Irish socialism' among the victims of the Easter Rising.[37]

Though O'Casey mentions Marx only once in the first three autobiographical volumes, it is in a highly symbolic context. It comes at the end of the chapter, 'In this Tent, the Rebubblicans' (an allusion not only to a circus but to Lady Gregory's slight speech impediment) in *Drums under the Windows*. O'Casey uses the entire chapter to mock those who claim the title 'republican', showing them up as facile nationalists with no understanding of history or of revolution. After this parade (a favourite O'Casey prose device) of pseudo-republicans, he demonstrates quite clearly that he is marching to the beat of another drummer:

> Sean sat on a pediment of a column keeping up the facade of the [General] Post Office, reading, reading the new catechism of the *Communist Manifesto* with its great commandment of Workers of all lands, unite! And in all the shouting and tumult and the misery around, he heard the roll of new drums, the blowing of new bugles, and the sound of millions of men marching [*DUTW,* p. 366] .

There are at least three reasons why O'Casey would have responded to Marx. First, Marx's 'workers of the world, unite' encompassed Tone's internationalism and his men of no property, an ethic O'Casey greatly admired in all his favourite writers. Second, Marx was the founder of 'scientific socialism', i.e. as opposed to the utopian romantics who believed socialism would one day magically appear. It was a speculative use of science, of course, but not unlike Darwin's forays into evolution. Third, the *Communist Manifesto* was a powerful message to the O'Caseys around the world. In this little pamphlet were compacted theories of history, philosophy, ethics and revolution. It exalted man as creator of and heir to all wealth, all resources; in short, the world. Moreover, it was written in a style familiar to O'Casey. Its language and form evoked colourful imagery in much the same manner as the Bible, and O'Casey came to admire it as much for its literary merits as for its political content.[38]

Influential as these people were on O'Casey's socialist vision, none matched the influence of James Larkin. It was not so much the influence of what Larkin wrote (for he wrote little of lasting importance) as the personal contact between the two and before that Larkin's heroic deeds. But before discussing Larkin's influence on O'Casey it is necessary to offer a brief comparison between Larkin and Connolly, as O'Casey saw them. This is important because both men have come to represent socialism in Ireland, and it is essential to understand why O'Casey rejected one and embraced the other.

There is no question that O'Casey's open antagonism toward Connolly dates from the year 1914. During its later months Connolly aligned himself with Constance Markiewicz, one result of which was O'Casey's ouster from the Irish Citizen Army. Moreover, a short time later the future Irish Free State trade union leaders successfully outmanoeuvred Larkin to install Connolly as head of the ITGWU. Later, of course, O'Casey bitterly chastised Connolly for his part in the Easter Rising.

Even before all this, though, O'Casey leads us to believe that his preference was always Larkin, and that Connolly was just another mediocre leader. For instance, O'Casey introduces Larkin in *Drums* with rhetoric worthy of Christ:

The rascals, cleric and lay, outtalked thee [Parnell], hissed thee, tore at Ireland to get at thee, and God remembered for many a year, silencing their voice till He grew sorry for the work-worn people, and sent another man into their midst whose name was Larkin. Through the streets he strode, shouting into every dark and evil-smelling hallway, The great day of a change has come; Circe's swine had a better time than you have; come from your vomit; out into the sun. Larkin is calling you all! . . . he caught them by the sleeve, by the coat collar, and shouted, Come forth, and fight with the son of

Amos who has come to walk among the men and women of Ireland. Let the sick look after the sick, and let the dead bury the dead. Come ye out to fight those who maketh the ephah small and the shekel great; come out that we may smite the winter house with the summer house; till the house of ivory shall perish, and the great houses shall have an end [*DUTW*, p. 276].

By contrast, O'Casey's introduction of Connolly stresses the labour leader's physical appearance, his isolation from the main-stream of Irish life, his dubious alliance with Arthur Griffith and his matter-of-fact speaking manner, offering words that 'circled noisily over the heads of forty or fifty people hunched together to oppose the chill of the wind' [*DUTW*, p. 12].

These two portaits are only partially accurate. No one seriously doubts that Connolly was one of Ireland's greatest thinkers, least of all O'Casey, and that Larkin was one of Ireland's greatest orators. At the same time, Connolly was not a very good speaker, lacking the charisma necessary for any leader of a mass move-ment, and alone he never made any serious inroads into the Dublin working class. On the other hand, Larkin was nowhere near Connolly as a theoretician, as a historian, or as a scholar. Connolly's strength was in his writings and in his willingness to see allies among all sections of the population. Larkin's strength was in his magnetic charisma and in his polemics.

Connolly did not fit O'Casey's image as *the* man for the time. In addition to the weaknesses already cited, Connolly did not have a successful record.[39] Although he formed Ireland's first socialist party and was highly visible during the protests against Queen Victoria's Jubilee in 1897, he was forced by economic circumstances to emigrate to the United States in 1903. His ISRP rarely had more than a small group of members, and these were fewer after he left Ireland.[40] Moreover, Connolly's ideas con-tributed little to the literary and language renaissance.[41] They did not influence the founding of Sinn Fein in 1905, nor could they be found exerting influence in the multitude of cultural and nationalist organisations that flourished during that period. Connolly's record in the United States was equally undistinguished. The Irish Socialist Federation and its organ, the *Harp*, which he founded in New York, languished because of a shortage of funds and members. Connolly returned to Ireland in 1910 and became known primarily for his *Labour in Irish History* and for several pamphlets. He became the national organiser for the SPI in 1910 and was one of the founders of the Irish Labour Party in 1912, but, as I have stated, these organisations made little impact on the Dublin working class. Additionally, when he was sent to Belfast in 1911 his efforts produced only more pamphlets and articles: this in stark contrast to Larkin's successful unionisation drive in the same city in 1907. Therefore, although Connolly would more than prove his capabilities in 1916 he was still groping and fumbling up to 1912. Though he influenced O'Casey he could not inspire O'Casey. That was left to Larkin.

In O'Casey's view Larkin had two major points in his favour. First, he was non-sectarian. He had combined Protestant and Catholic workers into a militant union in 1907 in Belfast, successfully defying both the narrow Catholicism of Joe Devlin and the bigoted Protestantism of the Orange Order. This unity would have had an enormous impact on O'Casey, who had urged the nationalist organisations to extend their recruiting to Protestants. Second, Larkin was single-mindedly working-class-oriented. He had little use for the Irish bourgeoisie whose money and favours exploited the poor on one hand and promoted Irish culture in the Gaelic League on the other. Larkin had forced the Irish capitalists into forming the Employers' Federation in 1909 in Cork to combat his efforts to unionise the workers, and it would have been ludicrous to imagine Larkin tolerating bourgeois influence on the board of his union. Moreover, Larkin appeared to O'Casey to be the living embodiment of the fired-up working class, out to avenge the slums, the poverty and degradation suffered by generations of Irish men, women and children. Like O'Casey, Larkin was a product of the working class. He knew their hopes and desires and their wants and needs, and he took their private anguish and articulated it into a public anger in a style all could understand. His oratory was meant to inflame, and it did.

Larkin's loyalty to the working class was highly important to O'Casey. Before, O'Casey was a Gaelic Sisyphus, striving to merely put the working class on the agenda. With Larkin and the union, though, the working class *was* the agenda, and everything was judged by their needs. This, then, was 'Larkinism', and it is not only a tribute to him as a labour leader; it is also an indication of his power and his influence. Nobody ever put an 'ism' after Connolly's name.

Larkin also fitted into O'Casey's early poetic and messianic view of world history. In the Irish context, Larkin was a working-class St Patrick, Brian Boru and Cuchulain rolled into one. Like St Patrick, Larkin was a former slave (wage-slave, anyway) who descended on to Ireland with a twentieth-century brand of radical Christianity and militant socialism, *Das Kapital* in one hand and the Bible in the other,[42] forecasting the expulsion of foreign enemies and the doom of native exploiters. Like Brian Boru he waged war against the legatees of the Danes, and like Cuchulain he placed his hopes with those whom he and O'Casey considered the real Men of Eireann — the working class. It is not that simplistic, of course, but what is important is that Larkin was within what O'Casey considered the finest tradition of Irish history and heroes: a man who represented O'Casey's view of the essence of what it meant to be Irish.

In a broader context, Larkin represented the heroic figures of literature and revolution, and the spirit of those who wrote of such deeds. Both he and O'Casey shared a love of Morris, Ruskin, Whitman, Emerson, Thoreau and other nineteenth-century prophets.[43] Larkin was O'Casey's Prometheus and Christ the man incarnate, defying the Zeusian money-changers in their Dame Street temples. He was the spirit of the French Revolution and the Paris Commune, and represented the triumph of man over tyranny, science over superstition, and future hopes over past glories. There was quite literally no one else like him in O'Casey's life, before or after 1912, and O'Casey would have willingly played Good Deeds to this Irish Everyman.

In this essay I have tried to show that O'Casey's judgements of nationalism, socialism and religion rested on the influence of labour. From his own experiences he knew the aches and agonies of long hours and low pay, and the fears and frustrations of unemployment and dependency. At different times religion and nationalism were panaceas for his personal problems, but he always viewed them through a class prism. Both religion and nationalism were therefore intrinsically defective and incomplete because their limitations were of greater prominence than their strengths. Only in the world of socialism did theory and practice coincide; only in socialism did the wealth belong to the creators of wealth; and only in socialism did O'Casey find the recognition for his class which he felt was long overdue.

Those first thirty years set the stage for his drama. His class dominated his plays, for he could no more write of another class than he could of another country. His world of labour, of struggle, of hopes, dreams, sorrows and songs was present in all his works, in all his days.

NOTES

1. See Sean O'Casey in Robert Hogan (ed.), *Feathers from a Green Crow* (London: Macmillan, 1963) which reprints O'Casey's *The Story of the Irish Citizen Army.*

2. As an historical document *Drums* should be judged by the same criteria as all other historical documents. The fact that it is autobiographical does not place it into a special category in this regard, and the over-riding question is primarily accuracy. Though the autobiographies have been challenged on many grounds I have seen nothing to seriously challenge O'Casey's accuracy, only his incompleteness. That they are incomplete is granted. It must, however, remain a primary source for this period of O'Casey's life.

3. The most complete chronology of O'Casey's life is found at the beginning of David Krause (ed.), *The Letters of Sean O'Casey,* I, (New York and London:1975).

4. Sean O'Casey, *Drums under the Windows* (New York: Macmillan, 1946) p. 93. Page numbers for references and quotations from this volume (abbreviated to *DUTW*) will be given in brackets.

5. 'God he felt proud all right. Felt as proud as he did when he first fell in step with Shakespeare. His body was now in fine alignment with his mind . . . He often inflated his chest now, forty-four inches round normally, often felt the sturdy muscles in arm and thigh . . . [*Drums,* p. 8].'

6. See the chapters beginning from 'Comin' of Age' to 'To Him That Hath Shall be Given'; 'Work While It is not Day' and 'The Cap in the Counting House'; and 'All Heaven and Harmsworth Too' in Sean O'Casey, *Pictures in the Hallway* (New York: Macmillan, 1942).

7. The experience on the railway figures in his play, *Red Roses for Me*.

8. O'Casey worked for a while for Delia Larkin, sister of James Larkin, in the early 1920s. His job was to clean up a hall every morning in time for use that night.

9. If the Anglo-Irishman can be characterised à la Behan as 'a Protestant with a horse', O'Casey's birth status was indeed Anglo-Irish. But from the age of six, after his father died, O'Casey and his family were merely Protestants. Later O'Casey was simply a Protestant working for a living, and had no relationship to the Anglo-Irish.

   The identity crisis is in the chapter 'Royal Risidence' (*Pictures in the Hallway*). The dialogue with his Uncle Tom, while noted for its comic overtones (which it surely has), also raised crucial questions regarding the contradictions of being British, Irish and Protestant: things the young O'Casey 'wanted to know', things 'he felt he must know'.

10. The first group consists of constitutionalists; the second group were revolutionaries who signed the Proclamation of 1916.

11. O'Casey became acquainted with Tone through street songs initially (see Sean O'Casey, *I Knock at the Door*, New York: Macmillan, 1939, pp. 273–4), though later he was to read the autobiography of Tone, which was edited by Tone's son (see *Pictures*, p. 328). Tone's autobiography contains all his political writings.

12. Quoted in Proinsias MacAonghuse and Liam Reagain (eds.), *The Best of Tone,* (Cork: Mercier Press, 1972) p. 4.

13. Quoted in *Labour in Irish History* in James Connolly, *Labour in Ireland* (Dublin: At the Sign of the Three Candles, n.d.) p. 75.

14. Idem.

15. *The Best of Tone,* p. 4.

16. O'Casey's primary job in the IRB was recruitment, for which see Leon O'Broin, *Revolutionary Underground* (Dublin: Gill & Macmillan, 1976) pp. 146–9.

17. O'Casey mentions this incident several times in *DUTW*. See pp. 19, 185, 197 and 213.

18. See the chapter, 'Song of a Shift', in *DUTW*, which is a simulated Gaelic League meeting.

19. One of the more interesting books about this phenomenon is Andrew Carpenter (ed.), *Place, Personality and the Irish Writer* (Great Britain: Colin Smythe, 1977), which tries to explore the manner in which writers drew inspiration from the west of Ireland.

20. *Letters* chronology.

21. As an example (a very small example!) thirteen chapter titles in the

first two autobiographical volumes have direct religious connections.
22. See O'Casey's heightened exaggeration in 'A Protestant Kid Thinks of the Reformation' in *I Knock at the Door*.
23. A line from O'Casey's play *The Star Turns Red* (1940) is almost surely autobiographical: 'It was the Brown Priest of the poor who started all this nonsense. He got the chap to cry out for the terms of the Rerum Novarum, and now Jack [read Sean] wants the Brown Priest to cry out in terms of the Communist Manifesto' [I].
24. See *Pictures*, pp. 285, 293 and 304, a conversation found similarly in O'Casey's play *Red Roses for Me*.
25. *Drums* pp. 252–3.
26. Sean O'Casey, *Under a Colored Cap* (London and New York: Macmillan and St Martin's Press, 1964) p. 263.
27. *Drums* pp. 127–9.
28. Compare O'Casey's statement 'though the Irishman refuses to be a subject of England's, he is proud to be one to the Vatican' in *DUTW*, p. 255. with similar statements in the preface to *John Bull's Other Island*.
29. George Bernard Shaw, *John Bull's Other Island* in *Collected Plays with Prefaces*, II (New York: Dodd, Mead & Co., 1963) p. 441.
30. In *Letters* p. 697, O'Casey writes of addressing a general meeting of the IRB to gain their aid in support of the labour movement. He appears to have been liason between the two organisations.
31. See for instance Anthony Butler's attacks on O'Casey in the Dublin *Evening Herald*, 4 October and 3 December 1976, and David Krause's reply, 26 November. The entire correspondence was reprinted in *Sean O'Casey Review*, III, 2 (Spring 1977) pp. 127–43.
32. A syndicalist expression which was used very often in the labour movement in the United States, but which also found in many issues of the *Irish Worker*. James Connolly was in the United States for several years as an organiser for the IWW, a radical syndicalist group.
33. Reprinted in *Feathers from a Green Crow*, pp. 88–100.
34. In 1914, Connolly wrote: 'This question of presenting socialism so that it will appeal to the peculiar hereditary instincts and character of the people amongst whom you are operating is one of the first importance to the Socialist and Labour Movements.' See James Connolly, *Socialism and Nationalism* (Dublin:, n.d.), p. 122. Similar statements can be found in the same writer's pamphlet 'Erin's Hope – Its End and Means' (Dublin: 1968), written many years earlier.
35. *The Story of the Irish Citizen Army*, p. 236.
36. O'Casey called Sheehy-Skeffington 'the living antithesis of the Easter Insurrection: a spirit of peace enveloped in the flame and rage and hatred of the contending elements' [*ibid.*].
37. *The Story of the Irish Citizen Army*, p. 236.
38. Many of Marx's works were available in English by 1908, including

The Eighteenth Brumaire of Louis Napoleon (1898), *Capital* (five editions to 1896), *Theory of Value* (1893, 1897, 1908), *The Poverty of Philosophy* (1900), etc.

39. Emmet Larkin (no relation to James) writes: 'During his seven lean years in Ireland, Connolly not only failed to interest the Dublin workers in socialism but made even less of an impression on the Dublin trade unionists' [Emmet Larkin, *James Larkin*, London: Routledge & Kegan Paul, 1965, p. 49].

40. There were eight founding members of the ISRP, though by 1899 they had about 100 members and branches in Cork and Dublin.

41. C. Desmond Greaves, *The Life and Times of James Connolly* (London: Lawrence & Wishart, 1961) disagrees, stating that the 'socialist emissaries' of the ISRP 'influenced the Gaelic revivalists, among whom W. P. Ryan, Standish O'Grady and Douglas Hyde were paying increasing attention to property questions' [p. 187]. Of course, the property question, or land question, was central to much of nineteenth-century protest in Ireland, and can be found most profoundly in Fintan Lalor's writings: a source probably more familiar to Ryan, O'Grady and Hyde.

42. Larkin is reported to have once said:

> There is no antagonism between the Cross and socialism! A man can pray to Jesus the Carpenter, and be a better socialist for it. Rightly understood, there is no conflict between the vision of Marx and the vision of Christ. I stand by the Cross and I stand by Karl Marx. Both *Capital* and the Bible are to Holy Books [quoted in Bertram D. Wolfe, *Strange Communists I Have Known*, New York: Stein & Day, 1965, p. 55].

43. One of Larkin's most famous speeches was made during his trial in New York in 1919–20 for sedition, when he said:

> How did I get the love of comrades, only by reading Whitman? How did I get this love of humanity except by understanding men like Thoreau and Emerson and the greatest man of all next to Emerson — Mark Twain [quoted in R. M. Fox, *Jim Larkin*, New York: International Publishers, 1957, p. 144].

4 O'Casey and Pearse

RAYMOND J. PORTER

While William Butler Yeats saw the Easter Rebellion of 1916 as a 'terrible beauty,' Sean O'Casey viewed it as a 'firey-tale, a die-dream,' and a 'deadly dreama.'[1] Although the poet was shocked by the destruction and bloodshed of the Rising and troubled by the question of what distinguishes dedication from fanaticism, he saw beauty in the self-sacrifice of the Irish rebels; and he expressed both the horror and the beauty of 'Easter 1916.' Not so O'Casey in *The Plough and the Stars*. He stressed the waste and brutality of war; beauty was confined to the humane actions of two non-combatants, Fluther Good and Bessie Burgess.

As in *The Shadow of a Gunman* and *Juno and the Paycock*, O'Casey in *The Plough and the Stars* undercut the notion that it is a glorious thing to die for one's country and affirmed that people are more important than national interests. This despite the fact that he was committed to and worked for the liberation of his country from English rule and despite the fact that earlier in his life he had not opposed the use of arms to attain Irish freedom. After all, he was for a time a member of the Irish Republican Brotherhood, a secret society dedicated to attaining Irish independence and prepared to use physical force to achieve that goal. However, as he indicates in a letter to Horace Reynolds, dated February 6, 1938, O'Casey, by way of the 'preaching of Jim Larkin and the books of Bernard Shaw,' became critical of 'pure nationalism' and the 'workings of the I.R.B.'[2] As he notes in *The Story of the Irish Citizen Army* (1919), not Connolly, Pearse, or Clarke, but Francis Sheehy-Skeffington, a non-combatant, was his 'hero' of Easter week: 'He was the living antithesis of the Easter Insurrection: a spirit of peace enveloped in the flame and rage and hatred of the contending elements, absolutely free from all its terrifying madness; and yet he was the purified soul of revolt against not only one nation's injustices to another, but he was also the soul of revolt against man's inhumanity to man.'[3]

O'Casey was interested in the movement to gain political freedom for Ireland, but not if that movement excluded explicit concern for economic and social freedom for the poor, the workers. The Easter Rebellion, so far as he was concerned, had no such aims. Furthermore, its immediate effect was to worsen the condition of the Dublin poor, bringing fear, violent death and destruction to the city's streets. It is not surprising, then, that the sentiments embodied in the emotional patriotic speeches of the nameless orator in Act II of *The Plough and the Stars* are ironically exposed as 'dope.'[4]

It is common knowledge that O'Casey borrowed the words of the unamed speaker of Act II from three works of Patrick Pearse: 'The Coming Revolution,' 'Peace and the Gael,' and a graveside oration for O'Donovan Rossa.[5] This is not surprising since Pearse was the leading spokesman for the physical force movement in Ireland for some two years prior to Easter 1916, and became the commander-in-chief of the rebel forces as well as the president of the short-lived Republic's Provisional Government. His works and his message of blood-sacrifice were quite familiar to the Irish public at this time; in fact, Mrs Hanna Sheehy-Skeffington, in one of her letters to the *Irish Independent* protesting against O'Casey's *The Plough,* was able to comment that the speeches in Act II were 'spoken in almost his [Pearse's] very accents.'[6] It was tricky enough that O'Casey was prematurely debunking the 'national myth'[7] of the Easter Rising, but in the process he was ironically undercutting the very words of Pearse, a man who by his exemplary life and martyrdom for Irish freedom had been raised to the status of sainthood in the minds of Irish Catholic nationalists. Gabriel Fallon has related that O'Casey, during the rehearsal period of *The Plough,* was worried about his use of the Pearse material, anticipating objections that would be raised by the Irish audiences.[8]

O'Casey's worries were well-founded, but the story of the Abbey riots is not the concern of this essay. Rather, I would like to consider O'Casey's attitude toward Pearse. Since Pearse's words embody a vision antithetical to that of the play and its author, one would expect to find that O'Casey was an ardent antagonist of Patrick Pearse. However, a reading of the auto-biographical *Drums under the Windows* and some of the dramatist's letters reveals a far different picture. There was more to Pearse than blood-sacrifice, and O'Casey was quite aware of it.

In the more than half-a-dozen references to Pearse — some brief, others quite extended — in *Drums under the Windows,* O'Casey on more than one occasion draws attention to the man's idealism, his tendency to dream of Ireland's glories, past and future. This view of Pearse as dreamer has been presented often by other contemporary witnesses and commentators. The first instance in *Drums* is a passage in which O'Casey describes a Dublin parade and demonstration of the Irish-Ireland movement; the time seems to be about mid-way through the first decade of the century: 'Trudging along in a wide space by himself came Padruig MacPiarais, head down, dreaming a reborn glory for Ireland in every street stone his foot touched . . . .'[9] At this time Pearse's efforts for Ireland were restricted to cultural and educational matters and channeled into the Gaelic League, and his bilingual Irish-oriented St Enda's School.

Between 1903 and 1909, Pearse served as editor of the Gaelic League's weekly newspaper, *An Claidheamh Soluis (The Sword of Light)*. During his tenure, *An Claidheamh* became an interesting and informative weekly, and it did a great deal to advance the Irish cultural movement from both a practical and esthetic point of view.[10] Surveying the nationalist scene, at this time, searching for a political leader, O'Casey assessed Pearse in the following fashion:

> Then there was Patrick Pearse, unknown but to a few, sitting at a desk editing the Gaelic League's *Sword of Light;* a dreamer pulled separate ways by two attractions, for one hand held on to St. Patrick's robe, and the other stretched

out to grasp the Spear of Danger held out to him by the singing, laughing, battling boy, Cuchullain. None of these would do.[11]

Pearse did grasp that Spear of Danger a bit later, but during the first decade of the century he was in no way associated with the forces of philosophy of armed revolt. However, in the October 1913 issue of *Irish Freedom,* he made it quite clear that religion and nationalism were not pulling him 'separate ways': 'I am old-fashioned enough to be a Catholic and a Nationalist.'[12] And in 1915, when his 'From a Hermitage' columns of *Irish Freedom* were gathered together and issued as a pamphlet, Pearse added a preface in which he made quite clear what his motives had been in undertaking the series: 'I commenced the series with deliberate intention, by argument, invective, and satire, of goading those who shared my political views to commit themselves definitely to an armed movement.'[13]

By June 1913, O'Casey had somewhat revised his earlier assessment of Pearse: 'This was the man whom Sean selected as the head and front of them all . . . .'[14] And he changed his earlier opinion that Pearse was pulled separate ways by religion and nationalism:

> Pearse was the one prominent Gael among the leaders of the militant movement who fought the battle of Ireland from the midst of the Faith, well in the stream, not of Gonzaga or DeSales or Loyola, but of Columcille, Aidan, Finbarr, Enda, Kevin, Columbanus, and Brigid. Such as he couldn't be near the swashbuckling canakin clink catholicity of Chesterton . . . .[15]

As to the man's idealism, or visionary side, O'Casey, although he continued to be amused by some of its manifestations, ultimately was attracted and moved by it:

> Beside Pearse, men might listen to the jangling bells, and think them musical; might watch men bend sleek, slick

knees, and think they honoured humility; might see men fast, and still think it sensible; might drink insipid water, and taste the wine; for your austerity was ever bright, your snowy mantle of rigid conduct was ever girdled by a coloured scarf, and golden buttons closed it over you; nay, on the very head of grinning Death itself you stuck a smiling star.[16]

As far as O'Casey was concerned, Pearse was one of the few militant nationalists interested in literature and art. In *Drums under the Windows,* the dramatist praises him as a lover of things beautiful, a modern thinker, and an advanced educator.[17] He also notes that Pearse, unlike many Gaelic Leaguers, defended Synge against the outcries of Irish public opinion: 'Gaelic Leaguers firing stones through the stream — save only that queer fellow Pearse, who ventured a trenchant word or two on behalf of the playwright.'[18] This was probably a reference to Pearse's column in *Irish Freedom* for June 1913. However, it should be noted that Pearse's attitude here is a revision of earlier, less favourable comments made during the *Playboy* demonstrations of 1907.[19]

O'Casey's enthusiasm for Pearse's St Enda's School venture took the form of active support in mid-1913. When Pearse founded St Enda's he included the acting and presentation of plays as an integral part of the school's program. From its first year, 1908–9, the St Enda's dramatic group produced plays and outdoor pageants every spring term, except in 1914, when the headmaster was lecturing in the United States. These productions, some in English and some in Gaelic, invariably received favourable reviews in the Dublin press, and, according to Maire Nic Shiubhlaigh, were comparable to the work of Dublin's better acting companies.[20] O'Casey helped to promote a week-long fete, June 9–14, organised by Pearse to raise funds for the school. Under the pseudonym *Craobh na nDealg* (The Thorny Branch), he wrote a letter to the *Irish Worker* (7 June, 1913), outlining the week's program — which included a three-act adaptation of *The Defense of the Ford* from the *The Cattle Raid of Cooley* —

and strongly urging Dublin's workers to support this Irish-Ireland undertaking. The letter concludes with words addressed to Pearse himself: 'Our hopes are your hopes; your work shall be our work; we stand or fall together.'[21] He also arranged through Jim Larkin that five thousand handbills announcing the event be printed — Pearse's budget allowed for a mere hundred — and 'these Sean handed out, day after day, in the busiest streets, ignoring his hunger, his aches, his grey-minded anxiety about his legs . . . .'[22]

However, a short time later, O'Casey's enthusiasm cooled when he discovered that Pearse rode the trams during the general strike and lockout of 1913. He specifically mentioned this in a verbal battle he was waging in the correspondence columns of *The Irish Worker,* in early 1914, over the relative merits of the Irish Volunteers and the Irish Citizen Army relative to the needs of the Irish labouring class. 'Pearse is worse than all. When the workers of Dublin were waging a life and death struggle to preserve some of the 'liberties' which ought to be common to all Irishmen, this leader of democratic opinion consistently used the trams on every possible occasion, though the controller of the Dublin tramway system was the man who declared that the workers could submit or starve.'[23]

Pearse may or may not have ridden the trams, but he was not opposed or indifferent to the workers' situation or to their cause. In the October issue of *Irish Freedom,* he pointed out the poverty, hunger, and terrible housing conditions endured by a large number of Dubliners. 'I calculate that one-third of the people of Dublin are underfed; that half the children attending Irish primary schools are ill-nourished . . . Twenty thousand Dublin families live in one-room tenements . . . There are tenement rooms in Dublin in which over a dozen persons live, eat and sleep.'[24] And then asserted that regarding this situation he could not be neutral:

> My instinct is with the landless man against the lord of lands; and with the breadless man against the master of millions. I may be wrong, but I do hold it a most terrible sin that there should be landless men in this island of waste

[vast?] yet fertile valleys, and that there should be bread-less men in this city where great fortunes are made and enjoyed.[25]

Concerning Jim Larkin, whom O'Casey enthusiastically fol-lowed and supported at this time, Pearse had some reservations, but his position in *Irish Freedom* was basically one of support. 'I do not know whether the methods of Mr James Larkin are wise methods or unwise methods (unwise I think, in some respects), but this I know, that here is a most hideous wrong to be righted, and that the man who attempts honestly to right it is a good man and a brave man.'[26] And a month later, in the November issue of the same paper he attacked William Martin Murphy and his colleagues. He included 'an employer who accepts the aid of bayonets to enforce a lock-out of his workmen and accuses the workmen of national dereliction because they accept foreign alms for their starving wives and children' in a list of 'incongruities which disgust, or ought to disgust.'[27]

Since O'Casey was a regular reader — and sometimes a severe critic — of *Irish Freedom* in addition to being an occasional con-tributor to its pages, he doubtless read Pearse's comments. Many years later in *Drums under the Windows,* he referred to Pearse in relation to the Irish labour movement circa 1913:

> . . . even Patrick Pearse, wandering softly under the Hermit-age elms, thinking, maybe, of Robert Emmet, the darlin' of Erin, and his low response to the executioner's *Are you ready, sir?* of *Not yet, not yet;* even he was to lift a pensive head to the strange new shouting soon to be heard in Dublin streets, loosening the restraining hands of St Patrick and St Laurence O'Toole, holding his girdle, to say, *No private right to property is good as against the public right of the people.*[28]

These comments indicate that O'Casey saw Pearse as somewhat removed from, but coming to some awareness of, the problems of the labouring man.

The words attributed to Pearse, and approved by O'Casey, at

the end of the above quotation are a paraphrase of a passage from a pamphlet the rebel leader completed on March 31, 1916, *The Sovereign People*. During the labour dificulties of 1913, Pearse began to study the writings of James Connolly, and Connolly's influence can be seen in the ideals espoused for Ireland in this pamphlet. The Irish people — all the people, rich and poor — were to be the nation, and they, through delegates, would make and administer laws and control the material resources of the country. All property was to be 'held subject to the national sanction,' but the nation, under the obligation to give equal rights and liberties to all, would determine 'to what extent private property may be held by its members, and in what items of the nation's material reources private property shall be allowed.'[29] Of course, Pearse said, all these matters would have to be discussed; the final decision was to be made by the nation as a whole.

However, O'Casey was always a bit suspicious of middle-class sympathy for the worker's cause. Having experienced considerable hardship after his father's death, he was never confident that anyone who had not endured similar experiences could really understand and be fully committed to improving the lot of his less fortunate brethren. Class differences inevitably stirred up his anger. A good example of this involving Pearse can be found in an angry exchange of letters he carried on with Maurice Leahy in the *Irish Times* in 1938. In one of his letters, Leahy mentioned Pearse as a 'Christian representative of Ireland,' and noted that 'Pearse saw in the tear-stained, dirt-stained faces of the dumb suffering poor people the Holy Face of God.[30] I fear I could not put Mr. O'Casey in such company.'[31] O'Casey replied quickly and angrily, hitting out at the middle-class status of both Leahy and Pearse. 'Here's a double edition of smug slobbering for you. Greystones rhapsodising over Gloucester street. Did Padraic Pearse see this wonder because of, or in spite of, the tear-stained, dirt-stained disfigurement on the faces of the "dumb suffering poor people"?'[32]

Pearse, of course, was never without food, decent shelter, and employment. His father was a successful ecclesiastical sculptor, and Pearse received a university education, earning both a

bachelor's and law degree. He, himself, granted that the problems of the poor were not a part of his immediate experience.
'It is always easy for well-fed persons to take detached views of
such things . . . If I were hungry, I should probably write with a
little more passion than I am displaying. Indeed, if I were as
hungry at this moment as many equally good men of Ireland
undoubtedly are, it is probable that I should not be sitting here
wielding this pen; possibly I should be in the streets wielding a
paving-stone.'[33] However, as noted above, he refused to remain
neutral in the matter of the strike and lockout of 1913, and
spoke up for the workers while attacking the inhumanity of their
employers.

O'Casey certainly would not have accepted Pearse's analysis
of the causes of social and economic inequity in Ireland: 'Before
God, I believe that the root of the matter lies in foreign domination.'[34] Although O'Casey was all for ridding Ireland of foreign
domination, he did not believe such action would necessarily
help the workers. He even numbered the 'most prominent members of the Executive of the Volunteers' among those 'who had
done all they could to snatch from the workers the right to join
the Trades Union of their choice . . . .'[35] The Irish Citizen Army
was the organisation O'Casey committed himself to in the fall
of 1913, when both groups sprang into existence. However, a
year later he resigned his membership when his motion that the
Countess Markievicz choose between membership in the ICA or
the Volunteers was defeated by a one-vote majority of the govern-
ing board of the ICA and he was requested to render an apology
for his action.

O'Casey disagreed with both organisations in their decision to
wear uniforms and to adopt a strategy of attacking, holding and
defending fixed positions. He argued for the tactics of guerrilla
warfare. In *Drums under the Windows,* he mentions that he sent
an article on the question to the *Irish Volunteer,* but it was
never published; and that he wrote to Connolly and Pearse pro-
posing a debate, but received no reply.[36]

With or without O'Casey, the Easter Rebellion erupted on
April 24, 1916, and the uniforms and strategy that the playwright opposed were much in evidence. So were death and des-

truction. O'Casey saw the rebellion as doomed from the start, and took no part in it. As he notes in *Drums under the Windows,* 'He didn't like this sort of thing at all. As he grew in grace and wisdom, he was growing less and less of a hero . . . he wanted to die in bed surrounded by medicine bottles.'[37] This, of course, contrasts with Pearse's attitude as expressed in a letter to his mother shortly before his execution: 'This is the death I should have asked for if God had given me the choice of all deaths – to die a soldier's death for Ireland and for freedom.'[38]

Furthermore, as indicated by Juno Boyle in *Juno and the Paycock* and Nora Clitheroe in *The Plough,* O'Casey did not believe that the women of Ireland willingly sent out their loved ones to die for Ireland. In a letter to the *Irish Independent* in February 1926, O'Casey stated, 'Nora voices not only the feeling of Ireland's women, but the women of the human race. The safety of her brood is the true mark of every woman. A mother does not like her son to be killed – she doesn't like him even to get married.'[39] Hanna Sheehy-Skeffington answered this assertion a few days later: 'Nora Clitheroe is no more "typical of Irish womanhood" than her futile, snivelling husband is of Irish manhood. The women of Easter Week, as we know them, are typified rather in the mother of Padraic Pearse, that valiant woman who gave both her sons for freedom.'[40]

In Pearse's play *The Singer,* the mother of the patriot hero who sacrifices himself for Ireland says, 'I do not grudge him,'[41] and later: 'Men of this mountain, my son Mac Dara is the Singer that has quickened the dead years and all the quiet dust! Let the horsemen that sleep in Aileach rise up and follow him into the war! Weave your winding sheets, women, for there will be many a noble corpse to be waked before the new-moon.'[42] It has frequently been claimed that Pearse put much of his own mother into the mother of *The Singer,* and Mrs. Pearse did echo the above sentiments in a letter of October 28, 1919: ' . . . I have only done what every Irish mother should do willingly as I did, give their beloved ones for Ireland and for freedom.'[43]

What we clearly have here on this issue are conflicting attitudes, two opposing philosophies. A similar situation prevails in Lady Gregory's *The Gaol Gate,* in which the mother is proud that her rebel son died rather than inform, but the young man's widow wonders how the daily necessities of life will now be provided. Undoubtedly, there was no unanimity of response among the women who lost loved ones in the action of Easter Week 1916 either.

What, then, of O'Casey and Pearse? They traveled the same road for a time, though they started from different locations and ultimately reached different destinations. O'Casey, with little money and few comforts, was active during the first decade of the century in the I.R.B. and the Gaelic League, and later in the Irish Citizen Army. He was always an enthusiastic worker in the Irish-Ireland movement, but invariably became disillusioned with the leadership and policies of the various organisations he joined and supported. At some point, there was always an argument followed by resignation. O'Casey attempted to reconcile and unite the claims of nationalism and labour. As he said at the end of his *Story of the Irish Citizen Army,* 'It is from these elements that Labour must build the future state, democratising the national movement and Irishising itself.'[44] He was not to realise such a reconciliation, and lived out his days across the Irish Sea in England rather than in his native land.

Pearse, from middle-class background, started from the cultural side of the national movement, the Gaelic League, and only in the last few years of his short life became a political activist, joining the Volunteers and then the IRB late in 1913. Essentially a quiet, retiring man with superior gifts as an educator and genuine talent as a writer and critic, he became the spokesman for, and one of the leaders of, the physical force movement in Ireland. This path brought him in front of a British firing squad early in the morning of May 3, 1916.

Both O'Casey and Pearse had a great love for their native land. O'Casey recognized this, and so he threw himself wholeheartedly into Pearse's cultural activities for St Enda's and Ireland. He also recognised Pearse's sensitivity to art and literature, and his sense of fair play. Although O'Casey was at times amused by Pearse's visionary and idealistic qualities, ultimately he was attracted by this side of the man. And although he had some doubts about Pearse's attitude toward labour, he did agree with the pronouncements in *The Sovereign People.* Where the two men were diametrically opposed was in the matter of the Easter Rising and the philosophy behind it. O'Casey viewed 'those who love Ireland so well that they have none left for themselves' as 'foolish.'[45] Pearse's countering view is contained in his poem 'The Fool': 'Ye shall be foolish as I; Ye shall scatter, not save;/ Ye shall venture your all, lest ye lose what is more than all.'[46]

O'Casey could not agree with the bloody sacrifice of 1916, but he respected and admired Pearse, one of the men who planned and executed it. This respect and admiration are clearly reflected in *Drums under the Windows* when the playwright re-creates the patriot leader's final moments:

> Ah! Patrick Pearse, when over the hard, cold flags of a barrack square you took your last stroll and wandered to where the rifles pointed to your breast, you never even paused, for that was what you guessed you'd come to; you came close to them; the stupid bullets tore a way through your quiet breast, and your fall forward to death was but a bow to your enemies. Peace be with you, and with your comrades too.[47]

NOTES

1. Sean O'Casey, *Drums under the Windows,* in *Mirror in My House: The Autobiography of Sean O'Casey* (New York: Macmillan, 1956) pp. 402, 407.
2. *The Letters of Sean O'Casey, 1910–1941,* vol. I, ed. David Krause (New York: Macmillan, 1975) p. 697.
3. Sean O'Casey, *The Story of the Irish Citizen Army,* in *Feathers from the Green Crow,* ed. Robert Hogan (Columbia: University of Missouri Press, 1962) p. 236.
4. Sean O'Casey, *The Plough and the Stars, Collected Plays,* vol. I. (London: Macmillan, 1957), p. 203.
5. W. A. Armstrong, 'The Sources and Themes of The Plough and the Stars,' *Modern Drama,* IV (December, 1961) pp. 234–42. In the process of locating the speaker's words in Pearse's works, Professor Armstrong made a few factual errors which should be cleared up here. Only one of the Pearse pieces — the Rossa oration — was a speech; and it was delivered not in July, but on 1 August, 1915. 'The Coming Revo-

lution' was an article in *An Claidheamh Soluis (The Sword of Light)*, the Gaelic League's weekly newspaper; and it appeared not in 1914, but in the 8 November, 1913 issue of the paper. 'Peace and the Gael' appeared as an unsigned article in the 19 December, 1915 issue of *Spark,* a nationalist weekly. It should be noted, of course, that Pearse probably used a number of phrases from the two articles in the many speeches he delivered for the Irish cause.

6. *Letters,* I, p. 172.
7. Saros Cowasjee, *Sean O'Casey: The Man Behind the Plays* (New York: St Martin's Press, 1964) p. 82.
8. Gabriel Fallon, 'The House on the North Circular Road: Fragment from a Biography,' *Modern Drama,* IV, (December, 1961) p. 232.
9. *Drums,* p. 161.
10. For a full discussion of Pearse's editorial and journalistic work, see Raymond J. Porter, *P. H. Pearse* (New York: Twayne, 1973) pp. 36–65.
11. *Drums,* p. 238.
12. Padraic H. Pearse, *From a Hermitage, Political Writings and Speeches* (Dublin: Talbot Press, 1952) pp. 176–7. From June 1913 to February 1914, Pearse contributed this 'From a Heritage' column to the Irish Republican Brotherhood's monthly newspaper, *Irish Freedom.*
13. Ibid., p. 141.
14. *Drums,* p. 352.
15. Ibid., p. 361.
16. Ibid., p. 362.
17. Ibid., pp. 351–62.
18. Ibid., p. 213.
19. See 'The Passing of Anglo-Irish Drama,' *An Claidheamh Soluis,* 9 February, 1907, p. 7; and Porter, *P. H. Pearse,* pp. 54–6.
20. Maire Nic Shiubhlaigh, *The Splendid Years: Recollections of Maire Nic Shiubhlaigh,* as told to Edward Kenny (Dublin: James Duffy, 1955) p. 146.
21. *Letters,* I, pp. 27–8.
22. *Drums,* p. 352.
23. *Letters,* I, pp. 40–1.
24. *From a Hermitage,* pp. 177–8.
25. Ibid., p. 177.
26. Ibid., p. 179.
27. Ibid., p. 183.
28. *Drums,* p. 281.
29. Padraic H. Pearse, *The Sovereign People, Political Writings and Speeches,* pp. 339–40.
30. This is an allusion to lines spoken by Pearse's hero, MacDara, in his play *The Singer:* Padraic H. Pearse, *Plays, Stories, Poems* (Dublin: Talbot Press, 1958) pp. 34–5.
31. *Letters,* I, p. 733.

32. Ibid., p. 735.
33. *From a Hermitage*, pp. 174–5.
34. Ibid., p. 180.
35. *The Story of the Irish Citizen Army*, p. 189. See also the correspondence in the *Irish Worker* between O'Casey and James MacGowan, *Letters*, I, pp. 34–50.
36. *Drums*, p. 403.
37. Ibid., p. 417.
38. Piaras F. MacLochlainn, *Last Words: Letters and Statements of the Leaders Executed After the Rising at Easter 1916* (Dublin: Kilmainham Jail Restoration Society, 1971) p. 33.
39. *Letters*, I, p. 169.
40. Ibid., p. 173.
41. *Plays, Stories, Poems*, p. 10.
42. Ibid., p. 42.
43. 'A Mother's Letter,' *Irish Press*, 27 April, 1966, p. 12.
44. *The Story of the Irish Citizen Army*, p. 239.
45. Ibid.
46. *Plays, Stories, Poems*, p. 336.
47. *Drums*, p. 362.

5 The Raid and What Went With It[1]

MICHAEL O'MAOLÁIN
Translated by MAUREEN MURPHY

My bed was along the north wall of the room, and Sean O'Casey's bed was more or less in the middle. There was a door in the south wall. I think that there would have been about three feet between the head of Sean's bed and the centre of the room when we slept, and there would have been the same distance between his feet and the door.[2] There was a sort of small library in the corner to the right of the door with Sean's and my books settled there. I never measured the room so I am guessing, but it is not a wild guess. The way we arranged ourselves, there wasn't an inch wasted. Sean's bed was collapsible, so he was able to put it between the two windows on the east wall of the room. During the day it wasn't necessary to move my bed out of its place. It was easy to arrange the two beds. Sean usually unfolded his bed first; then all we had to do was shake out the beds and straighten the covers. We usually went to bed about eleven o'clock at night, but then we would talk for an hour or so till midnight.

We had known each other for some years before Sean moved in to room with me. We were both active in the Irish language movement; however, we weren't in the same branch of the Gaelic League.[3] We were both very involved with the 1913 labour strike and we participated in other movements as well.[4] Occasionally, as we sat in our seats by the fire in that room, I would criticise those movements, and it was our difference of opinion — especially about movements and people — that caused our disagreements. It's fair to say each of us was stubborn about his own opinion!

We were in complete agreement about Jim Larkin and his work. Only for him there wouldn't have been a labour movement at all. He organised the workers and gave them hope. Before he burst like a thunderbolt over Dublin, nobody — native or exile — took the least interest in the working man's misery.[5] Now it seems his welfare is everyone's concern. We also agreed about Charles Stewart Parnell and that the Irish people were paying dearly for rejecting him as they had done. In the course of this country's history, from the defeat of the old Irish in Wexford (1169 Strongbow's invasion) until our own time, there were only three true statesmen, men who could beat the enemy at their own game. Alas! It didn't help them. The three of them: St Lawrence O'Toole, the one man in the midst of a group of children; Hugh O'Neill, who played with the English statesmen and who would have beaten them only for the Irish themselves; Charles Stewart Parnell who shook the English Parliament and those who were in it. Parnell and Biggar stood against the English and left them speechless.[6] Before that time, with the exception of Butt and perhaps one or two others, it was little wonder that the Irish Parliament were like lap dogs, constantly on their knees, arms extended begging alms.[7] Then Parnell came and he succeeded in Ireland, but he was cut to the quick by some of them, and they finally sold and killed the only person who was able to guide them safely. Whatever was their story, they rejected him. It's a forgotten story now and it's as well forgotten. Nobody who thinks of it today is happy about it, and throwing lime in his eyes at Castlecomer[8] in County Kilkenny — the tears burst from my eyes now when I think that there were Irishmen capable of doing such harm. Thinking of Zulu's action makes me envious. There was little danger that they would have done that sort of thing to Cetawayo.[9] If there were an excuse at all to ascribe to the action at Castlecomer, it would be that powder was wet in the same village against the Wexford heroes in '98.[10]

Sean used to rise rather early in the morning. He got up earlier than I did, folded up his bed, prepared his breakfast, and then did any straightening that was necessary. Almost every morning he would sing one of Burn's songs:

O'a the airts the wind cen blaw,
I dearly loe the west,
For there the bonnie lassie lives,
The lass that I loe best:
There wild woods grow and rivers row
Wi' many a hill between,
But day and night my fancy's flight
Is ever wi' my Jean.[11]

He had a sweet, soft, singing voice that would remind you of a robin — low without being too remote, and as the little red-breasted bird has a sweetness of his own, it was so with O'Casey. I often would purposely linger in bed listening to him singing that and others of Burns's songs.

One morning he called me to get up. As I recall, the morning was very cold, so I gave him this answer:

Up in the morning's no for me,
Up in the morning early;
When a' the hills are covered wi' snow
I'm sure it's winter fairly.[12]

'Have you read Burns?' he said to me. 'Do you think,' I replied, 'that I haven't read anything?' That started the sort of discussion we used to have about books and authors.

Long before Sean came to share my hearth, I knew he had a great interest in drama. He loaned me a sort of play that he had written about the leaders of the Dublin workers and asked for my opinion. I don't think he ever attempted to have it produced.[13] He was making fun of recognisable people and I would say he wanted nothing more from it than his own enjoyment and the enjoyment of others who read it. I remember there was a good deal of poetry in that play. He read one of the poems to me in the room, but I only recall the title.

He also read me the play he wrote about the national movement and how it interfered with the labour movement that was going at the same time.[14] He cleverly described the lives of women who discovered for the first time that they had a country to be saved and who urged the men they directed. The play was called 'The Crimson in the Tri-Color'. He asked me to leave the play in at the Abbey Theatre. I left it in, but the Abbey directors did not accept it.[15]

As for me, I never took much interest in drama. I was always blustering about nationalism and I admit I was that way about singing and reciting too. I often went to plays in theatres around Dublin especially those plays dealing with nationalistic themes. I spent evenings at the Abbey but I still think there was some sort of flaw in every play that was produced in that theatre. There was something that didn't satisfy me.

The nature of the Gael is in me and I'd rather a story by the fireside anyday to fashionable foolishness of the crowd who would make more of a play than appeared on the stage. Even today I'd prefer to sit among bawneens and red petticoats[16] than in the midst of gentry feasting and merry-making.

O'Casey read every line that Shakespeare wrote not once but 100 times. We had Shakespeare and the Bible memorised and there never was a man who had a scrap of that Book memorised who wasn't fluent and well-spoken. O'Casey made a real effort to learn and to speak Irish. He didn't just wear the kilt; he was so passionate about the fashion that he tried to make a rule in the Gaelic League that every officer, secretary and organiser of the society would wear the kilt all day long. I was present when the motion came up at the Árd-Fheis.

As well as Shakespeare, O'Casey read Bernard Shaw, and often heard bits of Shaw and other 'philosophers' from his lips. He was introduced to Oscar Wilde's plays then, too. As for myself I had read some Shakespeare. For a while I had *Julius Ceasar* memorised but it — and the two of us arguing about the English man and his work — has gone from my memory. I found Shakespeare difficult reading but if I finished one of his plays, I would have it. Since I am on this tune, it's just as well to reveal another secret about books and reading. I found it difficult to start a book and keep at it until the fourth, the fifth or the seventh chapter — fifty pages or so — but then it was mine. There are people who can be so hypnotised by a book that they don't eat or sleep till they finish the last page. I still regret any

ook I failed to complete. As far as Shaw and Wilde, I saw a
ouple of Shaw's plays years before I had O'Casey as a room-
nate and I didn't find them very interesting. It was the same
vith Wilde. I prefer Wilde to Shaw, but of all his works I think
The Ballad of Reading Gaol' is the most interesting:

> With a slouch and a swing around the ring
> We had the Fools' Parade!
> We did not care: We knew we were
> The Devil's Own Brigade
> And shaven head and feet of lead
> Make a merry masquerade.

t is not necessary for a person to be confined to a prison cell to
ee old prisoners walking in their ring for these lines hit one
etween the eyes.

There were books I had read that Sean hadn't: the poetry of
homas Moore and Walter Scott — every line of the latter. I read
good share of Byron's poetry and other poems — things I under-
tand O'Casey hadn't read. He hadn't read a word of Swift and I
ad a good knowledge of that author. I had also read a lot of
over-poetry and stories, and books by Lever, Wells, Birmingham,
heehan, Dickens, Stevenson, Mark Twain, all of Kickham, part
f Griffin, Banim, Carleton and other authors besides these. As
ar as Irish history and the heroes of that history, I read the lives
f O'Curry, the Young Irelander Davis, Mitchell and O'Leary to
ame but two or three and the old stories from the past.

O'Casey looked on Yeats as a kind of idol.[17] At the time I
ad a kind of pity for Sean in the midst of Yeats and the other
entry and the tightrope he walked for the silk hats. He admitted
t himself one night while we sat together by the fire. I think he
vas thinking aloud and I don't think he liked me to know that
e had that opinion.

Life was very uncertain in Dublin at that time. Our house had
ighteen visits from the police, the British Army, the Auxies
nd the Black and Tans. The last weren't too civil. They
ornered me one night at a place where there was an ex-
losion in a house and another time they made everyone

who lived in the district stand in two lines out in the square for a couple of hours. I don't think the story has been told yet. The English soldiers weren't too bad. The soldiers didn't use abusive language and the officers were very civil. I don't think they liked their work very much.

Sean and I used to discuss the uncertainty that was every where throughout the country and how frightened O'Casey would be when he would be returning from the hall where he worked.[18] The hall was near enough to the house. Sean worked there from dawn till sunset cleaning the place and setting out chairs for evening when the crowd came in to play the game. There would be so much to pay for each game, so the hall owners made a nice penny from the work. I don't think O'Casey had any connection with the gaming. We spent many evenings, from the time Sean returned from the hall till bedtime, debating various questions and comparing opinions about people we had met and movements we had taken part in together over the years. The neighbours thought that Sean was on the run and they tried to be obliging. They were happy to do any errand no matter how often they had to go out. I don't know whether he understood it all, but that's the way it was.

I never was reconciled to the ambushes that were in Dublin. It was one thing for them to be going on in the countryside or out in the open in places where there wasn't danger to ordinary people going about their business, but it was another thing for an explosion to go off without warning in the centre of a big town like Dublin with hundreds going about here and there. I didn't approve of it at all and I don't agree with it now. If there were any honour to be found in that sort of work, it wasn't deserved.

The time passed with discussions nearly every night about books, politics and people we knew, but somehow we kept clear of the offensive — the people in the house had sharp ears — and we came up to the midnight before Good Friday, 1921.[19] Sean would have been with me about five months and the two of us were accustomed to one another. Every night I went down on my knees to say my prayers, but Sean took no notice of it. We didn't often discuss religion. I do remember that he gave high praise to Wolsey one time — that he was very good to the poor but I think he got that from Shakespeare.

I never saw a prayer book, but Sean had a history of the Reformation. The odd time he'd read the little books that I had and I would say that he had a good knowledge of Catholicism. He had some books with him when he came to the place and I had some, too. Although they may have been in the public library, owning them was more effective for the two of us.

There were two large rooms on our floor and our room behind them. In order to open the door to the yard you practically had to close our door. The Volunteers (boys on the run) had access to those rooms which belonged to a person who was as deep in the independence movement as anyone in Dublin. A reasonable, easy-going man — God have mercy on him — no one ever heard him raise his voice; however, when there was work to be done, whoever flinched, poor Fred never did. Those on the run were in his room night and day. I saw them myself in the morning and in the afternoon — people I haven't seen for years.

We stopped talking that night at midnight. I turned over to the wall and it wasn't a quarter of an hour till I was asleep. Falling asleep I could hear the thunder of an explosion, but it didn't keep me awake. It would have been about an hour or two later that I woke from a sound sleep with a start to the awful blow of a crowbar. One blow followed another and I guessed that the Black and Tans were using three or four crowbars. Since it was the Tans, there was abuse, cursing, and vulgar language mixed together as they roared for someone to open the door. There were two glass windows on the sides of the door. The crowbar shattered the glass — we heard those burst early enough — but the door was firm till the crowbar broke it in. There was an iron bar near the top of the door and a bolt below it. As was usual with houses in the city, there was a latch about five feet up from the bottom and an iron chain half-way between latch and the bolt. The wood that was in the door could withstand gunshot but not the Tans who were outside. In the front room, the room closest to the street, there were two men asleep, men the Tans would have given anything to get their hands on. The men on the run knew that there had been a watch on the house the entire day before — often two of them keeping an eye on it, always at least one. I knew and the people in that room knew, but I don't recall that Sean did. I didn't inquire about anything I saw in those rooms as I went in and out. I don't think O'Casey noticed that they were in the house at all. He would go out every morning between nine and ten; I'd go to Mass at eleven. Sean wouldn't be back until, I'd guess, six. He would be very moderate in his evening meal as if he had had his fill at the hall in the middle of the day. I didn't draw down either way about this with him.

The Tans had a big car outside that night with searchlights that they started to shine all over the place. I'd guess it was now between quarter-past two and two-thirty in the morning. The light awakened one of the men in the other room who was sleeping in a bed with one of Fred's little boys. Hearing the noise and seeing the light in the room, he slipped down from the bed and crawled on his hands and knees towards the back wall, but the Tans outside seemed to notice something, a reflection perhaps, going through the hall. They increased their pounding on the door and if they had been talking first, now they were shouting.

Poor Fred was up and at the door before the two lads on the run. He told them to let themselves out into the back yard and that when they were away, he would open the street door.

O'Casey got a terrible fright when he heard the uproar at the front door. I admit I wasn't Cuchulain at the gap, but O'Casey was terror in the shape of a man. When he heard the first rap on the door, he asked me if I had heard it. I would have had to have been as deaf as a post not to have heard it. He begged me to unlock our door because they would be in on our necks thinking we were hiding.[20] I didn't think it would help. Since they were in our house, we had no other place and I thought it would be much worse without the lock because we could be encouraging anyone at all to come in to hide. In the end I consented and told him that he could unlock the door but to leave it closed. When the searchlight was gone I didn't have any vision and while I felt him move, I couldn't see Sean rising from the bed. Meanwhile we had no rest from the Brittania music at the street door. It wasn't long till I felt Sean's body stretched across me in my bed and his hands clawing and fumbling all over the wall above me. He was groping at the wall, his outstretched fingers taut with terror. I asked him what he was doing and he answered that he was looking for the door. 'Arah, you fool,' I said to him, 'isn't the door on the other side of the room.' Then he went over to the door and unlocked it.

About that time I heard footsteps coming towards us from the other rooms. Poor Fred was leading one of the men to the yard. Years later that fellow on his way to the yard told me that he saw Sean standing in the room while he was going towards the yard. The other man went into the second room. There was an awful noise and he didn't keep his head as well as the first man. With the rush, there was nothing to do but open the door to the yard and close it without bolting it. On his way back to the room Fred knocked at our door and asked did I hear them at the door to the yard. There wasn't any answer to give except that I heard them very well.

'Stay as you are, Michael,' he said and he went calmly to the door and opened it to the Tans. They seized Fred and ran into the room. Fred had left his wife and children in his room, the youngest child less than a month old.

The two of us stayed silent in our own room. I was afraid that they would spray the house with gunshot while I was blinded by darkness. There wasn't a puff out of O'Casey as he lay in his bed. I hardly moved. We both could hear two of the Tans coming towards our room. They stood at the yard door and noticed that the door was shut but not bolted. One of the Tans started to explain to the other that a door like that in this sort of a house would not be shut. It wasn't long before someone opened our door, flashed a light around and shouted to know who was there. He asked again. I answered that there were two of us who lived in the room and that we had been sleeping until he had awakened us. He only came inside the door then out he went to the yard again and looked the whole place over with his flashlight. I heard him come in again and return to the room where the rest were. I thought they would never come out of that room. Lord, weren't they slow hours! Would they ever end? What harm if a person could get up and move around, but I was bound to my bed as tightly as if I were tied hands and feet like a prisoner. It was hard to endure but I had to do it. If only I knew who was walking around.

There wasn't a peep out of O'Casey. He was so quiet that you couldn't hear him breathing.

The clock finally struck six. The Tans had been in the room for more than four hours. They didn't go anywhere else in the house, but they stayed in that room for the entire time. It was heavenly music to me to hear their cars go off. I threw off the bed covers quickly and went up to the room that the Tans had left. Fred's wife was sitting in her bed crying hysterically. The youngest child was in her lap and the other little ones were around her. It was an image of sorrow. When I went to the door, she burst into loud wails again saying through her tears that they had taken Fred with them. The Tan who was behind him had said, 'March to the gallows.' There was another young man in the room who had come in from the front room. Poor Fred was up against the wall with the Tans ready to shoot him. They accused him of making explosives and they questioned him about other things. They took the young man with them, too. He said he was Fred's nephew and that he had come from Glasgow the week before for a vacation. With every couple of words a fresh rush of grief came. There was a fire going so I said to her that I'd put down a drop of tea, that crying wasn't doing any good, that it would cure nothing and that it wouldn't bring Fred back. We noticed that there was a detail of soldiers outside the door and other soldiers here and there in the street outside. It seemed that they were not yet finished with the house.

When I had wet the tea who came into the room but the young man on the run who had gone out of the yard and who clambered over the high wall to the other yard followed by cats and dogs. He was bloody from scratches and cuts. 'Patrick,' I said to him, 'drink this tea and clear out of this house as soon you're done. There is a rank of soldiers outside and they will be in any minute.' He swallowed his drop of tea and was told what had happened to Fred and to the other man. He got away unnoticed. When the tea was shared round and when I had my cup, I returned to my own room. O'Casey was awake and there appeared

to be something bothering him in addition to the disaster that
was over the place. He spoke to me slowly and carefully.

'Michael,' he said, 'I have the minutes of the Citizen Army
here.'

'The-minutes-of-the-Citizen-Army-here?' I answered even
more carefully than he had spoken.

'She gave them to me to keep.'[21]

'Wasn't she nice.' I said sarcastically. 'Why didn't she keep the
book herself? Isn't her own place roomier than this place for
hiding it? The book will be wanted back when the danger is
over.' I knew well who the person was. 'Sean,' I said to him again,
'don't you know what kind of house this is? If you don't
know yet, you will know now. There are two keeping this house
under surveillance almost every day. There has been at least one
person watching the house for the last six months. Didn't you
ever notice that fellow in pale green frieze strolling on the east
side of the square? That's one of the bucks who has been watching the house. I don't think you knew it, but you know it now.
There are soldiers outside the door. If they search the house and
find that book, this room will go up in flames and you and I with
it.'

'What is the best thing to do?'

'Cover the book with a bag, take it down the hall and put it
under one of the floorboards. It won't be difficult to pull up a
floorboard and replace it securely. Go down now because it is
peaceful enough outside.' I went to the other room and Sean
went out. I never knew what happened to that book or where
he put it. I didn't care about anything as long as there weren't
soldiers in our room. Sean came back in about an hour.

A guard of soldiers was put at the street door but it didn't
interfere with anyone coming in or going out. The story had
spread around the district that our house was raided, that the
Black and Tans were inside for more than three hours, and that
they arrested people and took them to the Castle. It was all true
and the information didn't fail to get around.

The landlord came and when he saw the condition of the
front door, the windows on the side of the door smashed and
the fragments of broken glass here and there around the hall, he

was enraged. He started to complain to the poor woman whose husband had just been taken about opening the door to the Tans and allowing them to ruin the door and windows as they had done.

The officer in charge of the soldiers was in the hall and he attacked the officer in the same way. If he had had sense, he would have kept his remarks to himself. The landlord went through the house to the carpenter's shop at the back of the house. The officer followed him out. The landlord kept up the abuse and the soldier got very angry. Neither he nor his men had broken or ruined anything at all. The landlord's complaining lost whatever sympathy the officer had for him.

One of the soldiers spoke with the woman whose husband was taken. 'I have a wife and family myself at home in England and I don't like to hear anyone speak the way that man spoke with you.' That was an English soldier.

The poor landlord! I don't think he understood what was ahead of him that day. If he had let well enough alone and not said anything to the officer, I think the soldiers would have left after having had a look around; however, that was not what was in store for the place. When the landlord went to the door of the shop, he noticed that it too was smashed, and he complained some more to the authority. The Tan who had been out in the yard with the light was the one who had broken the door; the officer and his men had no part in the damage. In went the officer to the carpenter's shop behind my man and he saw a young man — the landlord's son — put his back against a chest of drawers that was against the wall. The officer ordered him to leave the place and he went over and pulled out a drawer. What did he uncover inside but five explosives. O Lord! I don't have to tell you that there was confusion all over then. Soldiers were everywhere. Sean and I were in our room and three soldiers were put at the door. They didn't let any one of us go outside the door even to go out to the yard. Cars, lorries, catapillar tanks came to the house and generals and officers beyond imagination came also. There were three steps on the way up to our room and the other rooms. Sean and I sat side by side without a murmer looking out through our door on to the entry.

There were three soldiers outside the door but they didn't interfere with us in any way. There was a single soldier here and there up from our room. Two or three of them were telling the others that they felt the weather very cold in Ireland as they had just come from Hong Kong. I smiled, I remember, when I saw a general with crosses and stars covering his chest approaching. He raised his knees so high they almost hit his chin. A soldier alerted him, 'Mind the steps, sir. One-two-three. Quite correct, sir.' He was as straight as a rule the whole time.

Then he saw the two of us in the room.

'Are these the pris-naws?' He was told we weren't.

The poor landlord and his son whom they had taken were in the carpenter's shop on the right side of the yard. The soldiers started to move all kinds of ammunition out of the shop: guns, explosives and all kinds of powder. I saw the soldiers coming into the yard and the two sitting inside the room. Were they able to look out on the yard through the two windows also?

'A regular awsenall,' said a soldier who was moving stuff out with another. I didn't laugh until I saw a soldier come out of the shop, stand next to the door of the yard, open his right hand and show something to the men next to him. He had succeeded in hiding a little pistol or revolver in his sleeve and all the time the officers were outside watching and giving orders every instant. 'The Sinn Fein mark is on this one,' he said to his mate. 'I'll get ten shillings for it.'

I guess it was about twelve o'clock that they softened a bit and allowed bread and milk and other messages to come to the house. Two people came early in the day but were told to leave; it wasn't a house to visit on this sort of day. Only those the guard allowed could come in.

About mid-day or one o'clock the young man came out of the shop surrounded by soldiers. There was a sort of cloth bag or rough kind of cover twisted around his mouth. They stood him against the wall opposite our window. Six soldiers were standing in line, their backs to the window, each holding his gun. An officer stood a little way off from them. The old man came out and stood by his son. He was a brave old man; there was no doubt about that. If he had understood the situation quickly that morning, maybe the story would not have been as bad as it was, but good or bad he was a valiant man at that moment. I myself was at the door looking out since we had been given permission a little while before to move around the house. In the course of the day the soldiers searched every room in the house completely. They didn't leave a place unknown, but they found nothing anywhere but in the carpenter's shop.

The officer gave an order to the crowd of soldiers, 'Ready — Present' and they aimed their guns at the two of them, at the old man and his son. A sort of weakness came over me and I leaned against the door. The thought that came into my heart was 'Oh, Lord. They're gone.'

When the Tans burst into the house and when they gathered around me and aimed their pistols at me, I didn't mind it as much as I minded this. Then the old man spoke. 'We're Irishmen. Shoot away.' The defiance to the English from the mouth of that old man! They didn't shoot. The officer was only trying to frighten them, but they didn't scare them, you see.

When Fred's wife saw the soldiers aiming their guns, she let out a scream to come inside to her little boys who were going around the house playing among themselves. One of the soldiers told her not to worry, that the officer wouldn't have them shot at all. He said to her, 'If the Tans were here, they would shoot without a doubt. But, woman,' he said to her, 'there is a big difference between the Tans and ourselves. We like the Irish people and want to be friendly with them.'

It was late afternoon before they were finished with the search. The senior officers spent the day coming and going. Some of them reminded me of the officers I saw in Wakefield Prison, especially one man who came to listen to any complaint the prisoners had.[22] The way he'd rub the bottom of his shoe against the stone he was standing on reminded me of an old horse on Aran, old horses that would be pressing their feet on the couch grass. It's likely that the complaints were very strong. One man said that the food was very bad. 'Ah,' said my man with a sort of wheeze as he wrote, 'we get the same food and so do the soldiers in the trenches.' 'No wonder, sir,' he answered my man impertinently, 'that the Germans are knocking the hell out of them.'

About five o'clock in the afternoon cars came to the house. The young man came out of the carpenter's shop. They weren't too careful the way they threw him into the cart. They put the father and the man who was working by day in the shop in behind the young man.

They closed the shop door and put some sort of a notice on it. By then, the raid has lasted more than fifteen or sixteen hours. O'Casey was in circles until he got out of the house that evening after the soldiers left. I think his heart was too full of raids and war. No matter what he wrote in his lifetime, it was always on his mind. Nothing further happened in the two or three weeks that he remained after that night. He left quietly without saying a word and I wasn't lonely for him.[23] I only saw him once after he left. He was on his way to the hall when we met at the northwest corner of the square. He offered me a cigarette. I said I didn't smoke cigarettes which was true. 'You won't accept anything from me,' he said. He needn't have told me that but everyone is entitled to his opinion. When his first play was produced, his old friends I heard received invitations to the theatre, but he forgot that my kind was alive. Maybe I wouldn't have gone, but I wasn't asked.

I heard that he was in Dublin years later, but I didn't see or hear anything until he had gone back again to England. I wrote to him a couple of letters over the years. I don't know now why I wrote the first letter, but the reason for the second was an essay he wrote in some English paper answering Stephen Gwynn about Aran people in Dublin.[24] He said Micheál MacRuaidrí — God have mercy on him — was from Aran. I wrote him to correct him. Micheál MacRuaidrí was from County Mayo.[25] Years later two American reporters came to ask me for my account of the play that O'Casey wrote. I wasn't happy about discussing the raid with them, but it was Sean who gave them the account and my name.

Robert Emmett was the first name of one of the two reporters and he was very careful to enunciate the 't' in Emmett. I told him about the name and I gave him permission to take photographs. He promised me that he would send a copy of the magazine to me as soon as the essay and photographs were published. He took a great interest in everything and gave me his name and address in New York. But after all the zealous promises, no paper ever came from America. I was overjoyed that there were two 't's in the American Emmett's name because the other Emmet never broke his word. Philpot Curran preferred his word to the vow of any man living.[26]

The young man who had the arms in his possession was brought before a military court a short time later. He took all the blame himself and was given a three to five-year prison sentence. His father and the workman who was taken with them were released after a couple of days.

After two weeks or so the youth who came from Glasgow — as it were — was also released. He had spent six weeks in the Castle and a week in Arbor Hill and if ever a person were lucky, he was. If they had known who they had, they would never have let him go. Poor Fred was sent to Kildare and his health broke there.

After all the searching by the Black and Tans and the soldiers, they finally found the guns that were hidden in Fred's room. I read the book that Michael Davitt wrote about the Boer War.[27] He wrote about a man going out to fight who lost his health guarding a train that was there. Poor Fred reminded me of that man. He was let out a month before the other prisoners to undergo surgery, but from that time until his death seven years later, the poor man was an invalid. He was out in 1916 and he was one of the first to go when they started the work up again. During those years he hid those who needed shelter and helped them in hard times. And what about the promises that were made to him? I saw him sitting by himself in the room where he sheltered many with nothing but his memory. Once he asked me to go with him to talk with a government Minister to see could he do anything for him. He had five children and he wasn't able to work. We saw the Minister at Leinster House. The recommendation that came from his mouth, I heard it myself, was to put an appeal before the Shaw Commission, the Commission started to compensate English property loss in Ireland. When I heard that Minister's recommendation for Fred and others like him, I remembered Parnell and how they threw lime in his eyes after all his work for this country. I also remembered the Irish who died of starvation and misery.

Ireland is an open, welcome place. Yes, for the Ministers themselves. It was as if those in power were finally shamed, because, they gave him a small pension of a pound a week. Fred lived for a month after that. When he died, his widow did not get his pension. She was left with five children and whether they lived or died gave small worry to those people.

They are grown up now and Fred's widow has her old-age pension. Politicians and their kind sometimes wonder why people are not interested in current public questions but this story and stories like it that go from mouth to mouth not only in Dublin but throughout the country explain the reason for that disinterest. That's enough.

NOTES

1. Late in 1920 Sean O'Casey moved into a room at Mountjoy Square which he shared with Micheal Maoláin (Michael Mullen), an Inishmaan man living in Dublin. See David Krause (ed.), 'O'Casey Chronology', *The Letters of Sean O'Casey*, I (New York: Macmillan, 1975) p. xxv. 'An Ruathar Ud agus a nDeachaigh Leis', O'Maoláin's account of his life with O'Casey and the Black and Tan raid that took place on Good Friday, 1921, was published in Irish in *Feasta* (Bealtaine, 1955) pp. 2–4, 6, 22, 24–5.

   O'Maoláin is of interest to O'Caseyans because he was the inspiration for Seumas Shields. See 'The late Mr. O'Maoláin was the original for Seumas Shields in *The Shadow of a Gunman*' [David Krause, *Sean O'Casey: The Man and His Work,* New York: Macmillan, 1960 p. 292]; 'Davoren is not the only character in the play to carry aspects of the playwright onto the stage; even Seumas Shields, although patently modeled after Michael Mullen, contains O'Casey characteristics'. [Bernard Benstock, *Sean O'Casey,* Lewisburgh: Bucknell University Press, 1970, p. 35].

2. There are a number of similarities between O'Maoláin's account, Sean O'Casey's 'The Raid', in *Inishfallen, Fare Thee Well* (New York: Macmillan, 1956, pp. 57–78), and Sean O'Casey's *The Shadow of a Gunman, Collected Plays,* I (London: Macmillan, 1950) pp. 93–154. The descriptions of the room with the stretcher bed are similar, the bitter cold, the Tans pounding on the door and shattering the glass, the

characterisation of the Tommies as decent men doing an unpleasant job, the carpenter's shop at the back of the house associated with explosives, and the defiance of the landlord and his son, of Charles Ballynoy and of Minnie respectively when they are taken off by the military all feature in these accounts.

3. O'Casey joined the Drumcondra Branch of the Gaelic League in 1906; he became its secretary in 1908. See Krause, *Letters,* I, p. xxv. The first mention of O'Maoláin's connection with the Gaelic League appears in an account of a meeting of the Inis Meadhoin Male Branch of the League. See *An Claidheamh Soluis,* I (19 Lughnasa, 1899) p. 359. By the autumn Mullen 'Inis Meadhoin' was active in the Central Branch of the Gaelic League in Dublin. He joined the St Brendan Branch in the spring of 1900 where his contributions to programmes were frequently noted: *An Claidheamh Soluis,* I, passim.

4. O'Casey joined Larkin's Irish Transport and General Workers' Union in 1911. When the Irish Citizen Army was formed in 1913 to protect the strikers, O'Casey became its Secretary. He resigned in October 1914. Michael Mullin is mentioned in the list of the Provisional Committee of the Citizen Army, as a speaker at a meeting in Finglas on 24 April 1914, and as a member of the Council who attended a special meeting about Citizen Army members who were involved in the Irish Volunteers: P. O'Cathasaigh [Sean O'Casey], *The Story of the Irish Citizen Army* (Dublin: Maunsel, 1919) pp. 15, 22, 45.

5. O'Maoláin may have taken this description of Larkin from O'Casey: '. . . and then this fiery human comet passed from the orbit of Irish life' [*Citizen Army,* p. 50].

6. Joseph G. Biggar, a Belfast merchant and Catholic convert, helped to found the Home Rule Party. Elected to Parliament in 1874, the year before Parnell, Parnell and Biggar joined obstructionist forces in the House of Commons. Biggar was a member of the Supreme Council of the IRB, but his parliamentary activity led to his expulsion in 1877, the year Parnell became President of the Home Rule Confederation.

7. Issac Butt founded the Home Government Association in 1870, a federalist movement that sought Irish control of the country's domestic affairs. A conservative nationalist, Butt found the obstructionist policy of Biggar and Parnell unacceptable. He finally lost his leadership to Parnell and Home Rule.

8. The Castlecomer incident occurred when Parnell appeared in Kilkenny to campaign in the bitter by-election that followed the Irish Parliamentary Party split. Something white was thrown at Parnell. Whatever the substance, it was a humiliating experience.

9. Cetawayo was a Zulu chief who rebelled against British rule. His Zulus destroyed a British regiment. He was taken prisoner, held in the Cape of Good Hope and taken to England in 1882. When the British government later tried to reinstate him as king of the Zulus, their attempt failed.

10. Miles Byrne, a 1798 hero, said that when the Wexford insurgents marched through Kilkenny they were joined only by the Castlecomer miners who deserted the next day with the rebel guns: *Memoirs,* I (Dublin, 1906) pp. 167-9. Samuel Lewis describes Castlecomer as a town partially rebuilt, 'It suffered greatly in the disturbance of 1798, from the violence of a party of the insurgents by whom a considerable portion of the town was destroyed' [*A Topographical Dictionary of Ireland,* I, London: Lewis, 1837, p. 292].

11. This is the first stanza of Robert Burns's 'I Love My Jean', also called 'Jean', See James Kinsley (ed.), *The Poems and Songs of Robert Burns,* I (Oxford: Clarendon Press, 1968) pp. 421-2.

12. These are the last four lines of the first stanza of Burns's 'Up in the Morning': *Poems and Songs,* I, p. 389.

13. The play about the Dublin labour movement may have been *The Harvest Festival,* which was submitted to the Abbey in 1919 and rejected on 26 January 1920: Krause, *Letters,* I, p. xxv. The play, now in the Berg Collection, New York Public Library, was published in 1979. Krause also mentions that O'Casey was 'writing comic skits which he read at club meetings': Krause, *Letters,* I, p. 4.

14. O'Casey's antipathy to the Irish Volunteers is well-known. He felt that the Volunteers, who were formed a month after the Citizen Army, were not sympathetic to the workers' cause.

15. If, as O'Maoláin says, O'Casey gave him *The Crimson and the Tricolour* to drop in at the Abbey, the Abbey would have had the play from early 1921 until they finally rejected it on 28 September 1922. There were at least two reasons for the long delay: Lennox Robinson misplaced the manuscript and there was an extended debate about the play among the Abbey directors.

16. Bawneens and red petticoats are the traditional dress of the Aran Islanders.

17. O'Maoláin says that O'Casey looked on Yeats as a 'Crom Cruach', an Irish pagan deity who has been associated with Magh Slécht (County Cavan). Modern archaeologists suggest that the story is an invention:

> 'In *Féilsgríbhinn* Eóin Mhic Néill (1940), 296–306, Michael Duignan has shown that the story of Crom Cruaich of Magh Slécht is largely the result of pseudo-learned invention working imaginatively on an etymological guess and a simple local legend, but he does not discount the possible existence in Magh Slécht (ancient name for the district in which are Baellaleenan and Derryragh) of a local center of a pagan cult [Maire MacNeill, *The Festival of Lughnasa,* London: Oxford University Press, 1962, p. 120 n].

That Crom Cruach is defeated by St Patrick in the legend suggests that he was a malevolent figure.

18. In 1920-1 O'Casey was working as a janitor at the Old Forester's Hall,

10 Langrishe Place, Summerhill. For his description of his job with Delia Larkin and the game that O'Maoláin mentions, see 'Drifting', *Inishfallen Fare Thee Well*, pp. 94–5.

19. The raid O'Maoláin describes took place on the night of 24 March 1921. It lasted through the next day which was Good Friday. In 'The Raid', Nellie Ballynoy says, 'An' it only a little way from Christmas too [*Inishfallen*, p. 69]. O'Casey sets *The Shadow of a Gunman* in May 1920.

20. 'He always left his door unlocked now, for past experience had shown him that the slightest obstacle to a swift entrance to a room always irritated them.' [*Innishfallen*, p. 64].

21. Robert Lowery has suggested that 'she' was probably Delia Larkin. Is Davoren's frantic search for the letter from Mr Gallogher and Mrs Henderson to the IRA a recollection of O'Casey's fear that the Citizen Army minutes would be discovered?

22. O'Maoláin's reference to Wakefield Prison, where 1916 insurgents were detained, suggests that he was in the Easter Rising.

23. O'Maoláin's suggestion that O'Casey left because of the raid is echoed in Davoren's line, 'There's one thing certain: as soon as morning comes I'm on the run out of this house' [O'Casey, *Plays*, I, p. 145]. Eileen O'Casey offers a more prosaic reason for his leaving: 'As he earned more money, he got his own room and it is this we see in the frontispiece of *Inishfallen, Fare Thee Well*' [Eileen O'Casey, *Sean*, New York: Coward, McCann & Geoghan, 1972, p. 78].

24. I haven't been able to locate this article. It does not appear to be in Ronald Ayling and Michael Durken, *Sean O'Casey: A Bibliography* (London: Macmillan, 1978).

25. Micheál Mac Ruaidrí was the gardener at St Enda's. A native speaker, he was influential with the students and a great source of support to the Gaeltacht boys who often were shy with the other boys. See Ruth Dudley Edwards, *Patrick Pearse: The Triumph of Failure* (London: Gollancz, 1977) p. 137.

26. Robert Emmet led an insurrection of United Irishmen in 1803. John Philpot Curran, the famous Irish orator, defended many of the United Irishmen but he did not defend Emmet because Emmet was in love with his daughter Sarah. When Sarah's letters to Emmet were discovered, Emmet withdrew Curran as his counsel.

    O'Maoláin is probably referring to Robert Emmet Girra, editor in chief, Little, Brown & Co., Boston.

27. O'Maoláin is probably referring to Davitt's *The Boer Fight for Freedom* (1902). Actually Davitt himself, with his willingness to continue Land League agitation in spite of great personal hardship, would also have reminded O'Maoláin of Fred.

6 Bernard Shaw and Sean O'Casey: An Unrecorded Friendship

E. H. MIKHAIL

When St John Ervine's biography *Bernard Shaw: His Life, Works and Friends* appeared in 1956, Dr Ronald Ayling, a very close friend of Sean O'Casey, wrote to Ervine saying that the one fault in his book was his failure to record O'Casey's relations with Shaw. Ervine wrote back in a letter dated 12 September 1957, saying that O'Casey was not one of Shaw's friends, and that he could not record something that 'never existed as an important fact'. Dr Ayling forwarded this letter to O'Casey, who said in his reply of 3 November 1957:

I wonder how and where St. John Ervine got his dogmatism? He is more dogmatic on everything under the sun than a newly-fledged Irish Bishop. I have no doubt that G. B. S. was a friend of his and of W. Archer; but, I imagine, in a limited way . . . As a matter of fact, St. John wouldn't have understood, and can't now, the bonds between me and G. B. S. Here are a few: He was a Dublinman, so was I; he was reared up a Protestant, so was I; he suffered the humiliation of living in the genteel poverty of the Irish lower middle-class, while I suffered the squalid, but more vigorous, poverty of the proletariat; Shaw was mainly a self-educated man, so was I; Shaw hated poverty in all its forms, so do I; Shaw fought against it most of his life, so did I, and still do; Shaw thought Stalin a great man, so did I, and so do still; Shaw was passionately devoted to the USSR and all the USSR did and was doing, so was I; Shaw hated all British Imperialism, so did I; Shaw rejected the Christian beliefs, so did I; Shaw saw through the Romantic idea of Irish nationalism, so did I; Shaw was a fighter, and he knew I was one, too (I've never heard that he ever said in a letter to St. J. 'Bravo, Titan!'); in almost his last words to Mrs. O'Casey he said, 'It is for Sean, now, to carry on the fight'; not St. J., but Sean; Shaw was a born Communist, so was I; Shaw called Jim Larkin 'the greatest Irishman since Parnell,' and Shaw knew how I had fought for the workers with Jim; Shaw was deeply interested in the Chinese Workers and Peasants' Red Army and its long and terrible march from Kiangsi in the south to Shensi in the north, wondering if they could do it, and if they did it, what effect it would have on the whole of China, so was I; . . . Shaw had a deep affection for Lady Gregory, so had I (I hope St. J. won't next say somewhere I was never a friend of hers; but he would hardly do that, for he disliked her, I imagine, or, certainly, she did him); his initials are carved on the great tree in Coole, so are mine, but I have never seen St. J.'s there; while St. J. mentions a number of American Drama Critics, I noticed he never mentions Nathan, yet Nathan had a deep reverence for Shaw, and Shaw thought highly of him, and so did, do, I; . . . Shaw was always delighted to see John Dulanty, the then High Commissioner for Ireland – it was he who brought the Roll of Dublin's Freeman to G. B. S.; Shaw loved his humor and his stories, and so did I; Shaw was always ready to talk about Ireland, and so was I.[1]

These affinities between Shaw and O'Casey, however, do not reveal the extent of their friendship, which lasted until Shaw's death in 1950. As early as 1916, during the time when O'Casey was a member of the Gaelic League and the Irish Republican Brotherhood, he maintained his interest in reading. He had bought and read works by Emerson, Zola, Whitman, Frazer, Darwin, France, and others. But it was not until his friend Kevin O'Loughlin introduced hin to Shaw's *John Bull's Other Island* that he was passionately moved. He devoured all the available works of Shaw, finding in him a man after his own heart, who

could view things objectively without drawing a romantic veil
over reality. Shaw, protesting against the executions carried out
by the British government, said that it 'was a fair fight in everything except the enormous odds My countrymen had to face'.[2]
And O'Casey, through Fluther Good in *The Plough and the Stars,*
reiterates this. Though O'Casey permits his characters to develop
in the roles allotted to them, at times he sacrifices their development in the interest of conveying his own views, an influence of
Shaw, for whom his affection had been one of the most domin-
ating passions of his life, and to whom he paid splendid tributes
in his autobiographies and critical writings. One of O'Casey's
early writings was a little book entitled 'Three Shouts on a Hill'.
It was a vigorous attack on the three movements for which he
had sacrificed so much: the Republican Movement, Irish Labour,
and the Gaelic League. The book consisted of three essays based
on his articles in the *Irish Worker* and *Irish Opinion.* After completing the book, which was never published, O'Casey sent the
manuscript to Shaw asking him to write a preface: Shaw returned
it with the following letter:

10 Adelphi Terrace WC2
[London]
3 December 1919

Dear Sir,

I like the forword and afterword much better than the
shouts, which are prodigiously overwritten.

Why do you not come out definitely on the side of Labor
& the English language?

I am afraid the National question will insist on getting settled before the Labor question. That is why the National question is a nuisance and a bore; but it can't be helped.

Of course the publishers will publish it with a preface by
me; but how will that advance *you* as an author? Besides, my
prefaces mean months of work. I'm asked for prefaces three
times a week. It is quite out of the question. You must go
through the mill like the rest and get published for your own
sake, not for mine.

You ought to work out your position positively & definitely. This objecting to everyone else is Irish, but useless.

In great haste — I am busy rehearsing.

G. Bernard Shaw

Shaun O'Casey, Esq.
18 Abercorn Road
Dublin

When O'Casey left Dublin for London on 5 March 1926 to attend the first night of *Juno and the Paycock* at the Fortune Theatre, he made friends with Shaw and Augustus John. During that time, and indeed ever since his marriage in 1898, the social side of Shaw's life was admirably catered for by his wife, Charlotte, There were regular luncheon parties at 10 Adelphi Terrace and later at Whitehall Court to which H. G. Wells, Bertrand Russell, Sean O'Casey, Sybil Thorndike, Lewis Casson, Rebecca West, and other famous writers, actors and actresses, politicians and economists were invited. O'Casey found Charlotte very trying at these lunches. She 'ate heavily, a great pile on her plate', and, feeling the cold keenly, sat hunched up over her food, a shawl around her shoulders and an electric fire beside her chair. And she would direct sharp criticisms at O'Casey during the meal. Asking him what he was doing then, when told 'nothing at the moment', she turned on him. 'Too busy quarrelling,' she said, rather viciously, he records in *Sunset and Evening Star.* 'I hear you have quarrelled with Agate now. You will have to learn a better way of conducting yourself. You will get nowhere with these senseless disputes.' The guests were 'mostly Mrs. Shaw's cronies', he notes, and Shaw was plagued to give his opinions on persons and things past and gone, by those who had come with pick and spade to disinter them and make them look lively again. Shaw said he found it a great strain to keep talking through lunch. 'Why the hell do you do it?' O'Casey asked. 'Is it vanity, is it just trying to shine?', to which Shaw replied: 'They all expect it of me. One can't sit in silence, staring at the others.'

Shaw stood by O'Casey's side during the controversy over *The Silver Tassie,* which the Abbey Theatre rejected in 1928. Yeats, as Director of the Theatre, sent O'Casey a letter stating his reasons for turning down his play. In his reply O'Casey, after pointing out his interest in the First World War, goes on to ask Yeats: 'Was G. B. Shaw in the boats with the French, or in the forts with the English when St. Joan and Dunois made the attack that relieved Orleans?' On another point raised by Yeats, O'Casey says: 'And was there ever a play, worthy of the name of a play, that did not contain one or two or three opinions of the author that wrote it. And the Abbey Theatre has produced plays that were packed skin-tight with the author's opinion — the plays of Shaw, for instance.' O'Casey took Yeats's letter to Daniel Macmillan. If, he said, after reading it, Macmillans would rather not publish the play, he would be willing to withdraw his contract. Daniel, who had read the play admiringly, examined the correspondence, did not agree with Yeats, and told O'Casey that Macmillans would be proud to publish. Just after this, Charlotte Shaw wrote from Passfield Corner where she and her husband were staying with Sidney and Beatrice Webb:

> Passfield Corner,
> Liphook,
> Hants.
> 17 June 1928

Dear Mr. O'Casey

G. B. S. & I have read The Silver Tassie with *deep interest.* We are both greatly impressed by it — I am most enthusiastic! — & we want to have a chat with you about it, & the whole business.

Could you, & Mrs. O'Casey, come & have luncheon with us at Whitehall Court on Thursday next, the 21st, at 1.30? Do if you possibly can. We would be alone so that we might talk freely (about our friends?! — *no* — about the play!)

Our flat is 130, & you come to Block 4 of the building & the Porter will send you up to us in the Lift.

Hoping to see you both on Thursday.

> *Yours sincerely*
> *C. F. Shaw*
> *(Mrs. Bernard Shaw)*

We are staying down here with the Sidney Webbs until Wednesday — so please write here.

Two days later Shaw's own letter reached 19 Woronzow Road, St John's Wood, NW8:

(4 Whitehall Court SW. 1)
Passfield Corner
19 June 1928

My dear Sean

What a hell of a play! I wonder how it will hit the public.

Of course the Abbey should have produced it – as Starkie rightly says – whether it liked it or not. But the people who knew your uncle when you were a child (so to speak) always want to correct your exercises; and this was what disabled the usually competent W. B. Y. and Lady Gregory.

Still, it is surprising that they fired so very wide considering their marksmanship. A good realistic first act, like *Juno*, an incongruously phantasmic second act, trailing off into a vague and unreal sequel: could anything be wronger? What *I* see is a deliberately unrealistic phantasmo-poetic first act, intensifying in exactly the same mode into a climax of war imagery in the second act, and then two acts of almost unbearable realism bringing down all the Voodoo war poetry with an ironic crash to earth in ruins. There is certainly no falling-off or loss of grip: the hitting gets harder and harder right through to the end.

Now if Yeats had said 'It's too savage: I can't stand it' he would have been in order. You really are a ruthless ironfisted blaster and blighter of your species; and in this play there is none righteous – no, not one. Your moral is always that the Irish ought not to exist; and you are suspected of opining, like Shakespear, that the human race ought not to exist – unless, indeed, you like them like that, which you can hardly expect Lady Gregory, with her kindness for Kiltartan, to do. Yeats himself, with all his extraordinary cleverness and subtlety, which comes out just when you give him up as a hopeless fool and (in this case) deserts him when you expect him to be equal to the occasion, is not a man of this world; and when you hurl an enormous smashing chunk of it at him he dodges it, small blame to him.

However, we can talk about it when we meet, which I understand is to be Thursday next week. This is only to prepare you for my attitude. Until then.

Cheerio, Titan,
G. Bernard Shaw

At luncheon Sean reminded GBS of the manuscript he had sent him some years earlier asking him for a preface, and told him that he had carried round his reply in his wallet for many years until it was creased and frayed. Charlotte tried to tell Sean that he should not be quite angry in the press, so firm in argument. Eileen O'Casey mildly said that

'Sean could hardly alter his personality, and that being naturally resentful about the whole thing, he must express his feelings. G. B. S., on Sean's side but not wishing to contradict Charlotte, did his best to smooth the problem over. There was no lull in a conversation that lasted until well into the afternoon.'[3]

Through the delicate fume of the conversation, Eileen suggested the compromise of Sean submitting any further letters to GBS, who, if he disapproved of a paragraph or sentence, could edit it into a more suitable expression. Charlotte vigorously applauded the idea, GBS approved, and Sean sat silent. The Shaws would come to lunch with the O'Caseys in a couple of days to push the plan further ahead. On 8 July, however, Eileen heard from Charlotte about the Shaws' difficulty in coming to Woronzow Road for a while:

Ayot St. Lawrence
8 July 1928

Dear Mrs. O'Casey

I am so *very* sorry, but I fear we cant go & see you now because we are just starting off abroad for a holiday & have got so terribly tied up with all the silly odds & ends we have to get done before we go. We have taken our sleepers for

Sunday, & are going to be down here until Thursday afternoon. Then there will be an orgie of business & packing!

I am the more sorry for this as I do feel 'Sean' wants a lot of looking after just now. He is going to be very naughty & fierce & resentful — & he is a terribly hard hitter!

That idea of letting G. B. S. see his letters to his 'friends' is a grand one. Do keep him up to it. Any letters addressed to 4 Whitehall Court will be forwarded *at once,* & I will send you our address the moment we are settled, & he must write about all he is doing, & G. B. S. will answer *quickly,* & try to act as a lightning conductor!

Directly we come back we will go & lunch with you, & see Brian, if you will ask us again.

Our very kindest & most friendly thoughts to you both.

Yours sincerely
C. F. Shaw

Mr. Yeats didn't come & see us about the play, but about the Irish Literary Academy they are trying to get up. He never mentioned The Silver Tassie. It was *I* who insisted upon talking about it — & he was rather self conscious & reluctant!

Sean was angry about the idea that Charlotte should look after any correspondence he received and was certain that GBS would never want to advise him about the way he should fight for his own work:

He had no wish to have his letters edited, even by such a man as Shaw. Yeats had hit as hard as he could, and Sean wasn't inclined to hold his punches. He had refused the counsel of Uncle Yeats, and he had no intention of taking the counsel of Auntie Shaw.[4]

So no more was done about it. *The Silver Tassie* event was of sufficient importance to bring another letter from Shaw. Writing to Lady Gregory he said:

[?] June 1928

Why do you and W. B. Y. treat O'Casey as a baby? Starkie was right, you should have done the play anyhow. Sean is now *hors concours*. It is literally a hell of a play; but it will clearly force its way on to the stage and Yeats should have submitted to it as a calamity imposed on him by the Act of God, if he could not welcome it as another *Juno*. Besides, he was extraordinarily wrong about it on the facts. The first act is not a bit realistic; it is deliberately fantastic chanted poetry. This is intensified to a climax into the second act. Then comes a ruthless return for the last two acts to give the fiercest ironic realism. But that is so like Yeats. Give him a job with which you feel sure he will play Bunthorne and he will astonish you with his unique cleverness and subtlety. Give him one that any second-rater could manage with credit and as likely as not he will make an appalling mess of it. He has certainly fallen in up to the neck over O'C. But this is not a very nice letter, is it? Consequently the very last letter I want to send you. So I will stop before I become intolerable.[5]

G. B. S.

In the meantime, O'Casey had written to Shaw to ask if a part of *The Silver Tassie* letter could be sent to Macmillans:

29 June 1928

Dear G B S—

May I send to Macmillans the following portions of your letter to me about the Silver Tassie?

'What a hell of a play! . . . a deliberately unrealistic phantasmo-poetic first act, intensifying in exactly the same mode into a climax of war imagry in the second act, and then two acts of almost unbearable realism bringing down all the voodoo war poetry with an ironic crash to earth in ruins . . . there is no falling off, or loss of grip — the hitting gets harder and harder right through to the end.'

When I got the quires of criticism from the Abbey, I galloped off to Macmillans and told them they could withdraw the book if they thought the criticisms more important, and though they held on to the book, I feel they got a shock, so when your letter came I sent it on to cheer them up, and they have asked me to seek your permission to print some passages.

Besides, as far as I can see at the moment, the coming year must be financially filled up with whatever the sale of the book may bring in and any help in this way is a gift from God.

I confirm my assurance that I have no vindictive feeling to the Abbey — I refused four offers to have the play produced in Dublin — and that I should be glad to have The Silver Tassie performed there subject to conditions mentioned which, I think, are fair and just under all the circumstances.

Warm Regards to you and to Mrs. Shaw.

Sean O'Casey

Shaw replied on the back of this letter on 3 July 1928, giving permission to quote from his letter, telling O'Casey that Lady Gregory was really on his side in the controversy, and warning him that 'Playwriting is a desperate trade' — 'Your wife must support you (what is she for?), and when she is out of work you must go into debt, and borrow, and pawn and so on — the usual routine. Such is life.'

The Silver Tassie was accepted for production by Charles B. Cochran and opened at the Apollo Theatre in London on 11 October 1929. On the first night, Eileen O'Casey sat in the stage box with Evelyn and C. B. Cochran, 'the three of us desperately nervous'. Lady Astor came with the Shaws. Far from being on edge, GBS was enthusiastic and eager; during the interval between the second and third Acts he made a point of finding Sean who had sat somewhere quietly on his own, far too wrought-up to show himself. GBS insisted again that it was a great play: an emotional moment for Sean after so vital an Act. Not long before the play closed, GBS, invariably loyal to Sean, wrote a letter to Cochran on 23 November 1929:

Whitehall Court
London

Charles B. Cochran
Apollo Theatre
London

My Dear Cochran,

I really must congratulate you on *The Silver Tassie* before it passes into the classical repertory. It is a magnificent play; and it was a magnificent gesture of yours to produce it. The highbrows should have produced it; you, the unpretentious showman, did, as you have done so many other noble and rash things on your Sundays. This, I think, will rank as the best of them. I hope you have not lost too much by it, especially as I am quite sure you have done your best in that direction by doing the thing as extravagantly as possible. That is the worst of operating on your colossal scale; you haven't time to economise; and you lose the habit of thinking it worth while.

No matter! a famous achievement. There is a new drama rising from unplumed depths to sweep the nice little bourgeois efforts of myself and my contemporaries into the dustbin; and your name will live as that of the man who didn't run away. If only someone would build you a huge Woolworth Theatre (all seats 6d) to start with O'Casey and O'Neill, and no plays by men who had ever seen a £5 note before they were 30 or been inside a school after they were 13, you would be buried in Westminster Abbey. Bravo!

G. B. S.[6]

The Silver Tassie was financially a failure: it ran for only eight weeks in London and did not pay its expenses. O'Casey had hoped that it would bring in enough to live on for one year, but all that it brought was extreme poverty. For five years after this play Sean had nothing on in London. The decoration of the house the O'Caseys moved to cost more than it should; like most artists, they let the money go as it came in. GBS insisted to Eileen

> that it was impossible for a writer or artist not to be finan-
> cially erratic, he was paid so irregularly. If he received a large
> cheque, he would spend it, not asking when the next might
> arrive, if at all. Rather he would look forward to the sale of a
> film or to the production of a play.[7]

The O'Caseys, therefore, seemed to be continually in money difficulties at Hillcrest, Chalfont St Giles. Samuel French & Sons, the play publishers, had asked often if they could buy the world amateur rights of the Abbey plays — *The Shadow of a Gun-man, Juno and the Paycock,* and *The Plough and the Stars* — for £300 and a half-share of all royalties for ever more. Sean hated to part with this property; equally, he hated to borrow. Samuel French also asked him to do prompt-copies, with a series of stage plans that Eileen produced with great labour after the O'Caseys had taken hours and hours to draw and measure them, a task they loathed. GBS disapproved of the bargain. He wrote: 'Three hundred pounds for half-rights for your lifetime plus fifty years is an absurdly hard bargain for you. My advice is to let wife and child perish and lay bricks for your last crust, sooner than part with an iota of your rights.'[8] Unwillingly, Sean accepted the offer for the play rights.

Recently published correspondence[9] shows that the O'Casey-Shaw friendship continued to develop. Sean, for example, wrote to Charlotte on 25 September 1928 thanking her 'for sending me Blake's Vision of Job'.[10] When *The Plough and the Stars* opened in London at the Duchess Theatre on 4 June 1930 for a limited run of six weeks, Sean again wrote to Charlotte on 23 June telling her that he was 'really gratified that you & G. B. S. thought so well of the play, & of the acting by little Kitty Curling,[11] who has talent, & who has had a pretty rough time of it in Dublin.'[12] When the Shaws knew that the O'Caseys had moved to Chalfont St Giles, Charlotte wrote to Sean on 27 August 1931 telling him that she was 'glad you are in the country as I know you both wanted to get away from London & it will be so good for you'; asking him if his new play was 'very far advanced'; and advising him not to be 'too belligerent!'[13] Sean replied[14] defending himself: 'God be my judge that I hate fighting.' Then on 28 October he wrote informing her that he and Eileen 'have settled in & are now breaking bread in our new little home . . . Any time you & G. B. S. . . . . chance to be in or near Mid. Bucks, we should be delighted if you would come to see us.'[15] Charlotte replied on 15 November:

I rejoice to think of you both in your own home with the garden and peace and quiet. Only I wish you were a little nearer . . . I am longing to hear you have a new play ready. Has the move interfered with one? G. B. S. has just finished his new one. It is called *Too True To Be Good,* and I call it a 'Super Farce'; I think you will like it.[16]

Sean answered[17] that he was looking forward to the publication of the play — 'it's a rare title, & contains in itself a terrible philosophy'. He described GBS as 'one of my great friends, anam — chara — soul-friend — as we say in Ireland, & has been so for many years, long before I met him in the flesh.' After telling Charlotte that the moving 'did interfere a lot with my work', he told her that he 'began last week to get back to the play or film[18] — or whatever it may turn out to be — & to the semi-biography to be called, A Child is Born.'[19]

In the meantime, W. B. Yeats had decided to form an Irish Academy of Letters.[20] A circular, signed by some prominent Irish writers, was sent out, appealing to others to become founder Academicians or associate members. 'The circular', O'Casey tells us in *Sunset and Evening Star*[21]

came to Sean signed personally by Bernard Shaw. Shaw was asking a favour from Sean; the first favour ever asked, and Sean saw himself threatened with the hardest refusal he had ever had to face. Shaw had fought by his side in the Abbey Theatre controversy over *The Silver Tassie,* and now Sean had to refuse the one favour the great man asked him.

Disliking institutions powered to decide what was good literature, Sean refused to join. The letter of refusal went to GBS, but no answer came back. 'No malice touched Shaw's nature; he was the most forgiving man Sean had ever met. Nothing mean ever peeped out of his thought or his manner; the noblest Irishman of all Irishmen.' Sean and GBS met many times again, but neither of them ever once mentioned the Irish Academy of Letters.

Sean's next play, *Within the Gates,* had its première at the Royalty Theatre in London on 7 February 1934. It brought the usual smart audience – the Shaws, the Cochrans, Lady Londonderry, Lady Rhondda – 'and we went on to St. James's Square for Lady Astor's supper-party to the cast. Though we did not believe the occasion had been a success, everybody tried to forget and to enjoy the rest of the evening.'[22] GBS, who was constantly advancing the interests of younger dramatists and who had the virtue of praising people behind their backs, wrote to Lady Astor on 9 February:

> Sean O'Casey is all right now that his shift from Dublin slums to Hyde Park has shewn that his genius is not limited by frontiers. His plays are wonderfully impressive and *reproachful* without being irritating like mine. People fall crying into one another's arms saying God forgive us all! instead of refusing to speak and going to their solicitors for a divorce.[23]

In spite of its American adventure, the play was not done again for any major production in England, though Sean continued to hope and had an idea once that Michel Saint-Denis might direct it at the Old Vic. GBS wrote to him about this in May 1936:

> There is no reason on earth why W. T. G. should not go on at the O. V. if Lilian Baylis wants it. But as she has a competent producer (Guthrie) on her staff there is equally no reason why you impose St. D. on her unless his qualifications are extraordinary and indispensable. An author can pick and choose his cast and even his staff for a West End production at a theatre hired ad hoc; but repertory theatres must be taken as they are, lock, stock (especially stock) and barrel. As to re-

hearsing, all an author can do is to produce the original performance so as to establish a tradition as far as possible; but
beyond that he cannot go without ruining himself.
We are still in arrears and confusion after our 11 weeks at sea,
and very old at that, Heaven help us; but we shall get straight
presently and see something of you twain.[24]

G. B. S.

The following year Sean, who had moved to Battersea, London SW11, 'wanted to keep in touch with' the Shaws and wrote
to GBS a long letter [25] on 24 November 1937. After sending his
'true sympathy' to Charlotte, who 'has been poorly', he told him
that he was beginning to read *Immaturity,* 'lent to me, by the
way, by a hard nut of an Irish Communist who was for a long
time assistant to Jim Larkin in Dublin . . . "Immaturity" is the
one novel of yours I've never read — never even heard of it . . . I
was struck with the idea that a Communist is born a Communist.'
He also told GBS that he was considering an offer from America.
'Anyway, I won't decide on anything till I finish, for good or ill,
the writing of 'The Star Turns Red'.'
The lease[26] of 49 Overstrand Mansions, Battersea, having been
broken, the O'Caseys decided to move to Devonshire to be near
the school, Dartington Hall in Totnes, which Eileen had chosen
for the children on GBS's emphatic recommendation. 'The trek
from here to Devon', Sean wrote[27] to Charlotte in September
1938, 'will, I'm sure, be a good thing for the two youngsters —
and that matters most.' But before the O'Caseys could rent the
only house that was vacant for miles around, they had to get a
friend to supply references and to guarantee the rent, a pre-
caution upon which the landlord insisted. 'The landlord didn't
like the look of Sean, or mistrusted anyone trying to make a
living by writing (small blame to him for that), and demurred
about agreeing to the tenancy.'[28] Not wishing to bother GBS,
Sean wrote to Charlotte asking her to do him this favour. Almost
immediately, a letter came back asking the O'Caseys to lunch in
Whitehall Court to talk about the matter.

But all for nothing. When Sean handed out the news that Mrs.

Shaw would stand as guarantor, the landlord let a snort out of him, jumped from his chair, ran to the farther end of the room, and almost shouted, It's no good; I'll not take any woman's guarantee! I won't let you into the house on any woman's name. I'll let no woman meddle in my affairs![29]

So Sean had to write to Charlotte telling her that her signature would not do. GBS then took over the guarantee, first indulging in a spicy correspondence with the landlord's solicitors, and a subsequent letter[30] told Sean that the business had been carried through:

> 4, Whitehall Court,
> London, S. W. 1.
> 17 October 1938

My dear Sean,

Your landlord, being a dentist, has developed an extraction complex. He proposed a lease in which I was not only to guarantee all your covenants, but indemnify him for all the consequences. I said I did not know his character, but knew enough of yours to know that the consequences might include anything from murder to a European war; so I redrafted the agreement. The lawyers, knowing that their man was only too lucky to get a gilt-edged (as they thought) security, and that his demands were absurd, made no resistance. I mention it as you had better watch your step, not to say his, with the gentleman. Anyhow I had a bit of fun with him.

I seem to have picked up completely. The anaemia was not really pernicious.

I am glad to learn that the two miniature O'Caseys are happy among the young criminals at Dartington, and that their mother is now one of the Beauties of Devon.

Charlotte sends all sorts of affectionate messages.

> G. B. S.

When a baby girl was born to the O'Caseys the following year, GBS sent fifty pounds as a birthday gift, with the following letter dated 4 October 1939:

My dear Eileen,

It is important that the boys should have a sister. Sisterless men are always afraid of women.

I enclose a birthday present for her. The next one will be only half-a-crown. The Budget — oh, the Budget! The end of the year will clean me out.

We take it that you are doing as well as can be expected.

G. Bernard Shaw

The Malvern Theatre Festival was an annual institution until 1939, when it was interrupted by 'the second Punic War'.

Though established to the glory of Shaw, it soon began to produce the works of other playwrights, past and present. On 22 April 1940 GBS sent a card from Ayot St Lawrence to Sean in which he said:

All well here.

I haven't been in a theatre for years: and I cant think of a new play, though the continuance of the Malvern Theatre Festival depends on my producing one. Can you oblige?

I should have gone to The Red Star[32] black-out or no black-out if I hadnt read it. It shewed up the illiteracy of the critics[33] who didnt know that like a good Protestant you had brought the language of the Authorised Version back to life. Splendid![34]

G. B. S.

Sean answered a week later:

Devon
29 April 1940

My dear G. B. S.

Fine to hear that all's well in Ayot St. Lawrence.

I've no play for Malvern. 'Purple Dust' has been taken by Eddie Dowling of New York,[35] & he'll be getting an option on the English License. He is very much struck with the play; & has, I believe, a part in it for himself. Dowling's father &

mother were Irish, & he is Irish, too! We're all Irish. Mr. Elmhirst[36] was telling me he had lunch with you lately. They're
doing part of your Film[37] here. Good luck. Don't worry
about Malvern & their mania for new plays. Haven't they hundreds to choose from. And a lot of yours, too.

> *God be wi' you,*
> *Sean*

Numerous Russian journals, *International Literature* and others,
had commissioned articles on such subjects as Shakespeare,
Tolstoy and the Soviet army. One asked Sean to do an appreciation of Chekhov, and to get other authors to join. He approached
several without success, including John Masefield, the Poet
Laureate. GBS sent what he called 'a Chekhov blurb'. Intermittently, he and Sean corresponded. Early in 1942, when
Sean was looking for a picture of Lady Gregory that might – he
thought then – go into a later volume of his autobiography, he
asked GBS about the Esptein bust and had this reply on a post-
card:

> The Epstein bust was a failure because E changed his plan
> when he was half-way through and ended with a muddle of
> the two. Besides, he was always seeking to reveal the abor-
> iginal savage beneath the civilised sitter; and nothing could
> change Augusta into a Brooklyn washerwoman, much less
> into a half humanized lizard.
>
> If I can find the negatives, I shall try to get some better
> prints for you.[38]
>
> G. B. S.

Towards the end of the same year, answering another letter
from Sean, GBS wrote from Ayot St Lawrence:

> 14th November 1942.
>
> My dear Sean,
>
> Dont on your life bring up your boy as that most despicable
> of all shams, a stage Irishman. A man's country is the one

whose air he breathes and whose people he knows. Breon is
an Englishman, born in British Battersea, bred in British Devon,
singing Drake's Drum and not Let Erin Remember, having
Raleigh for his local hero. To him his dad must always be a
funny sort of fellow, let us hope beloved and admired, but
still a curiosity. O'Flaherty, whom he calls O'Flayerty, is a
native of a savage island, who seems to take it as a matter of
course that his mother should be a thief and a liar who, by
way of being patriotic, claims that all great Englishmen were
Irish. Like Queen Victoria he is 'not amused'. Why should he
be? And arnt you glad he isnt? Why do you add 'strangely
enough'? The air has made an honest English lad of him: that
is all. Sixty six years of English air have not made an Englishman of me because I started with 20 years of Irish air. Battersea and Devon have by this time marked Breon for their own;
and nothing could be more wicked than to rob him of his birth-
right.

By the way, he will be greatly hampered by his father's
fame if he does not change his name. Think of Mozart's
son! of Wagner's son! of that unlucky Mendelssohn who said
'I have been son of my famous father and the father of my
famous son, but never myself.' If he intends to become famous
he had better call himself O. K. C. Totneson or Devonson.

Charlotte is an invalid now; and we are both damnably old.

Pearson's book[40] is all right as to the facts, and very read-
able. I helped him all I could.

Thats all for today. I am sorry I wasnt in London when
your consort came up. It is pleasanter to see her than it is to
see me in decrepitude.[41]

G. B. S.

Charlotte's illness was a sad shock to GBS: 'the gradual distortion of the stout body, the sinking away from association
with the companion she had loved and guarded so long. The great
and sensitive man had to watch the life of his wife declining day
by day; the flag of companionship slipping down the staff.'[42]
GBS wrote to Eileen telling her that Charlotte was very much
deformed; a disease of the bones that would affect the contours

of the face. He was looking after her, and would love to see Eileen; so would Charlotte, but it would be too painful and difficult for her. It was time, he went on in his facetious manner, that Sean produced a 'money-spinner'. Sean was greatly upset when he heard of Charlotte's death. He wrote immediately in consolation, and in October 1943 received one of the familiar GBS postcards:

> We came up to London, after an absence that ran into years, on the 26th July, my birthday (87); and Charlotte's death on the 12th of this month involves a heap of business that will keep me here for weeks to come. The spate of letters, 80 a day for a fortnight, was overwhelming; I had to acknowledge them in the lump by a notice in The Times; but still there were several that had to be answered.
>
> The end was to be expected at our ages (86 and 87). It was quite happy; and I was tempted to put into the notice 'No letters: no congratulations'.
>
> A letter has just come from Cosgrave — along with yours! Very friendly.[43]
>
> G. B. S.

Two or three times after Charlotte's death Eileen managed to get to Ayot St Lawrence to see GBS, who was lonely and told her that he was. One visit she made with John Dulanty, the Irish High Commissioner, who had business to discuss; GBS had thought it would be a chance for her to be taken by car from door to door. Dulanty wrote to Sean on 13 January 1950:

> As you will have heard, Herself and myself had a pleasant hour with Bernard Shaw, who greeted her with 'Well, Eileen, you've still got your good looks.' He was obviously glad to see her. (I wandered out of the room to give them the opportunity of a mild flirtation!) . . .[44]

In the early summer of 1950, GBS wrote to Sean telling him that

Eileen, still lovely as ever, gave me a photograph of the lot of you which pleased me so much that I have had it framed and look at it quite often. Your marriage has been a eugenic success: the Heir Apparent is a stalwart who must count me as a Struldbrug which is what I actually look like. I keep my wits about me much better than my legs; that is the best I can say for myself.

He concluded by saying: 'I have no news for you except the quite uninteresting item that I am having a bout of lumbago. They are trying to bake it out of me by Radiant Heat.[45] In July 1950 GBS was ill, having fallen while pruning an apple tree in his garden and broken his leg. In hospital he developed pneumonia, which set him back. Eileen journeyed to Ayot in October and found that they had turned the downstairs room at Shaw's Corner into a bedroom for him. She tried to persuade him that he would certainly get better and might yet see the hundredth birthday to which he had looked forward; 'but he said he was not sure that the time had not come to leave everything, for he could not bear the idea of being helped from his bed to the couch; the whole idea, in fact, of being obliged to depend on others'.[46] On her next visit to Ayot, GBS asked her: 'And how is Sean financially?' Thinking that that was hardly the time to worry him about their situation, she replied: 'Of course, we are perfectly all right.' GBS passed on to talk of his loneliness and the deaths of his contemporaries and friends, and appeared to be extraordinarily tired. A few days later, when calling at Dulanty's, Eileen had a compelling urge to go down to Ayot again. Dulanty was just coming downstairs. He exclaimed that he had telephoned Sean asking where Eileen might be found; GBS had said that he wanted to see her. At once she rang up Ayot, and they told her to come, if possible, that afternoon:

On arrival I found Shaw dozing and very pale indeed. Before he woke I had time to study the room in detail; except for its pictures of Stalin and Gandhi, it did look like a small room in a hospital, with its collection of medicine bottles by the bed. Finally G. B. S. opened his eyes. Turning to me, he said,

'I really think I am going to die.' His voice was weak and he spoke softly; one had to move close to him to hear what he was saying. But he rallied for a moment and began to talk in his old humorous way, asking what was going to happen after death and whom he would meet, treating it as a new experience instead of being in any sense frightened: 'If there's an Almighty, Eileen, I'll have a hell of a lot of questions to ask Him.' I said that perhaps he would be able to tell Sean what there was to meet. Sean, he answered, would have to carry on. 'No.' I said, 'Sean is too old'; and he replied. 'It's up to one or both of the boys if their lives aren't wasted in another war.'[47]

Softly, GBS stole away into a sleep, and quietly Eileen tiptoed out of the room, leaving him looking as if he were already dead. Outside, she talked for some time to a nurse. Then, suddenly, the bell, fastened to Shaw's shoulder, rang to bring attention. When the nurse went in, he asked her if Eileen had gone. When he was told that she had not but was about to go, he said he would like to say goodbye to her. She went back, sat down by the bedside, and with a lovely smile he said, 'Goodbye, Eileen, goodbye; give my love to all the O'Caseys.' Two days later, on the gate of the house at Ayot St Lawrence a notice was posted which read: 'Mr. Bernard Shaw passed peacefully away at one minute to five o'clock this morning, 2 November. From the coffers of his genius he enriched the world.'

NOTES

1. Letter in Dr Ronald Ayling's possession. Subsequent letters appear either in David Krause (ed.), *The Letters of Sean O'Casey: I: 1910–41* (New York: Macmillan, 1975) or in Eileen O'Casey (ed.), *Sean,* with an Introduction by J. C. Trewin (London: Macmillan, 1971).
2. *Daily News* (London), 10 May 1916.
3. Eileen O'Casey, op. cit., p. 85.
4. Sean O'Casey, *Rose and Crown, Autobiographies,* II (London: Macmillan, 1963) p. 280.
5. From a copy made by Lady Gregory and printed in Lennox Robinson

(ed.), *Lady Gregory's Journals, 1916–1930* (London: Putnam, 1946) pp. 110–11.

6. 'Letter to the Producer of *The Silver Tassie*', *The Times*, 26 November 1929, p. 14. Reprinted in Ronald Ayling (ed.), *Sean O'Casey; Modern Judgements* (London: Macmillan, 1969) p. 91.
7. Eileen O'Casey, op. cit., p. 111.
8. Ibid, p. 125.
9. Krause (ed.), op. cit.
10. Ibid, p. 313. The book Charlotte had sent to him was Joseph H. Wicksteed, *Blake's Vision of the Book of Job: A Study with Reproductions of the Illustrations* (London: Dent, 1910).
11. Who played the role of Nora Clitheroe.
12. Krause (ed.), op. cit., p. 410.
13. Ibid, pp. 432–3.
14. A copy of Sean's letter appears in 'Black Oxen Passing by', *Rose and Crown* (1952).
15. Krause (ed.), op. cit., p. 439.
16. Eileen O'Casey, op. cit., p. 113.
17. Krause (ed.), op. cit., pp. 440–1.
18. Of *Within the Gates* (1933).
19. 'A Child is Born' became the first chapter of his first autobiographical book, *I Knock at the Door* (1939).
20. For a concise account of the Academy, founded in 1932, see Stephen Gwynn, *Irish Literature and Drama in the English Language: A Short History* (London: Nelson, 1936) pp. 232–6.
21. Sean O'Casey, *Autobiographies,* II (London: Macmillan, 1963) pp. 179–80.
22. Eileen O'Casey, op. cit., p. 134.
23. Hesketh Pearson, *Bernard Shaw: His Life and Personality* (London: Collins, 1942) p. 390 n.
24. Eileen O'Casey, op. cit., pp. 144–5.
25. Krause (ed.), op. cit., pp. 684–5.
26. For the details about the broken lease, see O'Casey's letter to Gabriel Fallon, 25 August 1939, in Krause (ed.), op. cit., p. 812.
27. Ibid., p. 742.
28. *Sunset and Evening Star: Autobiographies,* II (London: Macmillan, 1963) p. 180.
29. Ibid, p. 181.
30. Ibid, pp. 181–2.
31. Eileen O'Casey, op. cit., p. 171.
32. Shaw means O'Casey's *The Star Turns Red,* which was first performed at the Unity Theatre, London, on 13 March 1940.
33. But it had an enthusiastic review from (of all people) James Agate, a critic with whom Sean was at odds.
34. Eileen O'Casey, op. cit., p. 177.

35. The play opened at the Cherry Lane Theatre, Greenwich Village, New York, on 27 December 1956, but had earlier been produced by Alec Clunes at the Arts Theatre in 1942.
36. Leonard Elmhirst of Dartington Hall.
37. Shaw's *Major Barbara,* directed by Gabriel Pascal, released in 1941.
38. Eileen O'Casey, op. cit., p. 185.
39. Breon was born in St John's Wood, not Battersea.
40. Pearson, op. cit.
41. Eileen O'Casey, op. cit., pp. 185–6.
42. O'Casey, *Sunset and Evening Star,* p. 182.
43. Eileen O'Casey, op. cit., pp. 206–7.
44. Ibid, p. 207.
45. Ibid, p. 208.
46. Ibid, p. 209.
47. Ibid, pp. 209–10.

7 'A Kinda Trinitarian Soul':[1] Sean O'Casey and the Art of Autobiography

WILLIAM J. MAROLDO

The *Autobiographies* of Sean O'Casey,[2] published originally from 1939 to 1954, at intervals of about three years, comprise six volumes — nearly ½ million words, by far the bulk of the Irish playwright's literary production. Yet only the first four, the Irish Books (*I Knock at the Door, Pictures in the Hallway, Drums under the Windows,* and *Inishfallen, Fare Thee Well*), exemplify autobiography as genre; the last two, the Books of Exile (*Rose and Crown* and *Sunset and Evening Star*), are not autobiography but blends of reminiscence and memoir differing in structure, point of view, and major theme from what precedes them. There are, moreover, signs in the fourth of the Irish Books which predict O'Casey's eventual abandonment of the genre.

Autobiography proper is a narrative of the variable length characterised by the author's expressed or implied *autobiographical intention.* It is fundamentally different from reminiscence, memoirs, diaries, letters and so-called autobiographical fiction. Furthermore, expressed autobiography is centrifugal; for it points outside the 'world' of the book for its validation and completion; its meaning is thus largely circumstantial and particular, rather than universal or general in the aesthetic sense. Once autobiographical intention is expressed in a given work, the work as a whole tends to be discursive, as its reader is more or less predisposed to seek facts, dates, polemic, and items of specific information. However, expressed autobiography can, and often does, function as a *confederation* of literary forms, each having independent statis as art once other requirements are satis-fied. Frequently, through the exploitation of distancing devices that hide or obscure the identity of the author, autobiographical intention is implied – or merely suspected; thereby it exerts less influence on the reader, who may now sublimate his desire for particulars and become, in consequence, more receptive of the general significance embodied in the work.[3]

O'Casey's autobiographical intention in the Irish Books is pre-dominantly implied. He achieves aesthetic distance from his material through the use of a persona and third-person narration; and he avoids mentioning dates, geographical details, and other particulars in the surveys of his childhood, youth and early manhood. Nevertheless, he is present as a distinct personality throughout the Irish Books; though O'Casey writes about himself in the third person, he writes, as a rule, in the brogue of the North Dublin slums; and he conveys it with suitable ortho-graphy.[4] This practice identifies the autobiographer, of course; but it serves also, as aural sign-symbol, to delineate other 'characters' in his book.

The persona of Johnny-Sean-Jack Casside, which is admit-tedly transparent, is the organising principle of the Irish Books; it helps to sustain their major theme, which involves O'Casey's succeeding, yet cumulative interests in traditional religion, Irish republicanism, and Irish trade unionism and socialism during the first forty-six years of his life. And the Irish Books end with Sean's self-exile from Ireland; phases of his trinitarian personal-ity have coalesced in his commitment to the life of artist; indeed, he has had his beginning with his first successes as an Abbey playwright.

The Irish Books cover a full range of literary forms – lyric, epic and dramatic – which show O'Casey as craftsman and artist. Though the Irish Books emerge as a confederation of such forms, the idea of common ground persists, attesting to the essential unity and coherence of the first four books of the *Autobiographies.* O'Casey's public accomplishment, which alone can aspire to art, results from his selection, rejection and moulding of materials available to him through memory and imagination and the *prism* of language (Joyce's term), in response to his most recent vision or reaffirmation of values.

What follows will attempt to substantiate and to validate, in a focal way, the foregoing pronouncements and assumptions concerning O'Casey and the art of autobiography. Form and content of four notable (and representative) sections of the Irish Books will be discussed: 'The Protestant Kid Thinks of the Reformation', in *I Knock at the Door*; 'Royal Risidence', in *Pictures in the Hallway*; House of the Dead', in *Drums under the Windows*; and 'Comrades', in *Inishfallen, Fare Thee Well*. These sections are chosen primarily because they can be abstracted from the *Autobiographies*, specifically, the Irish Books, as illustrations of the principle of confederation of literary forms. And when this discussion is over, much more will need to be said.

I Knock at the Door, the first of the Irish Books, closes some time in 1890; and it is clearly Johnny's book. But he himself is often in the background, and O'Casey the autobiographer frequently intrudes present thoughts, at the time of writing. Thus Johnny is a postfiguration of the ten-year old O'Casey might once have been, but probably not. From earliest childhood, Johnny gradually becomes aware of his family, his playmates and the time and place of his life. Away from privations of every sort and the careless activities of childhood, he is passive, usually in response to things he can only partially understand. He accepts life as it is; and adult thoughts about the way things ought to be confuse him at hime, in church and in Sunday school. Though he picks up notions about God and nation, he is yet neither advocate nor rebel. Nevertheless, Johnny's view of life is comprehensive and inquisitive; he tends to fill in the blank spaces with imagination and hope. As a child – indeed, like all children – he makes his own world, in which the present is of utmost importance; like, perhaps, the perpetual present of the drama.

Johnny, 'the Protestant kid', thinks of the Reformation in the midst of the wretched, vastly Catholic slums of North Dublin. And the theme, once again, is alienation; and it will permeate the Irish Books as its organising principle.

Johnny's glorious times of play and exploration end abruptly one fine day when the Reverend Mr Hunter, 'a shadow like the shadow of a monster crow' (*IKATD*, p. 135), comes upon him playing marbles. Johnny is accused of idleness. And O'Casey infuses gentle irony into the rector's words of Solomonic instruction, which are addressed now to a ragged, scarcely fed child of the North Dublin slums:[5]

> Don't you remember what the Bible says about idleness?
> No, sir.
> It says, John, the idle shall suffer hunger. Think of that, suffer hunger. Think of that, suffer hunger! That's what God says through the mouth of the wisest man who ever lived. The idle soul shall suffer hunger [*IKATD*, p. 137; cf. Proverbs, 19:15].

Convinced with pietistic simplicity that Johnny's eyes (always weak and often seared with pain and incidental blindness all the days of O'Casey's life) are well enough for school, the Reverend Mr Hunter talks to Mrs Casside about the matter. Johnny overhears his mother's submission to the rector's authority, as the rector insists that Johnny 'should be made into a firm protestant young man in this dark and roman land' [*IKATD*, p. 137]. Johnny protests, and this is the first clear note of rebellion in the Irish Books. But it is not the rebellion of a seven-year-old boy (at this juncture, in 1887); it anticipates more seasoned and more mature reflection: 'What past-gone long-gone dog-done thing had bred this dragging of him along at the backside of this soft-hatted stiff-collared chancer to be fitted into the life of a protestant day school?' (*IKATD*, p. 138.)

The language is a spirited medley of alliteration and assonance. The appearance of "dog-done" is unexpected and puzzling. Is it perhaps an allusion to Joyce's *dog-God* equation, coupled with the notion of God's having *done* it all? Indeed, the sound of 'dog-done' is closely equivalent to that of 'dog-dung', especially as it occurs before a consonant. Moreover, final *g*'s are usually dropped in North Dublin speech and in Johnny's. And, of course, 'ding-dong' rings a bell.

The selection continues without interruption, in a manner that suggests indirect interior monologue — so prevalent elsewhere in the Irish Books. Johnny seeks an answer to his question in remembered Sunday school lessons:

> Maybe, becauses Moses had stopped to have a gawk at the burning bush; or that the Isrealites were able to make mince-meat of the Amalekites; or that the followers of Christ were first called Christians at Antioch; or maybe, it was really because of *The Protestant Reformation* [centred, in italics, as a section, or chapter, heading] [*IKATD*, p. 138].

At this point, O'Casey intrudes directly into the chapter, inserting material which had appeared, in a slightly different version, in the *American Spectator* of July 1934,[6] five years before the first publication of *I Knock at the Door*. O'Casey sets aside both his persona and with it the task of autobiographer for the space of seven pages (*IKATD*, pp. 138–45). However, the material is shaped to fit into the context of the chapter. Deleting the last two paragraphs of the original version, O'Casey substitutes:[7]

> A wave or two of truth as it was in Luther splashed over Ireland, and so in process of time, The Reverend Hunter was born in protestant circumstances that make him a sky-pilot, and Johnny was born a protestant in circumstances that placed him in the position of being lugged along at the backside of this soft-hatted stiff-collared egg-headed oul' henchman of heaven, to be added to his swarm of urchins cowering and groping about in the rag-and-bone education provided by the church and state for the children of those who hadn't the wherewithal to do anything better [*IKATD*, pp. 145–6].

In the original version, the author's implied intention is clearly autobiographical; the essay, according to O'Casey, tells of one of the 'incidents I had experienced'.[8] But now it is essentially independent from its immediate context, which is here as elsewhere a confederation of literary forms. True, this section implies the thoughts of 'a Protestant kid', who is allegedly O'Casey himself when he was much younger; nevertheless, as a major portion of a chapter in *I Knock at the Door*, the inserted material does not add effectively to the unity and coherence of the book. In the present instance, though it is obliquely related in subject matter to the situation in which Johnny finds himself, the essay does not convey Johnny's thoughts, nor a plausible approximation of them, as he is lugged off to the 'inner gloom' of St Mary's National School.

It seems likely that the reader's recognition of the essay and possibly also his memory of its original context will influence his reception of it now. Thus it is like expressed autobiographical intention in that it may vitiate the self-sufficiency of the work in hand. However, the inserted material need not be recognised as such; and, in any case, its immediate pertinence in the Irish Books must depend on how it functions within its new context (like literary allusion, generally) or outside of it. Indeed, the essay may even here legitimately stand alone, a part of the confederation of forms which constitutes the Irish Books taken as a whole.

The essay is a compressed yet comprehensive survey of the Reformation, though it is predominantly an expression of feeling rather than an assertion of historical fact. It is, moreover, third-person exposition of mature, somewhat blatant criticism of the Christian Church before the advent of Protestantism. The language is seven-year-old Johnny's; it is heard as the speech of the North Dublin slums, and the sound of the Authorised Version of the Bible is invoked now and then. But the theme and the ideas stated belong to a mature O'Casey, who now speaks in his own voice.

> Then Luther decided to let things rip, and went at it, hammer and tongs, and made short work of the traffic of indulgences, a gilt-edged superstition that let anyone do anything from pitch-and-toss to manslaughter, so long as a suitable fee was dropped in the back pocket in the pants of a priest [*IKATD*, p. 143].

Moreover, Johnny, as a character, is thrust into the background for the duration of the inserted material. Though the newly written last paragraph of the essay manages to bring both the Reverend

Mr Hunter and Johnny within its purview, the temptation is strong to label this mere contrivance on O'Casey's part.

'Royal Risidence', now the third chapter of *Pictures in the Hallway*, the second of the Irish Books, which brings Johnny-Sean-Casside through to the end of the nineteenth century, appeared originally in the *Virginia Quarterly Review,* in 1940.[9] Thus its first publication followed that of *I Knock at the Door* (1939). In light of this, O'Casey's remark to the effect that it was in print 'before the idea of biography came into my head'[10] suggests little more than the possibility that 'Royal Risidence' had been reduced to its present form before he undertook writing the Irish Books, or, at least, before he began *Pictures in the Hallway*.

Like several episodes incorporated into the Irish Books, 'Royal Risidence' is self-contained; it is one of several disjointed incidents which tend to exemplify the principle of confederation of literary terms. As autobiography, they suggest 'moments' in Johnny-Sean Casside's growing awareness of the world around him; often they are lyrical interludes, which express feeling and emotion, but rely little on immediate external fact or chronology. They are phases of O'Casey's spiritual journey, frequently supported by patterns of literary and historical allusion.

Johnny is off to visit Kilmainham Jail, which is south of the Liffey, in the Inchicore Road, and west of the South Circular Road – a tram-ride through Dublin from Innisfallen Parade. Johnny is being taken there by his uncle, Tom Archer, his mother's brother, who is a wounded veteran of the Crimean War and now a pensioner of the Queen. Johnny is led forth 'to see the sight of a jail where men who did wickedly were kept safe from the temptation of doing anything worse than they had done before' (*PITH*, p. 33). There is irony in this appraisal of Kilmainham which will be recalled in focus later in the chapter and in the Irish Books, as Johnny comes to realise the nature of the wickedness committed by most of the inmates.

Kilmainham Jail is celebrated in modern Irish history, especially for its part in the struggles of Irishmen against English rule. It is a royal prison which houses predominantly political prisoners and militant Republicans; so there is added irony in O'Casey's dubbing Kilmainham 'Royal Risidence'. To him, perhaps, this mass of rough stone, more than Dublin Castle, symbolises British presence and power in Ireland. This attitude would have been shared by his comrades who were active in the cause of Irish nationalism later on in his career.

In as much as Parnell is acknowledged as dead in the course of 'Royal Risidence' (cf. *PITH*, pp. 38, 44), it is probable that the event described occurred sometime after 6 October 1891; that is, during Johnny's eleventh or twelfth year. Still, in a subsequent reference to the Phoenix Park Murders, which took place on 6 May 1882, O'Casey notes that 'something was dragging his [Johnny's] mind to dwell on things that had happened before he was born' (*PITH*, p. 52). This seems an implied insistence on the specious birth date of 31 March 1884, which hints that Johnny is now seven or eight years old, in keeping with the allusion to Parnell's death. Here and elsewhere in the Irish Books, confusion between O'Casey's two birth dates is evident now and then. But is has little effect on the development of autobiography, nor, especially, on the delineation of lyrical interludes.[11]

The description of the environs of Kilmainham Jail, 'where everything made the place look as if it were doing a ragged and middle-aged minuet' (*PITH*, p. 40), sets the tone of 'Royal Risidence'. It is reinforced almost immediately by a description of the prison itself:

There it was. A great, sombre, silent, stone building, sitting like a toad watching the place doing its ragged middle-aged minuet. A city of cells. A place where silence is a piercing wail; where discipline is an urgent order from heaven; where a word of goodwill is as far away as the right hand of God; where the wildest wind never blows a withered leaf over the wall; where a black sky is as kind as a blue sky; where a hand-clasp would be low treason; where a warder's vanished frown creates a carnival; where there's a place for everything, and everything in its improper place; where a hap-hazard song can never be sung; where the bread of life is always stale; where God is worshipped warily. and where loneliness was a frightened, hunted thing [*PITH*, pp. 40-1].

Quickly Johnny is 'installed as a freeman among the prisoners and captives' (*PITH*, p. 41). He is shown the tidiness and perfection of cells: 'A slop-pail stood to attention in a corner [of course, in proper military fashion] ; over it a tiny shelf holding a piece of yellow soap and a black-covered Bible, that cleanliness was next to godliness . . .' (*PITH*, p. 42). In each cell, there is 'a baby-tongues flicker of gas . . . the captive's little pillar of fire, the prisoner's light of the world, a light to them that sit in darkness, needing no light from the sun'. O'Casey reinforces the irony of this description immeditely: 'Lead kindly light, amid the circling gloom, lead thou me on till the day break and the shadows flee away' (*PITH*, p. 43). The allusion, to Cardinal Newman's 'The Pillar of the Cloud', is typical of many in the Irish Books.

Johnny is depressed, and the impulse grows to flee into the wholesome disorder and random freedom of the world outside Kilmainham. Here is unchanging alienation which he cannot tolerate: 'Stone and steel surrounding loneliness, pressing loneliness in on itself, with a black-coated Bible to keep it company and a jaundiced eye looking out of the darkness.' The Bible is now 'black-coated' − like a priest, and the 'flicker of gas' has become a 'jaundiced eye'. Here as elsewhere, O'Casey elects to personify nature and inanimate objects, the well-known fallacy notwithstanding, rendering them sensible forces against which man must contend. Ironically enough, there is a chapel in Kilmainham Jail which contains a small cabinet where 'the priest kept his God all the secular days of the week and took him out for exercise on Sunday' (*PITH*, p. 43). Not the God of the prisoners, certainly, but the God of the priest; the Eucharist, too, is a prisoner, with a somewhat special routine in this place of rigid routine − or a god or a pet, who exercises the seventh day.

Later in 'Royal Risidence', Johnny's thoughts take the form of indirect interior monologue; and what follows is a summary of the Phoenix Park Murders and their aftermath in Kilmainham Jail. O'Casey's presence is detected occasionally in the mature appraisal of what had happened; most of its content is quite beyond the scope of young Johnny Casside. Lord Frederick Cavendish, sent as Chief Secretary of Ireland to administer Gladstone's new policy, was assassinated with Thomas Burke, the

Irish Under Secretary, by a select group of Fenians:

> Beside the man in grey [Burke] he lay a memory now, covered
> soberly by a stately purple pall that the setting sun was slowly
> spreading over the sky, high above the rat [Burke] and the
> lion [Lord Cavendish, the Earl of Murray] as they lay in des-
> perate sleep together [*PITH*, p. 52].

Johnny has begun to fear the violent memories of the place: 'He
was sure that strange things strolled about in the dead of night
in the queer place.' O'Casey adds significantly a thought that is
young Johnny's which reflects the influence of his Catholic comrades: 'Had he been a roman catholic, he'd a made the sign of
the cross, but all he could say was, Jasus. Ay, Jasus help the In-
vincibles and the two men they slew' (*PITH*, p. 52). And once
again Johnny is lost in reverie. This time he follows the chase and
the capture of Brady, Curley, Fagan, Caffrey, and Kelly, their
brief interrogation in Dublin Castle and their trial in the Inns of
Quay Police Court, the conduct of their sentences, and their
burial beneath the flagstones in the yard of Kilmainham Jail.
Johnny's reverie blends with his awareness of his present situation: There was

> no crack of his [Brady's] voice as he went on through a
> gauntlet o' carbines, muttering the creed of the felon, poor
> oul' Ireland, poor oul' Ireland that was fadin' fast away from
> him; for it was time to be goin', goin' out of this sad place,
> goin' home before the heavy darkness came, an' he alone with
> the sleepin' warder [who has conducted Johnny and his Uncle
> Tom on their tour of Kilmainham] who looked for all the
> world as if he, too, was sleepin' the sleep of the dead, seemin'
> to say in his stillness that this was the only sleep that had rest
> in a place like this Tom's voice callin', in the corridor for me
> to come; and Johnny rose up and hurried out, leaving the hoary-
> headed oul' man asleep by the dying fire in the dusk, his head
> bent down in the dark of his trim blue coat [*PITH*, pp. 53-4].

'House of the Dead', the third chapter of *Drums under the*

Windows is given over to lyric, fantasy, and veiled assertion, which are sustained in a complex pattern of literary (and historical) allusion. The second part of the chapter (staged at the Richmond Lunatic Asylum) is, in effect, a nightmare, in which the loss of reality is subordinated to an organising principle presupposing order in chaos.

'House of the Dead' assembles innumerable moods, emotions, philosophical notions, opinions, and attitudes which may be attributed to moments of confused awareness in the life of Sean-Jack Casside, then in his early thirties, but which transcend his particular circumstances and perspective. Moreover, there is no attempt at verisimilitude; the chapter is emotive and suggestive of generalised experience, confusing throughout fantasy and actuality. O'Casey's memory of specific events is of no importance here; 'House of the Dead' is shaped by his imagination.

The second part of the chapter is a *tour de force*, replete with unrestrained exploitation of O'Casey's vast acquaintance with literature and stray fact and theory. Indeed, the emerging patterns of allusion, remarkable for their interrelationships and internal organisation, create many worlds of meaning and personal significance beyond those specified in O'Casey's rich prose. Though predominantly modes of third-person narration, the methods and techniques of exposition in 'House of the Dead' are varied and unexpected.

This chapter opens on a sun-filled day in the midst of wide vistas on the Portrane Peninsula, to the north of Dublin. Sean is at work along the Dublin-Drogheda Line of the Great Northern Railway, Ireland, at a point about thirteen miles from the Terminus, at Amiens and Sheriff Streets: 'It was grand to be out in the country and close to the sea (*DUTW*, p. 64). Several years have passed since Sean's first gruelling experiences with pick and shovel; and he now glories in physical exertion and abundant good health.

Sean catches sight of a field of growing corn (wheat), as a city-dweller seeing it for the first time, 'living and rippling before him'; and his thoughts wander to pictures that have served until recently in place of nature; Constable's *The Cornfield* and coloured representations of calendars are among them. Sean thinks of what the Reverend E. M. Griffin has said about corn during services and instruction, the story of Ruth and Boas coming inevitably to mind: 'But it was from a field of barley Ruth displayed herself to Boas, and this was a field of wheat. Was it wheat now? He couldn't tell: didn't know the difference between wheat and barley, so he'd call it corn.' Still within the context of the Bible and the rector's sermons: 'One could easily imagine Jesus Himself strolling softly through such a field as this on some peaceful Sabbath morning' (*DUTW*, p. 66).

He dreams on, lost in the beauty of nature, which is far different from the sombre atmosphere of the slums — with its solitary hawthorn tree and stray patches of ragged grass: 'Coloured peace was here; a gay peace; a merry stillness, undisturbed but for the ratchet-like call of the corncrake. Oh, blessed peace!' (*DUTW*, p. 67). The lyrical interlude is filled with the bright sights of summer in the country; and there is beauty, too, in its smells, which is nature's own, not at all like the dank smells of crowded cities:

> A strange smell full of sharp sweetness came to him, making him wonder, for he had never sensed such a smell before. New-mown hay, he murmured; ah! that's what it is, must be— new-mown hay . . . the scent of new-mown hay . . . imprisoned in the salty smell of the sea coming in the breeze that fluttered on to his sweaty, heated face [*DUTW*, p. 67].

O'Casey's 'stage-setting' is remarkable in its precision; he is now on a point along the railway line about one and a half miles from the Irish Sea, in a gently rolling landscape. About five miles from where he is standing and sniffing, eastward, is Lambay Island.

Suddenly, Sean's peace is shattered by a 'cry of lost laughter throwing itself into an icy wail that's taken the scent from the hay, the savour from the sea, and has thrust out peace from its tenancy of the sky. There it is again — good God! The sound comes from the Portrane Lunatic Asylum,[12] with its 100-foot 'modern round tower, erected on a summit of rising ground,'[13] less than a mile from where Sean is now standing. Sean is called back to the totality of life, of which beauty and tranquility are only parts:

So behind this fair, sparkling, laughing curtain that Nature let down before him many dark and evil things were lurking, or hung entangled in the bright colours and satisfying scents like decaying flies in the iridescent and lovely-patterned web of the spider [*DUTW*, p. 68].

It is apparent how well Sean remembers his excursions into Darwin (see *DUTW*, pp. 32-3) and into Darwin's nature – a wild, mindless, yet orderly struggle for survival, from which human sensibilities are banished. His thoughts echo a passage in *The Origin of Species*; the similarity between the two expressions seems to be more than mere coincidence:

We behold the face of nature bright with gladness, we often see superabundance of food; we do not see or we forget, that the birds which are idly singing round us mostly live on insects or seeds, and are thus constantly destroying life; or we forget how largely these songsters, or their eggs, or their nestlings, are destroyed by birds and beasts of prey; we do not always bear in mind, that, though food may now be abundant, it is not so at all seasons of each recurring year.[14]

And what of Tennyson's 'Nature, red in tooth and claw'?

Sean recalls not only Darwin, but also his own experiences in the slums of North.Dublin, where the best hopes of struggling humanity are often reduced to despair and death, denied fulfilment amid conditions resembling those of the jungle; indeed, Sean has once visited a madhouse: 'Forgotten for the moment, he had already seen these things with his own eyes, and his hands had handled them' (*DUTW*, p. 68). His memories obliterate what is left of the calm beauty of nature about him; and they introduce the second part of 'House of the Dead', which is antithetical to the first:

Out there, now, right in the centre of the corn, just where Jesus has passed by a few minutes before, floated the face of Ella, a white face of settled fear, tightened with a stony smile that had a seed of wild weeping in it [*DUTW*, pp. 68-9; cf. p. 66].

Some time prior to this bright day now bereft of brightness on the Portrane Peninsula, Sean had taken his brother-in-law, reduced to brutality and madness, to the Richmond Lunatic Asylum, in North Dublin. The 'lost laughter' heard now from the Portrane Asylum serves to connect the present with the past; however, for the balance of the chapter, Sean retains his vantage point beside the railway.

He thinks bitterly about the fate of his sister, since the 'smiling morn' (*IKATD*, pp. 101–15) of her marriage years ago: 'She had married a man who had destroyed every struggling gift she had when her heart was young and her careless mind was blooming' (*DUTW*, p. 69; cf. p. 115). Ella had six children destined to go the way of the slums, the last of whom died at the age of three, after the worst of care, 'leaving her to weep long over a thing unworthy a tear or a thought'. And Ella had settled more deeply into the squalor of her surroundings: 'Her home was a fanciful bastion of rags, bones, and bottles' (*DUTW*, p. 69). The promise of her youth and its bright acquaintance with literature and the better things of life has faded into forgetfulness and misery: 'All gone now; gone into the gloom of a night hiding gifts abandoned; gone, save in the resless memory of Sean's own mind.' (*DUTW*, p. 70) Thinking of Ella, and, perhaps, also of Tom, his dead brother, and other kindred unfortunates, Sean offers a prayer to a god in whom he can no longer believe; despite what he has come to know about the world's ills, he holds a hope suggestive of that voiced by the bereaved Mrs Tancred and later, by Juno Boyle, in *Juno and the Paycock*:[15] 'Oh, Ella, Ella! Oh. Jesus, have pity on us! If not in harmony with Thee, let the glow of something good be in the fragment of our life' (*DUTW*, p. 70).

Bugler Benson, who returned from service with the Queen's army about 1891, had fallen into idleness and decay, succumbing slowly to general paralysis of the insane (GPI). Only when he reached the final, desperate stage of the disease (*DUTW*, p. 73) did Ella sign the forms committing him to the Richmond Lunatic Asylum.

The trip to the asylum (reconstructed in Sean's memory this day on the Portrane Peninsula) takes place on a sunny, sparrow-filled evening: ' . . . better for Benson he'd been born a sparrow than a man' (*DUTW*, p. 75). He is beyond God's attention. A black cab, with its keepers of madmen, comes slowly up to No. 18 Abercorn Road (where Benson has spent the previous night), Benson is loaded aboard, and the trip across the city begins:

> Between the keepers, with Sean opposite to see him safe home, Benson, grinning helplessly, was driven to the house of strident shadows, to dress in the rough tweed of the loony pauper,[16] to wear the red woollen neckerchief so tied that when one became restless a keeper could seize it, pull, and choke all movement, quench all fire out of the gurgling, foam-lipped madman; to where he would be dust to dust and ashes to ashes before he was dead, withered grass that hadn't yet been cast into the oven, to Grangegorman [*DUTW*, pp. 75-6].

The world of the living, of actuality, is left behind; Sean's trip to the 'house of the dead' becomes quickly a trip to Hell — Hell blending the features and vistas of other Hells, notably those of Virgil, Dante, Milton, and, eventually, Shaw:

> Wide gates of heavy, dull, heartless lead opened to let them in, and the black cab rolled silently along the drive drawn by a horse with a sly and regular trot as if he felt and feared anything else might entitle him for companionship with the dread life of the still twitching dead [*DUTW*, p. 76].

The atmosphere thickens, quite palpably; and the reader is left to react in diverse ways to the details of ensuing description. And 'Royal Risidence' in outline, at least, is repeated with variation; however, literary allusion replaces historical allusion.

There are lunatics in groups about the asylum yards; and they seem to Sean to be like cloistered monks and friars: 'Dotted here and there were the dismal brothers of the disorders grey, their red mufflers making them look as if their tormented heads had been cut off, and pushed crookedly back on their necks again' (*DUTW*, p. 76). O'Casey's expression is thus reinforced: The 'disorders' are the species of madness that have put lunatics (like Benson) behind these walls; the 'grey' is their rough tweed —

without colour, without life, shorn from since-dead sheep; and the red line of the mufflers encircling their necks signifies the manner of their *dying*. Moreover, the oblique reference to cloistered friars persists; the unlucky mad are cut off from the world outside with its turmoil and its threat and its occasions for sin and life.

The dark building of the asylum (catching, perhaps, the last rays of the setting sun) is personified, Ruskin's pathetic fallacy notwithstanding, through O'Casey's use of rich, recurring sounds and images. All references to God become ironic; the world which Sean remembers having once visited is the antithesis of bright nature stretching out from either side of the Dublin-Drogheda Railway Line, on the Portrane Peninsula:

> The cab stopped slowly before the building, wide and long, built like a bully that had suddenly died shrugging his shoulders. Long rows of lifeless windows mirrored long rows of lifeless faces, their silence hymning a fading resurrection of Valasquez's idiots, a whole stonily grinning gallery of God's images turned to dull grey clay, the emptiness of a future in every face. Now and again, some of them would vent a laugh that ripped a shudder along the walls of the asylum [*DUTW*, p. 76].

The 'lost laughter' from the Portrane Lunatic Asylum is echoed in Sean's memory; and one hears, too, the mad nun's laughter in Joyce's *Portrait*.

The Richmond Asylum yard is an archetypical valley of death:

> The grass everywhere grew brown and long, and fell to dust whenever it was touched; the trees twisted their branches like limbs in pain, and grew grey leaves that never seems to move [movement=life+will+change], as if under the blight of the fig-tree Christ had cursed [Matthew, 21: 19–21]. Flowers that tried to grow beneath the windows were slimy stalks, crawling along the grey ground like slugs tantalizing the rim of a festering lily, lost amid the quiet storm of lunacy distilling a sour air everywhere. [The lily, here and in Joyce's 'The Dead', is the flower of resurrection; its meaning is subverted here, of

course.] In a corner a chestnut-tree dropped worm-worn fruit like leaden balls, and riven church bells rang out a raucous angelus [Millet's painting; Markham's poem] three times a day, carolling rakishly mid the mindless chatter and the rasping laugh.

O'Casey continues, without interruption, piling image upon image in surprisingly small space, as he develops his complex pattern of allusion: Here Homer, Virgil, Milton, and Keats are the principal contributors to the general effect. Indeed, there are echoes of what has gone before in the Irish Books:

> Only ghosts of things and men were here; nor in the sky above was any balm of blus, or fleecy solace from a drifting cloud; nothing but vacancy reaching to where God had gone from.[17] No gay bird sang [as in Yeat's 'Sailing to Byzantium'], no blazoned butterfly flew through the frozen sunlight, no gentle scent of gentler flower. No jocund dawn danced into sight over the hills of the morning,[18] no night came dreaming out of the slumbering sea; no big wind ever tossed the still trees, no tremor teased the earth, no fire blinked in the dead eyes waiting, and no still small voice stole upon the ears forgetting the sound of their own words, maimed and bewildered, vainly uttered [*DUTW*, pp. 76-7].

'Dead eyes waiting' — for what? A more unequivocal death, perhaps. Of course, this is a valley of death, or of death anticipated; and it is made hideous and forlorn by the persistent memory of life and of nature's proper glory.[19] Its inhabitants are the living dead (says O'Casey); nevertheless, there is dismal order here — and paralysing perfection.

The doctor in charge of admissions to the Richmond Asylum comes forward to greet Sean and his brother-in-law. He is Belial counseling 'ignoble ease and peaceful sloth' to Satan and others who would try to regain Heaven by purposeful action, whatever the odds against success, in Milton's 'Pandemonium[20] and Don Juan himself in Shaw's Hell.[21] Above all, he is Virgil, with quite different profession and intent, coming to meet Dante. Moreover, the doctor's humour is that of Mephistofeles advising the student come to learn:

> And out of the grey light and the noisy silence strutted a stout-bellied, loud-voiced, ruddy-faced man clad in loud-looking plus-fours, puffing stormily at a big pipe . . . [And] a gay smile on his face went about endorsing everything done by the sacred apes of god [*DUTW*, p. 77].

In his gay appearance and his words, the doctor contrasts with everything about him, and he is precise and determined in his actions, manifesting life and purpose in a place where they are absent.

Sean's childhood visit to Kilmainham Prison, 'where silence is a piercing wail', is recalled now; the two incidents share a common theme, the doctor-guide fuctioning in place of the warder, Tom Archer's Crimean comrade.

The doctor welcomes Benson's arrival:

> Aha! he said, when he saw Benson stumbling from the cab, 'here's another bright lodger for initiation into the brother-hood of Bedlamites [the 'disorders grey']. Well . . . what's this novice's *tour de force*?
>
> Bad case of G.P.I., doctor.
>
> Aha! Whores-de-combat, what? Well, lug him in, and regis-ter his name in the pigskin-covered book of the lie of the living [*DUTW*, pp. 77–8].

Sean reluctantly accepts the prideful doctor's offer to tour the asylum, like Dante about to begin his journey. And, again like Virgil, the doctor attributes reluctance to fear: 'Frightened, eh? Nonsense, man. Those outside are more dangerous than those who are here. The delusions, hopes, beliefs of those outside – unobtainable, man' (*DUTW*, p. 78). There is irony in such words, addressed to Sean as mortal 'man', which brings the asylum into contrast with the world outside once again. Moreover, Sean re-alises the truth in what he hears: both Tom and Ella have had their hopes and dreams blasted by the conditions in which they lived — and myriad bad luck. The doctor's assertions, which are platitudes, stress the privacy and self-sufficiency of the lunatic world:

> Here every man has all he wants. Outside a man lives in worlds created by others; here he lives in a world of his own. All's accomplished here, so it ceases to interest. Come with me to a land just over the border where those who live know nothing of their nearness — the Purple Land full of Druid moons, sleepy boughs, and voices of fire; where all are half awake, half silent, and half a world away from life [*DUTW*, p. 78].[22]

To the doctor, the boughs of dead and twisted trees found in the asylum yard are merely sleepy; but sleep is 'Death's counterfeit',[23] and O'Casey has already depected a 'house of the dead' in which sleep is death.

From this point on, the doctor becomes more clearly Virgil, as Sean begins his journey through an *Inferno* peopled with shades of Dublin's notables — literary, political, and casual in an Irish sense. The lunatics of Richmond Asylum recalls Dante's damned souls; and the circles of Hell as passed, though only dimly recognised as such. What is more, deadly sins and deadly sinners can be counted off, in grievous offence mostly of the spirit!

> A commonplace-looking man, with a bullet head, bulgy eyes, and straggly grey moustache, went whirling by, head over heels, head over heels . . .
>
> That's the holy whirligig,' said the doctor, hell-bent for Heaven. 'He's been given three thousand years to do the journey, and he has tightened steel hoops round his belly to keep him up to it [*DUTW*, p. 78].[24]

The Dantesque pattern continues to develop, largely at random (see *Inferno*, Canto IV); the doctor guides Sean:

> Here we are at the entrance of the Purple Land. Stoop! Here the higher-minded muck about, a kind of limbo [Circle I, the Virtuous Pagans], where they know neither pain nor joy, nor

can ever be at heartease, for all here are heart-tight and head-heavy with brooding; though all assume in company a jaunty mysticism of life's connection. Stoop! Mostly poets of a sort here, and fellows of lure [lore] and learning. Place of Masques. We've a long way to go yet [*DITW*, p. 79].

Leaving the *light* of Limbo, Sean and his companion enter the strange world of Irish myth and fable — 'all that never was'; colour, or, rather, shades of darkness in the absence of elemental light, ranges from 'dim violet to purple that was near to jet'. Sean should not be there; as a 'mortalman', he tends to reason, perhaps, to seek practical manifestations of nationality even here. The doctor warns him: 'Silence on your hollow head; silence on your dark body; silence on your dark brow. Make the sign of the seven-stringed harp of Aengus -- it's in the air' (*DUTW*, p. 79).

Abruptly, a transition is made to the actual world from this world of fantasy; the latter is merely a reaction to specimens of madness pointed out by the doctor: ' — Them dark things out there . . . are the bright spirits of the hills, where the Mountains of Dublin sweep down to the sea.' Sean becomes matter-of-fact, in reaction to what may be the figurative language of his guide: 'You mean the Mountains of Mourne, don't you?' (*DUTW*, p. 80.) However, the Mountains of Mourne are about fifty miles north of Dublin, close to the coast, in County Down, quite out of sight from the Richmond Asylum; so Sean's question seems beside the point. In fact, *all* questions are beside the point in this realm of moribund perfection and order: ' — No, I don't, snapped the doctor, nothing out of time or tune is allowed to enter here.' This is an ironic reference to Dante's '*Lasciate ogni speranza, voi ch'entrate*' (*Inferno*, Canto iii). Nevertheless, O'Casey sustains Sean's presence in the Richmond Asylum, managing at the same time to reinforce the unreal atmosphere of the place: 'Though they went a long way, they never stirred, the wide wings of numerous death's-head moths striking their cheeks and touching their eyelashes, frilling the violet air with tiny hovering skulls' (*DUTW*, p. 80).

Sean and his guide linger in the space of twilight, where the

myths of all nations have come together with those of Ireland:
' — What, is it the Keltic Twilight? questioned Sean, in a whis-
per.' Of course, he is warned to 'be simple, reverent, and understanding; and above all, be silent. The mysteries of the universe
are being solved here, including that of 'Cardinal Logue's Learning'. (How attentive Yeats would have been!) The figure of a
madman, who represents, among others, George W. Russell (AE),
comes towards them:

> He has a puce soul, whispered the doctor, and hence he thinks
> life is found only where everything is perpetually purple; and
> he indites hymns about mystical purple dew dripping from
> purple mystical trees, dim in a purple twilight that ends in a
> purple dawn [the span of night]. He gives the name of Dana,
> Donah, Dinah to the busy earth, and believes that his place in
> eternity is a faery seat among a thousand purple stars [*DUTW*.
> pp. 81–2].

The reference to his 'puce soul' seems to bring the madman into
the context of the *Inferno* (Canto iii, still); however, allusion to
Dante's Neutrals is inappropriate here, unless we think of vir-
tuous pagans at home in *Tuatha de Danaan*, which suggests
Laocoon's unheeded warning: '*Timeo Danaos et dona ferentes*'
(*Aeneid*, ii, 49), but to small end.

The doctor continues to sport with the mad, who think that
they know, assigning great meaning and wisdom to their words
of nonsense. Here there are philosophers, poets, and painters far
greater than any in the outside world: 'They soar above all
others in thought, see only through eyes of dream that pierce
straight through the veil of blank' (*DUTW*, pp. 83–4). All the
greatest contributors to the world's art and thought have their
counterparts here; and what they have to say to Sean and what
he learns about them in the 'House of the Dead' reduces the
world 'outside' to parody and dross. Sean fears that he will join
them in their flights of perfect fantasy:

> And Sean turned swiftly and fled away from the happy scene;
> back the way he had come, through the purple twilight into

the violet gloom, through the darting grasshoppers, murmuring as he ran, Oh, Lord, oh, my Lord! Oh, my good Lord, keep me from risin' up!

A litany of sorts, no doubt; but both prayer and aspiration point in the opposite direction, to be brought, once again, down to earth. The night before his trip to the Richmond Asylum, Sean contemplated Benson's raging madness with a different prayer, with precisely the same meaning: 'Oh, Lord, keep me from sinkin' down; oh, Lord, keep me from sinkin' down!' (*DUTW*, p. 74.)

Sean's proper station — like that of all 'mortal men', including awakened Dante — is in the precarious centre of life, between the heaven of the mad and the hell of the damned. His is a world of chance, of disorder, of life. The world of the mad, like that of the dead, does not tolerate error or change; and, accordingly, the human will has no place there. It is an amalgam of absolute answers (of Platonic reality, perhaps), where nothing happens; it is beyond process (space and time, the co-ordinates of becoming). The world to which Sean flees is of the living, full of uncertainty and doubt, full of pain, disappointment, and compromise with truth. According to the doctor, who commands silence and forbids questions, the mad enjoy unrestrained freedom and desire nothing; but this is not freedom at all, nor is it life. It is a mode of anarchy, perhaps, making due allowance for private worlds where everything *is* the way it ought to be. Only questions (doubt), will and choice build an actual world in which hope is possible. The madmen of the Richmond Asylum in worlds of their own making, without questions and the power to discriminate, are frozen (like the dead) in an unchanging reality; and this testifies to the madness. A living man is limited by his thoughts and his perception of what he shares with nature and other beings; the mad are confined to themselves. Man must give up solipsism to guarantee a world in process.

Through Sean's rejection of the orderly realm of the mad, O'Casey asserts once again his own unqualified acceptance of life; it is an existentialist appraisal, wherein the expanding consciousness of the individual can recognise no limits, joining that of others, yet retaining its persistant centre of self. Yet he seeks re-affirmation of human values and atonement in a vaster scheme of which he is a part.

'House of the Dead' closes with a last look at Benson; Sean observes a subverted maypole dance, which heralds not spring and new life, but death. Thus O'Casey rather melodramatically restates the theme of the last section of this chapter, still maintaining the atmosphere of fantasy:

> As he ran towards the leaden gateway, he beheld a grey circle of forms going round and round a black stake driven strongly into the darker ground; On the top of the stake sat a dazzling white skull, and black ribbons, tied to the stake, encircled the necks of the forms moving around it so that it looked like a maypole dance in a garden of death; and one of the grey forms was Benson grinning greyly as he plodded crookedly after the grey form in front of him [*DUTW*, pp. 90–1].[25]

In further support of the principle of confederation of literary forms, 'Comrades', the eighth chapter of *Inishfallen, Fare Thee Well*, the fourth of the Irish Books, does not contribute significantly to the autobiographical design of general work. It is essentially an interlude set in the Civil War; and Sean (the last phase of his trinitarian nature), as a 'character', is either peripheral or entirely absent in the course of its development. Still, 'Comrades' is remarkable in several ways. It emerges as the most carefully worked out of the segments comprising the Irish Books, showing O'Casey as a craftsman and as a formal experimenter. The chapter is constructed architecturally or orchestrated; and its meaning is unequivocal. O'Casey speaks directly to his reader, and what he has to say is simple and forthright.

'Comrades' is thematically an indictment of man's cruel, senseless treatment of his fellow man which contrasts ironically with the pretentions of traditional Christianity and of blatant nationalism. The theme is peculiarly Irish, then in the Free State and now in Ulster, and always familiar. O'Casey sees a subversion of human values and hopes for a better world in the recurring spectacle of war, brought now into focus in the Irish Civil

War. Former comrades, who fought together against England for a common good that neither understood completely, are now at each others throats, still ignorant of the issues involved, as Free-Stater and outlawed Republican. Moreover, there is throughout an insistence that man is corrupt in his general betrayal of life andnature. The theme is developed in an interesting point-counterpoint pattern which resembles, in musical terms, the two-part *fugue*.[26] Sustaining this is an *easy rhythm* in prose, which is prevalent in the Irish Books, which E. M. Forster defines as 'repetition plus variation',[27] and the result is both pleasing and effective.

Apparently to reinforce his treament of theme, O'Casey uses as leitmotif an echo of Azucena's poignant aria from Act IV, Scene ii, of Verdi's *Il Trovatore*, '*Ai nostri monti ritorneremo*' ['We shall return to our mountains']; but with a change of mood and emphasis. Indeed, with respect to this allusion, the universal tragedy of civil war, which brings brother against brother in bloody strife for vague political principle, is epitomised in the opera with its own sad resolution of conflict between Conte di Luna and Manrico, who are ignorant of the fact that they are brothers. A faint notion persists that Azucena, the old gypsy woman who witnesses the tragedy in *Il Trovatore*, stands now in the place of *Seanbhean bocht*, 'the Poor Old Woman' of Ireland, who must witness civil war.

Consistent with their structural similarity to a two-part *fugue*, the three sections of 'Comrades' may be designated (1) the *exposition, or enunciation*, where the single theme is introduced, and the components ('voices') of the composition appear in suitable relationships: (2) the *episode*, or development of theme, which is a basic point-counterpoint pattern, involving 'subject' and 'answer'; and (3) the recapitulation of the theme, in this case, the *stretto*, 'which consists of a piling up of the theme at a closer interval of time than that which separated the subject and the answer in the exposition'.[28]

'Comrades' opens abruptly in the spring of 1923; Sean is 'on his way to a sit-down in Stephen's Green, where he could dreamily deny the tale of a God existent, and test the woe of the world with thought' (IFTW, p. 134). An old comrade of his, a former drover of cattle down the North Circular Road, now a colonel in the Free State army, claps his hand on Sean's shoulder. He is Mick Clonervy, according to Sean a poor choice for either an officer or a soldier: 'The smart, elegant uniform fitted the body, but failed to fit the spirit of the man.' Indeed, the Free State army falls far short of Sean's standards; and his appraisal recalls Sean's past associations with the ICA and his flair for military tactics: ' — This new corps of officers, thought Sean, will never do. Utterly unaware of the elements of military life, and has no desire to learn them. How are things, Mick? He asked, hardly knowing what to say' (*IFTW*, p. 135). This is an instance of merged dialogue, commonplace in the Irish Books, where Sean's thoughts accompany his direct statement to another character in the development of a scene.

Sean and his former comrade chat about things in general and in particular about a recent meeting between Clonervy and Yeats, at Donnybrook where the poet had visited a country house then under military guard. In this way, the stage is set for the ensuing action:

> Sean's glance followed the colonel's eyeing casually a young man cycling smoothly past them, his face turned toward the Green, away from them, humming *Home to Our Mountains* from *Il Trovatore*, the cyclist's hand moving emotionally to the gentle swing of the tune [*IFTW*, p. 136].

Suddenly, the 'lilting cyclist', pausing at the curb, throws a home-made bomb into a house opposite St Stephen's Green, which serves as a barracks for Free State troops. There is a loud explosion, 'tempered by screams of agony from the room where the bomb had burst' (*IFTW*, p. 137). Clonervy (an inept soldier) experiences some embarrassment when he discovers that his pistol is empty; but soon he and two plain-clothes men, on their own bicycles, are in pursuit of the fleeing bomb-thrower.

This section of 'Comrades' (the *exposition*) ends amid the confusion following the explosion in the Free State barracks:

> An ambulance came tinkling up to sort out things; while Sean

hurried to the Green to sit in serenity beside the lake to try to sort things out, too, among the indifferent ducks and drakes. [*IFTW*, p. 138]

Again Sean looks to nature for the solutions to problems besetting him; but nature, like the ducks and the drakes, is indifferent to human strife. Sean's reference to the wounded soldiers as 'things' to be sorted out tends to reinforce this attitude of indifference, which Sean himself shares in some measure throughout the chapter, while maintaining his passive role of observer from his bench in St Stephen's Green. Though the theme may be still somewhat obscure, thus ends the exposition in the emerging structure of 'Comrades'.

The theme of 'Comrades' develops along two separate yet interwoven lines of narration, which, in effect, correspond to 'subject' and 'answer' (in the *episode*) in a point-counterpoint pattern. In 'Comrades', two *flights* are recounted; and a single theme is explored, in a manner which suggests emphatically the two-part *fugue*.

The cycling bomb-thrower heads in the direction of the Dublin Mountains ('Back to Our Mountains'): a distance of approximately four miles — from St Stephen's Green southward, by Waterloo Road, the Appian Way, Belgrave Road, through Rathmines, Rathgar, and Dartry, along the River Dodder (Lower Dodder Road), into Rathfarnham. The colonel and his two companions are in close pursuit, and it is now apparent that the fleeing cyclist will eventually be caught. By this time, the colonel has recognised the Republican bomb-thrower: 'Lanehin, Captain of the crush [company] I was in when we were fightin' th' Tans. Lanehin — a bastard!' (*IFTW*, p. 139.) Kevin Lanehin and Mick Clonervy are thus former comrades, now on opposing sides in the Civil War; but there is little love lost between them. In fact, Clonervy is determined to settle old scores with his one-time superior. There is irony in this separation of vague political issues from personal hatred which strips most of the significance from accepted notions of civil war. Thus O'Casey emphasises aspects of more general warfare between man and fellowman. Irony is reinforced as Lanehin, abandoning his bicycle to continue on foot through the rough terrain, reaches an old stone wall: 'He'd wait here. Here in the hills ['Back to Our Mountains']. Just as he was he'd stay. He had no gun, no gun.' The young Republican curses his commanding officer, as, perhaps, Clonervy once cursed him: 'Damned fool, that O.C. of his who advised him to go on the mission without a gun. He's all right — curse o' God on him!' (*IFTW*, p. 141.) Lanehin is overtaken; thereupon, he recognises Clonervy, now only thirty feet away. In desperation, he requites the colonel's hatred: 'Jasus! sitting down, resting, and staring at him! Mick Clonervy, Sergeant of his company when they both fought the Tans; a colonel now in the Free State army; promotion sure. Sell his own mother for a yellow tab' (*IFTW*, p. 142).

Lanehin is ordered to stretch his arms along the top of the wall, while Clonervy and his two companions casually eat their lunches and drink from a flask. Lanehin's posture against the wall suggests that of the crucified Christ; and the colonels repast, less clearly, suggests the Last Supper, as a prelude to sacrifice. The impression will become more distinct as the scene develops. Knowing that it is futile, Lanehin, none the less, begs for his life:[29]

I'm an old comrade of yours, Mick, the young man pleaded.
    Sure I know that well, said the colonel heartily, and I'll say this much — for the sake of oul' times, we won't let you suffer long.
    Jasus! whimpered the half-dead [i.e. *exhausted* and *soon-to-die*] kid, yous wouldn't shoot an old comrade, Mick!

    . . . .

    Be Jasus!   We would, he [Clonervy] said, and then he pulled the trigger [*IFTW*, p. 144].[29]

The mention of 'Jasus' throughout this flight is, of course, ironic; and so are the implications of 'Be Jasus!' — that God's commandment is fulfilled in death — in murder made *legal* within the non-moral context of war. O'Casey's meaning is clear: Lanehin's flight (the 'subject') ends in a consummation of per-

sonal hatred which leaves little room for politics. One line of
narration in the exploration of the theme of 'Comrades' is completed – with a pistol shot.

The second line of narration begins simultaneously with the
first, at St Stephen's Green, where Sean sits quietly observing
nature and reducing it to thought; and it (the 'answer') pro-
gresses in a point-counterpoint relationship with the details of
Lanehin's flight. It is a second flight, which, though independent from the first, is woven into it as a series of interruptions
– given on the pages in *italics* (*IFTW*, pp. 138, 139, 142, and 144).
From his vantage point, Sean witnesses successive stages in the
courtship of drake and duck: *'On the top of the pensive lake a
modest brown duck came swimming shoreward from a pursuing
drake . . . '*(*IFTW*, p. 139). Thus the nuptial flight ends: *'The
drake had reached his goal, and he was quivering in the violent
effort to fulfill God's commandment to multiply and replenish
the earth'* (*IFTW*, p. 144).

Within 'Comrades', the two lines of narration and simultaneously, completing the *stretto*, with the colonel's pistol shot
and the drake's triumph. However, there is an ironic contrast
between man's response to God's commandment ('Be Jasus!'),
which ends in death, and the drake's response, which sustains life.
It is a reassertion of the fact that both death and life are inevitably part of indifferent nature, beyond politics and man-made
conventions; one flight ends in the hills south of Dublin, the
other in a green park.

NOTES

1. In a letter to the present author, 18 October 1961, O'Casey remarks:

    [You] yourself have unconsciously gathered me together in three
    words – I am a kinda trinitarian soul: Johnny, Jack, Sean – one in
    three and three in one, and it isnt easy not to divide the substance
    or confound the persons; for there is one person in Johnny, another
    in Jack[,] and another in Sean; yet these three persons make one
    man.

See William J. Maroldo, 'Lines from Torquay — Letters by and about Sean O'Casey', *Sean O'Casey Review*, III, 2 (Spring 1977) pp. 117–126. Letters cited below are to be found in this collection.

2. *Mirror in My House*, 2 vols (New York: Macmillan, 1956). This edition contains the six autobiographies: *I Knock at the Door* (1939); *Pictures in the Hallway* (1942); *Drums under the Windows* (1946); *Inishfallen, Fare Thee Well* (1949); *Rose and Crown* (1952); and *Sunset and Evening Star* (1954). These volumes were issued separately by Macmillan (New York) during the years indicated; but bound together, they retain their original pagination. Henceforth in this essay, they will be cited, by suitable short titles, as they are found in the combined edition.

3. For an expanded definition of autobiography as a literary genre and an aesthetic mode, see my 'Sean O'Casey and the Art of Autobiography: Form and Content in the Irish Books', unpublished doctoral dissertation (Columbia University, 1964) pp. 1–94.

4. In the letter to the author 18 October 1961, cited above O'Casey observes:

> There are two reasons why we speak as we do — D before a broad vowel in Gaelic is always thickened to dh, and the effects of Gaelic speech lingers on the tongue of many Irish-Dublin persons; and remains of the Elizabethan manner of speaking. When I was young, poor Dubliners pronounced 'Murder' as murther or murdher, 'door' as doore, floor as flure dure, tea as tay, just as in Shakespeare . . .

5. See David H. Greene, 'Great Dramatist's Approach to Autobiography', *Commonweal*, LXV (25 January 1957) p. 441, and David Krause, *Sean O'Casey: The Man and His Work* (New York: Macmillan, 1960) p. 2.

6. 'A Protestant Kid Thinks of the Reformation', *American Spectator*, II, 21 (July 1934) p. 3: O'Casey concludes his article reiterating Beverly Nichol's appeal, in press and on radio, that Christians should resume church attendance and close reading of the Bible; the tone is ironic and unconvinced. O'Casey, in a letter to the present author dated 9 April 1962, remarks, 'By the way, our daughter (21) is now reading the Bible for the first time!'

7. Ibid., p. 3.

8. In a letter to the present author dated 10 August 1962.

9. 'Royal Risidence', *Virginia Quarterly Review*, XVI, 1 (Winter 1940) pp. 51–67.

10. In the letter of 10 August cited above. It is possible that the selection was received by the editors as a completed chapter of *Pictures in the Hallway*, then a work-in-progress.

11. O'Casey's birth certificate is recorded at the Irish Registrar's Office, Dublin: He was born on 30 March 1880, the son of Michael and Susan (*née* Archer); and he was christened John Casey. *Who's Who 1955* lists

O'Casey's birthdate, which was absent from previous editions, as 31 March 1884, and continues to do so until 1960. However, in 1961, the birthdate is given correctly as 30 March 1880. See Sean O'Casey, 'Delicate Art of Growing Old', *Harper's Magazine,* CCXX (August 1959) pp. 65–6, where O'Casey subscribes to the latter date: 'I am now seventy-nine and the days are all too short for me to hear, see, and touch the things around me [p. 65].'

12. See *Handbook for Travellers in Ireland*, 4th edn (London: Murrary, 1878) p. 27, where the site of the Portrane Lunatic Asylum, once an extensive deer park, is placed fifteen to sixteen miles north of Dublin – its city limits at that time.

13. Weston St John Joyce, *The Neighbourhood of Dublin* (Dublin & Waterford, M. H. Gill, 1912) p. 298.

14. Charles Darwin, *On the Origin of Species: A Facsimile of the First Edition* [1879], with an 'Introduction' by Ernst Mayr. (Cambridge, Massachusetts: Harvard University Press, 1964) p. 62.

15. See Sean O'Casey, *June and the Paycock*, Acts II and III, respectively, in *Collected Plays,* 4 vols (London: Macmillan, 1957), I, pp. 1–89, especially pp. 54–5 and 87. One is inclined to equate Mary Boyle and her prospects (in Act I) with the youthful Ella and her hopes in *I Knock at the Door*; both girls, of course, are products of the same environment. And one always thinks of Emma Bovary.

16. 'Loony pauper', see Joyce's *Ulysses* (New York: Modern Library, 1946) p. 710 (part of Bloom's 'cross multiplication of reverses of fortune'): 'Nadir of misery: the aged impotent disfranchised moribund lunatic pauper.'

17. General paralysis of the insane (GPI) is a degenerative disease which follows syphilitic infection of the brain, probably what is now called *paresis*, a symphilitic infection of the cerebral cortex, not involving other parts of the cerebro-spinal system. In the case of Nicholas Benson, the disease is no doubt a souvenir of his days in the army, hence the doctor's specification of GPI may be apt. For an interesting account, which is only peripheral to the contents of 'House of the Dead', see T. P. C. Kirkpatrick, *A Note on the History of the Care of the Insane in Ireland Up to the End of the Nineteenth Century* (Dublin: Dublin University Press, 1931).

18. A first allusion to the Mountains of Mourne, north of Dublin? See the *Aeneid*, vi, line 441, Virgil's Fields of Mourning (*Lugentes Campi*).

19. Compare *Paradise Lost*, ii. lines 624–7:

> Where all life dies, death lives, and Nature breeds,
> Perverse, all monstrous, all prodigious things,
> Abominable, unutterable, and worse
> Thank fables yet have feigned or fear conceived. . .

20. *Paradise Lost*, ii, line 227. Instances of Satan's *non serviam* are always worth noting; see especially, ibid., i, lines 249-55, 261-4. Such celebrated rebellion shares much with that of Sean-Jack Casside and Stephen Dedalus.

21. See *Man and Superman*, in *Complete Plays,* with Prefaces, 6 vols (New York: Dodd, Mead, 1962) III, pp. 483-743, especially Act III, Scene ii, *Don Juan in Hell,* pp. 600-50, not 607: '*Don Juan* ... [There] is plenty of humbug in hell (indeed there is hardly anything else); but the humbug of death and age and change is dropped because here we are dead and eternal.' And p. 613: '*The Devil* . . . There is a notion that I was turned out of . . . [Heaven] ; but as a matter of fact nothing could have induced me to stay there. I simply left it and organised this place.' But Don Juan, in search of another sort of perfection, rejects Hell; see ibid., p. 616; '*Don Juan* . . . Heaven is the home of the masters of reality: that is why I am going thither . . . Hell is the home of the unreal and of seekers for happiness . . . There are no special questions here, no political questions, no religious questions, best of all, no sanitary questions.'

22. The Purple Land often designates the Land of Youth or the Land of Dreams, in Gaelic, *Tir na n'Og*: the allusion, perhaps overplayed, is consistent with O'Casey's implications throughout the section.

23. *Aeneid*, iv, lines 278-9.

24. The holy whirligig is Matt Talbot, a martyr of Dublin and a sort of religious opportunist. For a sketch of his life, see Desmond Ryan, *Remembering Sion: A Chronicle of Storm and Quiet* (London: Barker, 1934) pp. 79-80. O'Casey comments on Matt Talbot in *Inishfallen, Fare Thee Well,* pp. 224-6. Cf. Dante, *The Divine Comedy,* translated by John Sinclair. 3 vols (Italian with English translation) (New York: Oxford University Press, 1961) I, passim.

25. Cf. *DUTW*, p. 76: 'Wide gates of heavy dull, heartless, lead opened to let them in'. The word *lead*, which is figurative, suggests mindlessness and more, remotely, *saturnalia*, the licensed disorder of the Romans. Moreover, in a chain of associations (appropriate within the context of 'House of the Dead'), *Saturn* implies Chronos or Time. Further, the mention of lead calls to mind other metals and their significance: *gold*, wisdom; *silver*, the higher mental activities; *iron*, the lower mental activities; and *brass* and *bronze*, the physical — all absent from 'House of the Dead'. It seems likely that O'Casey wished to convey by the word *lead* the dull lifelessness of the asylum, and he succeeds. In a similar vein, he will use variations of *lead* and *leaden* throughout the Irish Books. In any case, O'Casey's use of colours and metals is usually reflexive and casual, having but incidental reference to extraneous connotation.

26. One is, of course, reminded of Aldous Huxley's *Point Counter Point*,

where decisive points in the lives of the characters are matched in an essentially polyphonic manner. O'Casey's use of point-counterpoint in 'Comrades' is far less complicated.

27. E. M. Forster, *Aspects of the Novel* (New York: Harcourt Brace, 1954) p. 168.

28. Edwin John Stringham, *Listening to Music, Creatively* (New York: Prentice-Hall, 1943) p. 413, n. 8. Stringham adds that the *stretto* is 'often used to build up or to intensify the emotional effect in general'. O'Casey accomplishes this in 'Comrades', where 'Subject' and 'Answer' end on the same note: the shot from Clonervy's pistol and the drake's triumph are simultaneous.

29. Lanehin's words echo those of Johnny Boyle in the third act of *Juno and the Paycock: 'Johnny*. I'm an oul' comrade — you wouldn't shoot an oul' comrade' (*Collected Plays*, I, p. 84).

8 On Fabrications and Epiphanies in O'Casey's Autobiography

DAVID KRAUSE

> 3 The road of excess leads to the palace
>   of wisdom.
>
> 4 Prudence is a rich ugly old maid courted
>   by Incapacity.
>
> 44 The tygers of wrath are wiser than the
>   horses of instruction.
>
> 57 Damn braces. Bless relaxes.
>
> William Blake, 'Proverbs of Hell'

> Its soul, its whatness, leaps to us from the
> vestment of its appearance. The soul of the
> commonest objects, the structure of which is
> so adjusted, seems to us radiant. The object
> achieves its epiphany.
>
> James Joyce, *Stephen Hero*

> He was at home among the mortals. His epiphany
> was the showing forth of man to man. Man must
> be his own saviour; man must be his own god.
>
> O'Casey on Shaw, *Sunset and Evening Star*

Autobiography no less than fiction is the art of supreme fabrication, and it is therefore as a supreme fabricator of his life that I wish to consider Sean O'Casey's creation of himself and his world in his autobiography. Since no deep portrait of a life, and certainly no self-portrait of the artist, can be reduced to a realistic mirror-image, whether in an autobiography or a novel, the symbolic Johnny Casside must be seen as a fabricated or mythic expansion of the living O'Casey, just as the symbolic Stephen Dedalus must be seen as a fabricated or mythic expansion of the living Joyce. What this means is that these two Irish writers, working with similar transmutations in different but related genres, were compelled to invent their lives in extravagantly fictive terms in order to achieve the aesthetic distance which distinguishes art from life. It also means that in the Irish experience, where reality is often a nightmare and the truth must be mythologised before it can be recognised, everything must be transmuted if it is to be endured, with the result that most fiction is autobiographical and most autobiography is fictional. Fabrication is sublimation in Ireland. In autobiography as well as fiction, the vital statistics of life are less significant than the vital imagination of art; the creative process must function as more than a reflex mirror for the imitation of life. The artist as fabricator makes something that did not exist before; he invents a new vocabulary, a new form. And when he reconstructs his own life, which presumably did exist before, what he makes is a symbolic projection of that life which has not yet been seen, which was waiting to be discovered.

In subject nations like Ireland where the historical betrayals have produced an excess of human misery, the impulse to fabricate or create new forms can be urgent, and the literary transmutations of necessity mitigate and even supersede the grim realities of life. Since the pervasive mood of Irish fatalism is a state of mind conditioned by seven centuries of frustration, it is no accident that the folk imagination has fabricated the second law of thermodynamics into Murphy's law or the Celtic version of entropy: if things can possibly get worse, they always will. Perhaps the intensity of the national anguish provoked the Irish people, consciously and unconsciously, to fabricate, to wear ironic masks in order to fool John Bull and the lord of the big house. In the relevant terms of R. D. Laing, the Irish have consistently had to invent survival games, fabricated strategies 'in order to live in an unlivable situation'.[1] When nations like Ireland develop advanced symptoms of frustration and fantasy, and the people have difficulty trying to hide their centuries-old repressions and daily illusions, they may seek relief in acts of physical aggression, or they may turn to the artistic process which, by providing a compensatory release of verbal aggression, becomes an act of faith in a fatalistic world. Under the yoke of an unrelieved history of master-slave relationships, then, and while abortive political attempts to liberate the nation offered only compromises and defeats, the Irish people were forced to create a superabundance of sublimating oral and written literature which helped to transfigure and disguise reality. The uninhibited glory and freedom of words became the primary ritual of catharsis for the country.

The fine art of verbal fabrication has always been a sword of the spirit in Ireland, and I would therefore venture to suggest that psychologically the transubstantiated words of literature have for centuries functioned as a secular Mass, or a liturgy of Joycean epiphanies. In the beginning there was always the liberating word in Ireland. I call upon Blake, as well as Freud and Joyce and O'Casey, to guide me here, the apocalyptic Blake who in his towering epic *Jerusalem* celebrated the sanctity of art as an aesthetic gospel when he wrote:

> I know of no other Christianity and of no other Gospel than the liberty of both body & mind to exercise the Divine Arts of Imagination, Imagination, the real & eternal World of which this Vegetable Universe is but a faint shadow . . . What is the Divine Spirit? is the Holy Ghost any other than an Intellectual Fountain?[2]

I would only add that in Ireland, even more than in Blake's Albion, the Holy Ghost is the Fountain of Art.

The extreme tensions of life in Ireland have always demanded extreme fictions. It is therefore emblematic that the twin artifices of talking and writing creatively should have become the divine instruments of psychic release in a disordered world. The compulsive appeal of words to the eye and ear, the two spiritual senses, as they have been called, helped the people survive in a frustrated and paralysed nation, a nation in 'a state o' chassis'. No one understood and dramatised these symptoms of frustration in the national character more effectively than the modern Irish fabricators, Joyce and Yeats, Wilde and Shaw, George Moore and Lady Gregory, Synge and O'Casey, Fitzmaurice and Behan, Clarke and Kavanagh, O'Connor and O'Faolain, Flann O'Brien and Edna O'Brien, all of whom, along with many of their fellow countrymen and women, in fiction, poetry, drama and autobiography, invented the extravagent and redemptive literature of Ireland. In that country a powerful or poetic word has invariably been a weapon worth 1000 pictures.

Ireland is now a partially independent but still partitioned and beleaguered nation, and the racial memory of 700 years of subjugation cannot be rubbed away in a generation. Even De Valera's republic of frugal shopkeepers, who after the sacrificial rhetoric and bloodshed of 1916 somehow managed to pre-empt Connolly's mad vision of a Workers' Republic, to add yet another frustration, were unable to forget that Irish art is always superior to Irish life. The mythic art of the word is the unreal McCoy in Ireland, where the vegetable universe of reality is but a faint shadow of the divine art of the imagination, and this phenomenon may help to explain why Irish life endlessly strives to imitate Irish art.

Perhaps no one understood the mysterious relationship between art and life more shrewdly than Oscar Wilde, that supreme fabricator and most flamboyant Dubliner of them all, Wilde who proclaimed what Blake and most Irishmen knew when he insisted that the divine gift of lying was the essence of all art. In his brilliant dialogue on 'The Decay of Lying' – a decay which may have begun to fester in England but has seldom been evident in Ireland – Wilde stated that 'No great artist sees things as they really are. If he did, he would cease to be an artist.'[3] The artist's mendacious and unfettered imagination, therefore, must liberate him from what Wilde called 'the prison-house of realism'; it must help him find the vision beyond reality, the Yeatsian mask or anti-self, the aesthetic vision that can only be discovered through the mythic power of lies or fabrications. Art is a magic 'veil' not a reflex 'mirror', Wilde argued, and along the way he corrected a common misconception about Hamlet:

They will call on Shakespeare – they always do – and will
quote that hackneyed passage about Art holding the mirror
up to Nature, fogetting that this unfortuante aphorism is deliberately said by Hamlet in order to convince the bystanders
of his absolute insanity in all art-matters.[4]

Hamlet himself was an artist in his calculated fabrication of
madness, and literalists who take delight in his aphorism, or
take his disguise as a mirror of life, are no more reliable than
Polonius in their failure to distinguish between art and reality.

Artifice in Elsinore and Ireland is not 'the real thing', it is the
thing beyond reality, the most ingeniously fabricated thing.
Ireland like Elsinore was tainted by tyranny, and the Irish artists
play variations of Hamlet's game of fabrication and disguise,
though without his consummate resolution. In the extension of
Wilde's illuminating symbolism, which echoes the aesthetic
mythology of Blake and Yeats, the 'forms' of art are 'more real
than living man', they are 'the great archetypes of which things
that have existence are but unfinished copies'.[5] It is in precisely
this paradoxical sense that those two supreme fabrications,
Dedalus and Casside, are the archetypes of the living and therefore unfinished shadows of Joyce and O'Casey. And the symbolic Dublin that both writers fabricated in their works was the
archetypal city, of which the geographical city was but an
unfinished copy.

Dublin was the uncommon denominator for both men, the
uniquely irreducible focus, and their conceptions of the city
grew out of similarly ambivalent attitudes of love and hate,
compassion and arrogance, kinship and alienation. Again we
must return to Blake for his theory of creative contraries to
account for the ironic reconciliation of these opposites: 'Without
Contraries is no progression. Attraction and Repulsion, Reason
and Energy, Love and Hate, are necessary to Human existence.'[6]
All contraries are necessary for existence in dear, dirty Dublin.
The paradoxical impulses of attraction and repulsion prevented
Joyce and O'Casey from succumbing to the easy temptations of
the Celtic twilight or nationalist moonshine that always threaten
to sentimentalise the frustrated Irish, and therefore both men
were free to fabricate the life of their city with a gritty tone of

sceptical reverence. They revealed all the profanations and epiphanies of their holy city; Joyce in his tragic-ironic short stories and symbolic novels, O'Casey in his tragi-comic plays and epic autobiography.

There were also many contraries between Joyce and O'Casey which separated and united these half-blind and percipient, raging and affirming giants. Joyce's milieu was middle-class Dublin, O'Casey's milieu was working-class Dublin, and therein lies a social and economic distinction that partially accounts for the contrasting methods they used to take the measure of their city. University-educated and already a self-conscious artist in his twenties, the Thomistic and agnostic Joyce was an intense aesthete with his pedantically neo-classical principles all mapped out, a literary mandarin in complete control of his lyric and comic destiny. A self-educated common labourer not fully conscious of himself as an artist until he was in his forties, the Marxist and agnostic O'Casey was an intense socialist with what could only vaguely be called romantic or Promethean principles, a literary primitive who had to improvise his dramatic and comic destiny. In their various mock-heroic ways both men profaned the excessive pieties of Cathleen Ni Houlihan and attempted to recreate the conscience of their people. And although they were both alienated figures while they were living in Dublin, similarly alienated by church and state politics, their Dublin roots were never more evident than when they left the city in self-exile and pursued their indomitable Irishry on foreign soil.

Joyce was the pure artist: his genius was a calculated, finely controlled instrument which seldom played a wrong note, and he always knew where he was going with his cunning craft. O'Casey was the impure artist: his genius was an instinctive, roughly hewn instrument which sometimes played outrageous notes, and he had to make his artisitic discoveries by trial and error. Joyce's bold and innovative techniques made him a more significant figure of universal influence, as the groping O'Casey himself was often quick to acknowledge. Nevertheless, there are many instances where O'Casey is at the top of his fictional form in his autobiography, for example, in the way he exploits the strategies of comedy and epiphany and invents a flexible structure of picaresque fabrications to accomodate the adventures and initiations of Johnny and Sean Casside. In his autobiography as well as in his plays, O'Casey revealed that, like Joyce, he was a master of comic irony and had few peers in his rendering of the mock-heroic absurdites that frustrated his vainglorious countrymen.

I am not at the moment concerned with O'Casey's giddy attempts to play with Joycean puns and neologisms, in which comic and satiric extravaganzas he can sometimes parallel the master and sometimes sound like the sorcerer's apprentice. Specifically, what I have in mind are the instances when O'Casey in his autobiography successfully adopted and modified for his own purposes the technique of the Joycean epiphany. In the penultimate chapter of *Stephen Hero*, Joyce defined the literary epiphany as an attempt to reveal the '*quidditas*' or 'whatness' of an unexpectedly luminous experience, the very quintessence of the mysterious thing itself. Stephen explained it in the following manner:

> By an epiphany he meant a sudden spiritual manifestation, whether in the vulgarity of speech or gesture or in a memorable phase of the mind itself . . . The moment the focus is reached the object is epiphanised . . . Its soul, its whatness, leaps to us from the vestment of its appearance.'[7]

The spark that ignites the epiphany is always something unpredictable, something outside the artist, or something hidden in his mind, something he hears or sees, a vulgar colloquy or fragment of speech overheard, a gesture or object observed in a room or in the street; and suddenly, miraculously, there it is, the heart of the encounter, the thing in and beyond reality is epiphanised as the artist looks *into* rather than *at* something or someone. Wilde might have insisted that all art epiphanises life through the divine process of lying or fabricating. Blake might have seen the epiphany as the creative force that is radiated by a divine excess of love and wrath, wisdom and folly. Yeats might have caught the flash of an epiphany at critical moments in his poems or whenever he responded to the vibrations of his daimonic anti-self. O'Casey would have agreed with all of them,

but he was not consciously imitating them when he was instinctively touched by the Holy Ghost and created his own variety
of epiphanised experiences.

What distinguishes O'Casey's use of the epiphany is the
astonishing degree of visual imagery which he brings to his
moments of illumination. He is a word-painter in contrast to
Joyce as word-poet. He is so graphically visual he often thinks
in dream-pictures, he seldom hides his verbal brush strokes, and
he creates a powerful sense of dramatic movement and
immediacy on the page. Joyce, on the other hand, transfixes his
epiphanies, freezes them into images of statis and imbues them
with a powerful sense of eternity. In his Introduction to the
first edition of *Stephen Hero*, Theodore Spencer pointed out
the static and timeless aspects of Joyce's theory of the epiphany:

> A theory like this is not of much use to a dramatist, as Joyce
> seems to have realized when he first conceived it. It is a theory
> which implies a lyrical rather than a dramatic view of life. It
> emphasises the radiance, the effulgence, of the thing itself re-
> vealed in a special moment, an unmoving moment, of time.[8]

Spencer was right about Joyce, but he was apparently not aware
that someone like O'Casey, a playwright working in a fictional
form of autobiography, could open the theory to dramatic as
well as lyric possibilities.

Now, before going on to examine some of those possibilities,
those heightened moments of dramatic *quidditas* in O'Casey, I
want to suggest a theory about how I think his verbal and visual
techniques are structured by acknowledging a special debt to
the noted art historian and iconologist E. H. Gombrich. In a
luminous discussion of sensory symbolism in painting,
Gombrich points out some synesthetic correspondences between
technique and taste in art by suggesting that what goes on the
palette or paint-mixing board is directly related to the response
of the palate or taste-buds. In order to illustrate how these
correspondences work, Gombrich introduces two metaphoric
and catalytic agents that are always available to the painter, and I
believe that similar agents are available to the writer, especially to

Joyce and O'Casey. The first agent is a distorting surface of wobbly or rolled glass, the second is an abrasive surface of crunchy or gritty texture. Believing with Wilde that the artist is an image-maker not an imitator, one who constructs fabrications rather than representations, Gombrich asserts that the working artist, in the first instance, figuratively holds a sheet of wobbly glass in front of his canvas to wrench or distort the natural and symmetrical shape of things, to avoid what is too representational and predictable. In the second instance, which is part of and overlaps with the first, the artist includes a texture of crunchy or gritty pigments and brush strokes to break up the soft or smooth surfaces, to avoid what is too literal and sentimental. In both instances the artist tries to liberate himself from everything that is too facile in order to achieve an aesthetic distance from reality. He has, in Gombrich's words, struggled 'to get away from skill and sentiment', and as a result 'we are constantly brought up against tensions and barbs, as it were, which prevent our eyes from running along smooth lines'.[9]

In support of the artist's need to create visual tensions and barbs, Gombrich cites the Browning poem in which the too smooth and too realistic Andrea del Sarto, trapped by the fault of his faultlessness, tries to correct a purposely mis-drawn or wobbly arm by Raphael. Then, in a direct experiment Gombrich takes an 'atrocity' or realism painted by Bonnencontre, the excessively sentimental and symmetrical 'Three Graces', and holds a sheet of wobbly glass in front of it, suddenly transforming a tasteless piece of 'sloppy mush' into a symbolic image that is gratifyingly vigorous and crunchy. Thereafter Gombrich goes on to point out the metaphoric varieties of wobbly glass and crunchy texture in modern art, in the paintings of the French Impressionists, in the violent and primitive distortions of Van Gogh and Gauguin, in the tensions and barbs that emerge in Cezanne, in the passionately savage and sophisticated canvases of Picasso.

I believe, therefore, that there are significant connections between the visual and verbal art forms, that similarly metaphoric constructs of wobbly glass and crunchy texture can be found in the symbolic prose of O'Casey's autobiography. In spite of the fact that O'Casey the dramatist is often put down as a naturalist or realist, a misleading critical platitude that is unfortunately evident in most anthologies and surveys of drama, he is in everything he wrote a verbal and visual image-maker who brings the passionately savage eye of the modernist painter to the printed page. All his work, from his early journalistic and historical essays to his late farcical fantasies, was fabricated through a symbolic conceit of wobbly glass with tensions and barbs of crunchy comedy and irony. The Daumier-like scenes of the ragged poor of Dublin during the 1913 General Strike in *The Story of the Irish Citizen Army* are distorted with contraries of pain and hope. The tone and structure of the Dublin trilogy are calculated to break down the lines of smooth and symmetrical action, and the mock-heroic language of the characters is limned with rough and gritty strokes that deny stock responses to historical events. The surrealistic second act of *The Silver Tassie*, the park-world metaphor in *Within the Gates*, the comic disintegration symbolism in *Purple Dust*, the miraculous transformation scene in *Red Roses For Me*, the cock-catalyst revolt in *Cock-a-Doodle Dandy*, the sardonic Prerumble in *The Drums of Father Ned* — all of these asymmetrical and apocalyptic, savage and farcical fabrications are designed to reach far beyond 'the prison-house of realism' in order to create verbal and visual correspondences.

Now I want to examine some of those synesthetic correspondences in the autobiography by concentrating on two types of fabrication that are directly associated with the initiations and discoveries of Casside, the secular epiphanies. The first type is the introspective moment when O'Casey looks at himself and creates personal epiphanies for Johnny or Sean. The second type is the perspective moment when he looks at Ireland or the world and creates historical epiphanies for us. There are many ways to read a work as complex and multi-dimensional as the autobiography, and for my present purposes I have chosen to read it as a book of revelations, a wobbly and gritty kaleidoscope of private and public visions.

If epiphanies, like discoveries, only come to those who are looking for them, young Johnny Casside finds them even before he has reached the age of full understanding because he is so eager to confront the strange and hostile world around him. For example, his first confrontation with death came when he was six and his father died. After the funeral, while the mother sorrows in silence, the sister and the brothers get into a series of sharp arguments, with one another about Parnell, and with the innocently irreverent Johnny who sings about the death of cock robin and asks interminable questions about which colour God likes best. The impact of their grief is deflected by the heated arguments, until the others leave angrily and Johnny is left alone with his mother. O'Casey sets up the moment of epiphany with a comic crunch when Michael, just before he leaves for the pub with Tom, aims some mocking barbs at little Johnny:

I wonder, said Michael, how you'd get to know whether God Almighty likes blue, green, yellow, or red the best?

Oh, shut up, Mick, said Tom, and let the kid alone.

Red, I think, went on Michael, red like the red on a monkey's arse.

No more talk like that in front of the kid, said Tom tittering.

Oh, shag the kid! said Michael, he'll have to learn about these things some day [I, p. 54][10]

And Johnny begins to learn about some of these things as he looks out of the window and watches them leave, watches the lamplighter creating a string of yellow lights in the street, and finally sees the first sign of his mother's grief in the reflection of the fire in her tears:

Johnny watched the little lamplighter running, with his little beard wagging, carrying his pole, with a light like a sick little star at the top of it, hurrying from lamp to lamp, prodding each time a little yellow light into the darkness, till they formed a chain looking like a string of worn-out jewels that the darkness had slung round the neck of night. His mother returned to the room as he was stretching to see how far he could see down the street, and how many of the lights he could count. Going over to the fire, she sat down, and gazed steadily into the blaze.

I was thinking, Mother, he said, that green must be a great favourite of God's, for look at the green grass, and the leaves of bushes and trees; and teacher said that green stands for life, and God loves life.

He waited, but his mother did not answer him. He turned, and saw her gazing steadily into the blaze of the fire. He stole over and sat down beside her, and took her hand in his. And there they sat and stared and stared and stared at the flame that gushed out of the burning coal. Suddenly he looked up and saw the flame from the fire shining on tears that were streaming down her cheeks [I, p. 55].

Johnny has shared a sudden moment of communion with his mother by innocently releasing her pent-up grief. Without realising it he prepares himself for the epiphany by watching the grotesque little lamplighter create a string of yellow lights in the darkness outside, and then by wondering if green is God's favourite colour since it represents the life that God creates. At that point, as she stares at the red flame of the fire, the stricken widow's reverie is broken by her son and she finally seems to realise that she has been touched irrevocably by death not life. The sudden stab of grief is epiphanised for mother and son. And more, it is totally visualised for us in finely etched nuances of darkness and light. If Johnny sees more than he entirely understands in that reflection of the fire in his mother's streaming tears, he has come face to face with one of God's mysteries that will touch him often in the years ahead. He has shared a sacred moment with his mother, the sheet-anchor of his life, and he has played out with her the theme of the song he was humming at the start of the chapter, 'We all go the same way home', the song in which all mankind clings together, the symbolic song that gives the chapter its title. The whole chapter is a fabrication of dramatic barbs and lyrical dissonances which O'Casey couldn't have remembered realistically from his childhood, but which he has invented with brilliantly contrasting tones of visual imagery, all seen as through a wobbly glass darkly. This chapter, as a work of supreme fiction, like so many others in the autobiography, could well stand beside the finely wrought stories of lyrical and gritty paralysis in Joyce's *Dubliners*. It should be apparent that, like Joyce, O'Casey could be the pure artist as word-poet as well as word-painter when the fictive moment demanded his total effort.

Now I want to shift to the more crunchy and comic O'Casey, to look at another early chapter just before Johnny's unusual encounter with a tired cow on the North Circular Road, and I only want to examine two paragraphs at the start of the episode. It is a typical day of unrelieved pelting rain in Dublin and Johnny, whose impressionable mind is full of Bible stories, wonders if the deluge of rain is a sign that God has decided to punish wayward mankind with an annihilating flood. This time the whole incident takes place in Johnny's uninhibited imagination and we get an extended interior monologue in the vivid lingo of a shrewd Dublin 'chiselur' who is convinced that he has witnessed a miracle, the imminent damnation and suddenly merciful salvation of the world in a comic epiphany of joy:

How 'ud it be, thought Johnny, if God opened the windows of heaven, an' let it rain, rain like hell, for forty days an' forty nights, like it did when the earth was filled with violence, an' it repented the Lord that He hath made man, causin' a flood till the waters covered the houses an' the highest tops of the highest mountains in the land? There'd be a quare scatterin' an' headlong rushin' about to get a perch on the highest places, to sit watchin' the water risin' an' risin' till it lapped your legs, and there was nothin' left to do but close your eyes, say a hot prayer, slide in with a gentle splash splash, an' go to God; though you'd hardly expect to find a word of welcome on the mat in heaven, if God Himself had made up His mind you were better dead. But that could never happen now, for God had promised Noah, a just man and perfect in his generation, there'd never be anything like a flood anymore; and as proof positive, set His bow in the cloud as a token of a covenant between Him and the earth, for Noah to see when, sick an' sore, he crept out of the ark to start all over again with what was left of himself an' family, with the beasts of the earth, all creeping things, and all the fowls of the air, male an' female, that he had carried with him all the time the flood remained over the surface of the earth.

There was the very rainbow, now, sparklin' fine, one end restin' on the roof of Mrs. Mullally's house, and the other end leanin' on the top of one of the Dublin Mountains, with the centre touchin' the edge of the firmament; an', if only our eyes were a little brighter, we'd see millions an' millions of burnished angels standin' on it from one end to the other, havin' a long gawk at all that was goin' on in the earth that God made in the beginnin', an' that had to make a fresh start the time that Noah an' his wife, an' his sons, an' his sons' wives came outa the ark with the elephants, the lions, the horses, and the cows that musta given Noah the milk he needed when he was shut off from everything, till the dove came back with the olive branch stuck in her gob [I, p. 70].

It could only be achieved with a grand design of wobbly glass and crunchy texture. It could only be constructed by one of the merry monks who might have illustrated the Book of Kells with a fantastic procession of angels and animals, or perhaps by the visionary Blake as he contemplated a child's dream of the salvation of man, or yet again, on a vast allegorical canvas by a Picasso or a Chagall. Only such divinely inspired fabricators might have matched O'Casey's cosmic mural of damnation and salvation as it took shape in the comically transcendent mind of Johnny Casside, from the hand of God to the rainbow crowded with millions of angels gawking in amazement at the earth, to the ark of Noah and all his animals, to the mountains and streets of Dublin and the roof of Mrs. Mullally's house, to the dove of peace arriving 'with the olive branch stuck in her gob'.

But all things move by contraries for O'Casey and that is only the beginning of his parable, which ends on a dark note when Johnny is soon confronted by a tired and stray cow who wasn't saved in the ark, a rebellious cow who refuses to follow the herd in the frantic run through the Dublin streets from the cattle market down to the pens at the North Wall from where they would be shipped to the slaughter houses in England. That stubborn and weary Irish cow, Johnny thinks, has apparently been abandoned by God: 'a sthray cow lyin' on a rain-wet street is not enough to make God bother His head to give a thought about it' (I, p. 73). So we move from a song of innocence to a song of experience as O'Casey rings the changes on the recurring motif of Irish aspiration and frustration, and finally paralysis in the image of that tired and lost cow. The private nature of Johnny's original epiphany broadens to become a hint of an historical epiphany for us, with more to come later on the symbolic fate of Ireland. The angry drovers who have kicked and beaten the cow to no avail finally go after the rest of the herd, leaving Johnny to guard the stubborn beast. He feels a strong sense of empathy for the poor animal but he can't help or save it in any way, and since night is falling he must run home to his mother. The fate of the lost cow, like the fate of Ireland, remains unfinished, unresolved, as the departing Johnny looks back and transfixes a scene of epic sorrow in a forsaken cow:

At the end of the road he looked back, and, in the purple of the twilight, he saw the dark mass of the cow still lyin' on the path where everybody walked, starin' straight in front of her as if she saw nothin', while the rain still kept fallin' on her softly; but the sun had stopped her shinin', and the rain was no longer golden. [I, p. 74].

This pattern of epiphanised contraries runs throughout the autobiography; for example, in *Pictures in the Hallway,* in the chapter on the hawthorn tree where the spicy scent of the hawthorn blossoms collides with the filthy work of the dung-dodgers, and Johnny proudly holds his sprig of creamy hawthorn as a sacred emblem in the battle of Dublin's poor against the inevitable slime and ashes of life. Again, in the final and title-chapter of this volume the teen-aged Johnny discovers the world of painting in an epiphany of bright colour and design amid the grimy smoke and cinder heaps of northside Dublin:

Colour had come to him, had bowed, laughing, and now ran dancing before him . . . now that colour had come to him, he longed to be a painter, and his very bowels yearned for the power to buy tubes of cobalt blue, red lake, chrome yellow, Chinese white, emerald green, burnt sienna, and a deep black pigment [I, p. 387].

But he cursed the poverty that prevented him from becoming a painter and he had to be satisfied with looking in a shop window in Dawson Street at some watercolours that ravished his eyes; and in a secondhand book barrow he discovered and bought for a few pence two old books that illustrated the paintings of Fra Angelico and Constable, and it was 'like a sudden burst of music' for Johnny, a revelation of heaven and earth seen through a wobbly glass lightly:

With all he had learned from the Bible and the Prayer Book it was but an easy jump into the brightly-tinted world of Angelico; and from the little church of St. Burnupus, in its desolate seat among the dust of the dowdy streets, the cinders of the bottle-making factory of North Lotts, for ever pouring out its murky plumes of smoke, the scarred heaps of mouldering bark and timber chips round Martin's timber yard, the dung of the cattle, passing in droves down to the quays, the smell of the beer-soaked sawdust, floating out from the wide-open doors of the pubs, blending its smell with that of the foul rags of the festering, fawning poor, Johnny ferried himself safely to the circle of delicate blue showing forth Angelico's golden-haired Saviour clad in a robe of shimmering creamy grey, a shining orb in a beautiful left hand, a halo of heavy gold, transversed with a crimson cross, encircling His heavenly head; or, there He was, standing in a purple arch of the heavens, staff in hand, looking with love on two Dominican brothers, one of whose hands timidly touched the Saviour's, the two of them dressed in robes tenderly cream, covered with sombre black cloaks cunningly tinged with green, standing there gazing at Christ with a look that reverently called God their comrade. Again, with Angelico, he wandered through clouds of angels, a little stiff with innocence, thronging the skies like gaily-coloured Milky Ways, crimson or green or blue-gowned, powdered with stars or roses or golden fleurs-de-lys. Sometimes he chanted hymns softly to himself, strolling towards heaven through a field of pinks and roses, meeting often on his way more lovely angels, blowing with fattened cheeks through golden trumpets, or stringing delicate white fingers over graceful psalteries or zithers, sounding in honour of the Blessed Virgin, while her Son fixed another gem in her crown of glories.

Again, under the green, sunlit, or dewy trees, planted by Constable's imagination, giving shade and gracefulness to an eager sun, he wandered afield; or looking down where the ripening corn was striding upward to a golden grandeur, he wandered down quiet paths rimmed with vivid green, touched in with lavish blossoms, shyly forcing forward to kiss a greeting to the careless passer-by; while red-brown cattle, drowsing in the field beyond, stood knee-deep in the sappy grass, the honeyed smell of clover brooding delicately over the sleepy meadow, soothing the sweating brows of boatmen poling barges down the placid river full of sunny nooks making the green shades greener; gentle houses peering out from among the stately elms, the plumy poplars, and the proudly-nurtured ash with its sweeping foliage, moving in the wind, like a dancing Fragonard lady, coy with pride, and fancying herself the gem of the world around her; and over all the greying silver and the tender blue of a fresh and beaming sky.

So, through these two men, beauty and colour and form above and beside him came closer; came to his hand; and he began to build a house of vision with them, a house not made with hands, eternal in his imagination, so that the street he lived in was peopled with the sparkling saints and angels of Angelico, and jewelled with the serene loveliness Constable created out of the radiance of uncommon clay [I, pp. 387–8].

This may well be the seminal passage on the synesthetic technique of visual and verbal fabrication O'Casey used in the autobiography, for it is apparent here that he intended to create his story with the magic of words as pigments, building his own house of vision out of the uncommon clay of Dublin, from the mouldering dust and smoke and cinders to the epiphanised glory of something akin to Angelico and Constable. But the glory is usually tempered in the gritty contrast of poverty and radiance. In an early chapter of *Drums Under the Windows*, when the grown-up Johnny, who has now become Jack to his labouring comrades and Sean to his Gaelic friends, is mixing cement on a railway job and finds himself in the country for the first time. Amazed at the golden sea of growing corn, and the sharp sweet smell of new-mown hay, he immediately thinks of 'the glory of Constable's *Cornfield*', and he fancies he can see 'Ruth standing there in that field, up to her middle in the corn, a creamy face, rosy cheeks, and big brown goo-goo eyes staring at poor Boaz' (I, p. 444). His imagination runs wild as he next sees Jesus strolling through the corn field, chewing grains of corn as he thinks about some parable, while the Scribes and Pharisees are hiding and whining behind the hedges. Suddenly his reverie is interrupted by a horrible cry, a repeated cry of lost and mad laughter that comes from the nearby Portrane Asylum, and this quickly brings to his mind the image of his poor sister Ella whose life is being destroyed by her mentally deranged husband now locked up in the Dublin Asylum at Grangegorman:

> Out there, now, right in the centre of the corn, just where Jesus had passed a few moments before, floated the face of Ella, a white face, a face of settled fear, tightened with a stony smile that had a seed of wild weeping in it. He went back to his work of tempering the mortar and of carrying his hod of bricks to the mason; but whenever he turned his eyes to the growing corn, there was that damned white face, stony with fear, a swaying stem of corncockle at times empurpling an eye, or the scarlet shadow of a poppy giving it a bloodily splashed mouth, watching his work; watching, watching him work [I, p. 446].

So often something terrible and irrevocable is happening at the same time that something simple and glorious is taking place. During the 'terrible beauty' of the Irish Civil War in 1922 when Free Staters and Republicans were savagely killing one another for the greater glory of Ireland, O'Casey damned both sides and remained loyal to the lonely flag of labour, the Plough and the Stars. In the chapter titled 'Comrades' in *Inishfallen, Fare Thee Well*, O'Casey records one episode of the ritualistic slaughter with an ironic detachment that heightens the revelation of horror. While Sean sits on a bench in Stephen's Green watching the ducks on the lake, he meets an old friend, drover Mick Clonervy, a man who had regularly helped his father herd his cattle down the North Circular Road to be slaughtered in England. Mick is now Colonel Mick, dressed in the uniform of the Free State army, and he is slaughtering Republicans, who are slaughtering Free Staters. While he and Sean talk a Republican on a bicycle suddenly throws a bomb at a near-by building along the Green where Free State troops are being quartered, and in the midst of the explosion a wild chase begins as the colonel leaps on his bicycle and, with the help of two plain-clothes men, sets out in frantic pursuit of the bomber, whom he recognises as Kevin Lanehin, a young lad who only a few years earlier served with him when they were both under the same flag and cheerfully killing Black and Tans. After an ambulance arrives to take care of the dead and wounded, 'Sean hurrie[s] intò the Green to sit in serenity beside the lake to try to sort out things, too, among the indifferent ducks and drakes' (II. p. 87).

At this point in the narrative O'Casey adopts a double focus, alternately showing us how Sean uneasily watches the mating ritual of the ducks, at the same time that Clonervy gets ready to perform the ritualistic execution of Lanehin. The terrifying chase leads out towards Rathfarnham and the Dublin hills, with innocent children cheering as the mad cyclists go racing by, and Lanehin's 'life rolled off behind him like thread unwinding from a turning spool'; and at the same time *'The brown duck, like a maid hid in a Franciscan habit, spurted forward when she felt the pursuer coming too close'*. Finally, O'Casey fabricates a double confrontation for us as Lanehin, exhausted and cornered in the hills, begs for mercy; as Sean, tense and abstracted, waṫches the ducks come together; and suddenly there is a grotesque consummation of death and life;

I'm an old comrade of yours, Mick, the young man pleaded.

Sure I know that well, said the Colonel heartily, and I'll say this much – for the sake of oul' times, we won't let you suffer long.

Jesus! whimpered the half-dead lad, yous wouldn't shoot an old comrade, Mick!

The Colonel's arm holding the gun shot forward suddenly, the muzzle of the gun, tilted slightly upwards, splitting the lad's lips and crashing through his chattering teeth.

Be Jasus! We would, he said, and then he pulled the trigger.

Looka, Ma! shrilled a childish voice behind Sean; looka what th' ducks is doin'!

Sean turned swift to see a fair young mother, her sweet face reddening, grasp a little boy's arm, wheel him right around, saying as he pointed out over the innocent lake: Look at all the other ducks, dear, over there on the water!

The drake had reached a goal, and he was quivering in the violent effort to fulfil God's commandment to multiply and replenish the earth [II, p. 91].

It isn't only the fact that the shocked and amused O'Casey is on the positive side of the ducks and drakes here, but that he understands how the destructive and creative impulses exist side by side and reveal the tragi-comic cycle of life. This ironic revelation is strikingly similar to the one presented in Auden's poem, 'Musée de Beaux Arts', where the tragic fall of Icarus in Brueghel's painting takes place while the dedicated ploughman goes about making his fields fertile, and 'a boy falls out of the sky', just as an Irish lad crashes in the Dublin hills. Auden and Brueghel and O'Casey, they knew all about it:

About suffering they were never wrong,
The Old Masters: how well they understood
Its human position; how it takes place
While someone else is eating or opening a window or just
    walking dully along;
How, when the aged are reverently, passionately waiting
For the miraculous birth, there always must be
Children who did not specially want it to happen, skating

On a pond at the edge of the wood:
They never forgot
That even the dreadful martyrdom must run its course
Anyhow in a corner, some untidy spot
Where the dogs go on with their doggy life and the
     torturer's horse
Scratches its innocent behind on a tree.

But how did it come to all this in Ireland, the debauch of
dreadful martyrdom ironically mocked by the innocent ducks
or dogs, going on with their ducky or doggy life in the midst of
suffering, why did it happen? O'Casey is seldom slow to answer
such questions. He not only understands suffering, he can roar
out his wrath about it, he can make gritty observations on it
that are calculated to cut deeply into the conscience of those
who caused the suffering; and when he comes to the causes of
the fate of Ireland the outrageous folly of the Irish is only
superseded by the even more outrageous folly of the British. In
the title-chapter of *Rose and Crown* he happens to meet Stanley
Baldwin in London, and after teasing him with slyly irreverent
comments that bewilder the 'toby-jug mind' of the Prime Minister,
and 'Sean's belly fill[s] out with the ecstasy of secret mis-
chievous laughter', it is the time for an O'Casey drum-roll of
injustices, an historical epiphany for Baldwin and England and
all of us, an ultimate revelation of why the Irish have always
been forced to play slaughter games while the animals play at
ducks and drakes. 'There is in Ireland, sir, a political catechism
as well as the one coined by the Council of Trent,' O'Casey
begins with a rumble; and he goes on, with a devastating wobble
and crunch, to paint an indicting mural that could be an Irish
version of Picasso's 'Guernica':

The ministers of the Rose and Crown have never known, and
know not now, anything about the ways and means that have
made the Ireland of today. Knew nothing, know nothing,
about her folk-art in story, song, music, legend, and dance;
know nothing about her struggles to perpetuate her life with
something else besides a potato; know nothing even about

the later things that tingle the Irish nerves, fire the Irish blood, provoking one section into wearing an orange sash, and another into wearing a green one. . .

Yet the predecessors of these men ramped over the land for hundreds of years; shot, hanged the leaders of the Irish who couldn't agree with them, and jammed the jails with the rest; when every tenant-farmer in the land lost the right to live; when hunger rose up with them in the morning and went to bed with them at night; when, at one go, in one place, seven hundred people were flung from their homes, poor mud-made homes at that, but homes all the same, by an absentee landlord, because the tenants couldn't give him enough for an extra fit of whoring; when the peasants were bound to pay six pounds an acre rent and work for their landlords at fippence a day; when an English earl was forced to explain, *If the military force had killed half as many landlords as it had the revolting Whiteboys, it would have contributed more effectually to restore quiet*; when in eighty-five years eighty-six coercion acts were passed to keep the Irish peasants toeing the landlordian Christian line; when to have a pike, a lance, or a knitting needle constituted an offence worth a term of transportation for seven years; when everyone or anyone found walking the roads, or standing at a corner, an hour after sunset in a proclaimed district was liable to the long holiday of fifteen years' transportation; when every judge to be a judge had to be a landlordian lover, and, finally all were made to act as jurymen as well as judges; when the catholic peasant of the south and the protestant peasant of the north of Ireland spent their lives sowing their own graves that stretched from the river Lee and the river Boyne to the shores of Lakes Ontario and Erie and far beyond them; when every government minister, every privy councillor, every magistrate, was a landlord, or a landlord's brother, or a landlord's friend; so that the threat, as recorded in the holy Bible, made by the King of Assyria to the people of Israel that he would reduce them to eating their own dung and drinking their own piss, fell upon the catholic peasant of the south and the protestant peasant of the north; while the perfumed voice of Lord

Beaconsfield applauded, and Lord Salisbury declared, with a
clapping of cold hands, that very soon the Kelt in Ireland
would be as scarce on the banks of the Shannon as the Red
Indian on the banks of Manhattan [II, pp. 323–4].

Contrary to the common view still prevalent in Ireland and
elsewhere that O'Casey left the source of his genius behind
him when he went into self-exile, the mighty anger etched in
this pictorial scroll of his nation's anguish indicated that he could
never forget his Celtic roots. On every page of the autobiography
there is evidence that although all six volumes were written in
England, he never really left Ireland. In so many special and
symbolic ways the autobiography is an epiphany of Ireland itself,
and particularly working-class Dublin. His Dublin memories
always come back no matter where he is. When he and his wife
try to enroll their son in a convent school in England and are
turned away because they haven't enough money, he invokes
the spirit of Fluther Good with a touch of comic grit:

> Imagine Fluther Good, if he happened to be a father, going
> up this drive, his heavy hand holding the light one of his son;
> Fluther's shoulders squared, his walk a swagger, his lips for-
> ming the words of *The Wedding o' Glencree*; on his way to
> interview the reverend mother. – How much, ma'am for this
> little fella? How much? Jasus, ma'am, that's a lot to charge a
> chiselur for his first few lessons, an' makin' him into an
> ordinary, orderly Christian man [II, p. 369].

When he is in Devon brooding about original sin – 'Original sin
has got us all by the short hairs' – he looks at the red earth of
Devon and remembers something from his childhood in Dublin
and invents a wobbly and crunchy scene that only a lively little
Dublin 'chiselur' could have fancied on the fall of man:

> Here, in Devon, they were anchored on the real red earth,
> rich earth, and very fruitful. Here, maybe, Adam was made,
> for in a bible Sean had had when a kid, he remembered a
> marginal note telling the world that Adam meant red earth;

so here, maybe, Adam was needed into life. Adam filled a vacuum. All he had to do was keep his feet, and all would have been well, and all would have gone on living. God, what a grand world it would have been! The brontosaurus would have been a pet, and pterodactyls would have been flying in and out of our windows, chirruping just like robins! But the man had to fall down. The woman done it, sir – pushed me down; caught me off me guard. Couldn't keep his feet for all our sakes; fell, and ruined the whole caboosh [II, p. 514].

All the passages I have chosen are seldom mentioned or recognised for their special qualities, and they are only a fragmentary illustration of O'Casey's unique ability to fabricate extravagant pictures with words. It should also be evident that I have purposely avoided mentioning what might be called the big bow-wow revelation scenes, like the surrealistic creation of his own birth as the third and last Johnny to survive at the beginning of the first volume; the spectacular transformation scene when dirty Dublin is temporarily resurrected and redeemed on the banks of the Liffey in the second volume; the tragi-comic and gritty portrait of Mild Millie as his Cathleen Ni Houlihan of the Dublin slums in the third volume; the ultimate epiphanisation of Lady Gregory in half-stained and half-wobbly glass in the fourth volume; the crunchy epiphanisation of New York as the sacramental city of Whitman's glorious masses in the fifth volume; the Blakean epiphany for all suffering children, that they might escape 'the mind forg'd manacles' and be free, in the 'Childermess' chapter of the sixth volume.

At one point in the last volume as he thinks about the story of his life and how he first began to write it, O'Casey dreams his way back to his beginning and wonders how he was able to recapture it: 'His own beginning would be the first word, the little logos born into the world to speak, sigh, laugh, dance, work, and sing his way about a day, for tomorrow he would die . . . Only in sleep might he dream it back; never again, except in sleep' (II, p. 515). Thus, the story of his life, as if seen through the magic of a Wildean veil or a Yeatsian mask, unfolds with the freedom of a dream, a series of dream pictures for those two spiritual senses, the eye and the ear, a vision that moves beyond death in eternity. He dreams his way back through half a million visual words and he is instinctively following in the Celtic tradition of the *aisling*, the genre of the dream-vision or poem of revelations; the intricately fabriated *aisling* which can only be perceived through a druidic or metaphoric image of wobbly glass, as in the *aisling* of MacConglinne, the *aisling* of Earwicker, the *aisling* of Casside.

Yeats was always a writer of revelations, visions, *aislings*, and sometimes the early Yeats dreamed his way back to the daimonic power of art more feelingly than the later Yeats. It was the later Yeats who urged O'Casey to create art in which 'the whole history of the world must be reduced to wallpaper',[11] which fortunately O'Casey refused to do. It was the early Yeats of 1905 in a moment of supreme insight who must have had a perfect vision of the kind of art O'Casey would go on to create in his autobiography when he wrote: 'All good art is extravagant vehement, impetuous, shaking the dust of time from its feet, as it were, and beating against the walls of the world.'[12] This is precisely what O'Casey does in the story of his life and why it is good art: he is extravagant, vehement, impetuous; he shakes the dust of time from his feet; he beats against the walls of the world; and as a result he fabricates his synesthetic book of revelations with a mighty wobble and crunch.

NOTES

1. R. D. Laing, *The Politics of Experience* (New York: Ballantine, 1968) p. 115.
2. William Blake, 'Jerusalem', in *Poems and Prophecies* (New York: Dutton, 1954) p. 255.
3. Oscar Wilde, 'The Decay of Lying', in Richard Ellmann (ed.), *The Artist as Critic,* Critical Writings of Oscar Wilde (New York: Vintage, 1968), p. 315.
4. Ibid., p. 306.
5. Idem.
6. Blake, 'The Marriage of Heaven and Hell', op. cit., p. 43.
7. James Joyce, *Stephen Hero*, edited with an Introduction by Theodore Spencer (London: Cape, 1956) pp. 216–217.
8. Spencer, Introduction to *Stephen Hero*, p. 23.

9. E. H. Gombrich, 'Psycho-Analysis and the History of Art', in *Meditations on a Hobby Horse* (London: Phaidon, 1963) p. 41.
10. Sean O'Casey, *Autobiographies I, II* (London: Macmillan, 1963). All quotations are from this edition and page references are indicated in parentheses.
11. Allan Wade (ed.), *The Letters of W. B. Yeats* (London: Hart-Davis, 1954) p. 741.
12. W. B. Yeats, *Samhain: 1905*, in *Explorations* (London: Macmillan, 1962) p. 193.

9 The Autobiographies as Epic

CARMELA MOYA

Sean O'Casey's *Autobiographies,* whatever their unevenness and occasional blatant defects, are obviously far more than what is generally understood by the term, both in form, with the third-person novelist approach, and in the multiplicity of levels. Moreover in the first four volumes we find not only a national as well as a psychological evolution conveyed with artistic restraint and yet with a sense of personal involvment, but also a historical sweep which gives breadth to the narrative with all its shifting perspectives and structural tensions. This epic quality is further enhanced by the panoramic effect, innumerable characters and the intensity of vision: as O'Casey relives the Troubled Years, he gives form to 'the darkest depths of slumland and the agony of the unsuspected years of turmoil and terror',[1] dealing more in fictionalised truth than in the narration of bald facts.

From the outset individual events take on a universal significance, for in the opening lines of *I Knock at the Door,* the dramatist's birth is seen not as that of John Casside, but as that of one of the anonymous children of the innumerable poor flung into a world of flagrant contradictions:

In Dublin, some time in the early 'eighties, on the last day of the month of March, a mother in child-pain clenched her teeth, dug her knees home into the bed, sweated and panted and grunted, became a tense living mass of agony and effort . . . and pressed a little boy out of her womb into a world where white horses and black horses trotted tap-tap-tap-tap-tap-tappety-tap over cobble stones.

The date of birth is imprecise; the nameless woman in child-pain becomes The Mother, and in the first sentence the reader is led from the bed of confinement into the bustling streets of the world with all their colour, movement, and sounds. O'Casey then goes on to paint a fresco of the 1880s with all their brio, illusions, religious hypocrisy and social inequalities. A world of parades and battles; cardboard kings and uncompromising virgins; bibles and tracts; 'fashions, fenians and fancy fairs; musk, money and monarchy . . . where it was believed that when children died of the croup or consumption and fever, they were simply not, for God took them'. Then, with the second sentence of the book we are jerked back to the confinement:

> And the woman in child-pain clenched her teeth, dug her knees home into the bed . . . and pressed and pressed till a man-child dropped from her womb down into the world . . . and gathered to itself the power, the ignorance, the desire, and the ambition of man.

Here, in spite of (or perhaps because of) his aggressive individualism, his irony, anger and compassion which already burn through these introductory pages, O'Casey asserts his sense of oneness with humanity, though in true Blakean fashion he could damn and bless in the same breath.

Many excellent studies have already been written on the social and political upheavals of the Troubled Years,[2] therefore suffice it to say that in the Dublin of O'Casey's youth, infant mortality was the highest in Europe, higher even than in Egypt and India, due to infectious diseases, malnutrition and foul housing conditions which the dramatist denounces all through the *Autobiographies* and notably in 'The Hawthorn Tree', (*Pictures in the Hallway*) and in 'First the Green Blade', (*I Knock at the Door*). Working conditions were just as bad: it was a common enough phenomenon for men to earn 14s. for a seventy-hour week, and women 5s. for a ninety-hour one. As David Krause observes: 'The lower class Dubliners had little to look forward to beyond disease, drunkenness and death';[3] worst of all, perhaps, to the incessant humiliations to which the poor were subjected and which O'Casey subtly communicates in 'The Hill of Healing', 'A Child of God' (*I Knock at the Door*) and 'Behold, My Family is Poor' (*Drums under the Windows*), to quote only a few instances. Politically speaking, after centuries of British rule and mismanagement, it was also a time of great unrest: Home Rule seemed a far-off dream, and dissension, even among the Irish themselves, was the order of the day. It is not surprising, therefore, that the social conscience of O'Casey, born rebel of exacerbated sensitivity, should have been awakened at an early stage. As he himself remarked, commenting on the Dublin slums:

> Frequently he wandered, hurt with anger, through these cancerous streets that were incensed into resigned woe by the rotting houses, a desperate and dying humanity, garbage and shit in the roadway . . . where the ruddy pictures of the Sacred Heart faded into a dead dullness by the slimy damp of the walls oozing through them . . . Many times, as he wandered there, the tears of rage would flow into his eyes, and thoughts of bitter astonishment made him wonder why the poor worm-eaten souls there couldn't rise in furious activity and tear the guts out of those who kept them as they were.[4]

And rise against all forms of injustice he did, both in word and deed. As the initial pages lead the reader to expect, the revolt against social inequality constitutes as much the woof and the warp of the epic as the fight for national independence, the anonymous heroes being the slum dwellers and the Knights of the Pick and Shovel, while James Larkin, their leader, is given the stature of a demi-god of mythology. Another hero (and the heroes of the six books are few) is Charles Stewart Parnell, the champion of Home Rule, who makes an appearance in the opening chapter (before O'Casey's own birth). The potential explosiveness of the political scene is suggestively evoked by the cab driver who remarks to Mrs Casside contemplating her stiffened child, her second Johnny to have died of the croup: 'I'd sell me hat, I'd sell me horse an' cab, I'd sell meself for [Parnell], be Jasus . . . if he beckoned me to do it. He's the boyo'll make her ladyship, Victoria, sit up on her bloody throne, an' look round a little, an' wondher what's happenin'.' O'Casey, therefore, censuring oppression in all its aspects, shuttles back and forth: backwards to the death of his brother in an imagined and dramatised sequence which implies some degree of continuity in life, as he himself, the third Johnny of the name, was destined to survive; forwards, by implication, to the impending tragedy of Parnell in a compendious vision of space and time, which is characteristic of the *Autobiographies* as a whole.

Another way in which the dramatist attempts to recreate his early childhood in the Dublin of 1880–91 is by using a series of microcosms where his 'vision of innocence', couched in terms of devastating child logic and insouciance, again denounces social and religious injustice, national inconsistencies, and colours major political events. A good example of this procedure is to be found in the chapter entitled 'The Red Above the Green', (*I Knock at the Door*). Mrs Casside takes Johnny on a grand tour of Dublin to admire the city lights, the festivities 'in honour of something to do with the Majesty of Victoria', for all 'respectable' people should show their love and manifest their loyalty to her. The tram conductor sings, half to himself and half to those in the tram:

> Once I lay in the sod that lies over Wolfe Tone,
> And thought how he perished in prison alone
> His friends unavenged, and his country unfreed –
> Oh, bitter, I said, is the pathriot's meed.

Johnny, moved to see the tears trickling down the cheeks of the conductor whispers: 'Who was Wolfe Tone, ma?' The mother explains that he was a Protestant rebel who had gone over to France nearly 100 years before and had brought back a great fleet to help to drive the English out of the country, but a mighty storm had scattered the ships from Bantry Bay. Johnny wants to know what happened to the rebel and is told that he fought on a French warship till it was captured, then was put into prison and executed by the English. The boy expresses surprise that the Irish didn't save him, but Mrs Casside finds no explanation. All that happened so long ago, so what is the point in bothering their heads about things that don't matter any more? Johnny, however, convinced that such things *do* matter, will, perversely, go on bothering his head about them all through his long, turbulent life.

In this chapter, the tram is a microcosm of Ireland with all her complexities, the passengers representative of different political and religious tendencies. The vehicle is full to overflowing, and the conductor, exasperated by the obstreperous spectators come to admire the festivities and trying to 'turn the pushing into an orderly parade', snaps viciously:

> A man'ud want St. Pathrick's crozier to knock a little decency into yous . . . I don't know why th' hell Parnell's wastin' his time thryin' to shape yous into something recognisable as men an' women. . Honest to Jasus, I'm gettin' ashamed of me life to mention I'm Irish . . . And all of yous riskin' the breakage of your bodies to do honour to a famine queeen rollin' about in a vis-à-vis at a time the Irish were gettin' shovelled, ten at a time, into deep an' desperate graves.

At this, one of O'Casey's expressionistic characters, 'the man with a wide watery mouth with a moustache hanging over it like a weeping willow' retorts, incensed, that neither he nor the other 'personalities' on the tram are out to give a show of loyalty to anyone who would go against the Irish Party fighting for them 'on the floor of the House of Commons'. He himself has urgent business to deal with in the centre of the town and even 'if the illuminations were brighter than even all the comets terrifyin' the sky [he'd] sit with [his] face fast in front of him, seein' only the need for Home Rule'. But the tram conductor, O'Casey's *porte-parole*, who periodically puts in an appearance throughout the first four books, is no dupe. 'A prime lot of pathriots yous all are', he observes sarcastically, for all of them delight in the revelry in the streets 'alive with the flags of all nations, save Ireland's own'.

Johnny, of course, is no exception: dazzled by the lights and the banners, he feels a glow of pride at being an integral part of these festivities. He and Mrs Casside are barely troubled by the sight of a 'rowdy' shaking his fist at a window of the Orange Lodge, for it only needs the sight of Dublin turned into 'a glitterin' an' a shinin' show' to bring the people, who are 'frantic for quietness' to their senses. Suddenly, however, the chorus figure of the man with the weeping willow moustache, who up to now has acted as echo to Mrs Casside's dithyrambs, creates another dissident note. Law and order, with the crown at the head of all the people would have been established long ago had it not been for that 'ruffian' Parnell whose aim was to become the uncrowned king of Ireland. Johnny's mother, momentarily leaving aside her enthusiasm for the Queen, replies that the country couldn't have a better one, and murmurs of approbation are heard in different parts of the tram. The man with the wide, watery mouth, forgetting his former pleas for moderation screams that 'An unbelievin' Protestant's no kind of man to be the leadher of the Irish race', to which the conductor, the symbol of sanity and common sense, retorts that if his passenger is as loyal as he is anxious to show himself, he ought to be able to keep the Queen's peace! O'Casey, the mature man looking back in this double-level narrative smiles sardonically, but Johnny, his former insouciant self is more preoccupied with the rippling lights making a 'laughing day' of the night. The silver glitter of the helmets of the police in the streets below, the College boys intoning 'God Save the Queen' with vigour and fervour seem reassuring until a low booing from the crowd becomes a threatening roar of anger, a swelling river in full spate as the nationalists chant

> The jealous English tyrant, now, has banned our Irish green,
> And forced us to conceal it, like something foul and mean;
> But yet, by heavens! he'll sooner raise his victims from the
> dead,
> Than force our hearts to leave the green and cotton to the
> red!

A great green flag is raised, the crowds surge forward and attack the college boys, the Royal Standard is yanked down from a big bank building (yet another ironical symbol) and is torn to pieces, while the tram stands 'like a motionless ship in a raging sea'. The man with the wide, watery mouth stutters, slavering with rage: 'Why don't the polish [sic] do somethin'?', and as though in answer to his prayer the mounted police charge the stone-and-bottle-throwing crowd, where screaming mothers are separated from their children, and bring their batons down on the head of the man carrying the green flag. The last image Johnny will see as the tram crawls away is that of a huddled figure in the street half-way between the bank and the college, 'almost hidden in the folds of a gay green banner'.

It is, of course, this incident which inspired the chapter heading: the red of England above the green of Ireland; the blood of the demonstrators spattering the national flag, thus inverting the words of the patriot song: 'The Green Above the Red'. The tone, ostensibly, is that suited to the 'vision of innocence'. The day is relived with a sense of dream-hazy excitement, colours are heightened, bewilderment and insouciance follow each other with disarming rapidity. It is only at the end of the chapter, where fear is the predominant emotion, and the lone, maculated standard-bearer lies still in the street, that all the hidden implications become clear. Here O'Casey refrains from preaching (which, unfortunately is not always the case) and consequently is all the more telling. He appeals more to the reader's instinct than to his reason, the analysis of the ambivalence and contradictions of the Troubled Years being more implicit than explicit, an integral part of the narrative.

The characters represent a cross-section of a supposedly politically conscious society: some, admittedly, are caricatures, such as the fat woman 'with a big bustle on her big behind', so, in a way, is the man with the wide, watery mouth (who might have stepped straight out of *Within the Gates*). He is, nevertheless, given a specific identity, being referred to – not without malice – as 'Georgie Middleton's da; as it is 'Georgie Middleton's ma who wears the pants of Georgie Middleton's da', his patriotism and his enthusiasm for Home Rule are written off in a single phrase. Then there is the conductor, who will make a second appearance in 'The Sword of Light', a Catholic Fenian who has the courage of his convictions and who acts as the voice of national conscience, as the upholder of a heroic past which he evokes in his lament for Wolfe Tone. Moreover, this eighteenth-century rebel, along with Parnell, is felt as an actual presence through the greater part of this chapter, which not only throws the petty egoisms of the passenger into relief, but also establishes a kinship with the bearer of the green banner, seeming to hold out – at this stage of the *Autobiographies* at least – some tenuous hope for Ireland's future.

But naturally enough, the truly three-dimensional figure in this passage is Mrs Casside, a sincere loyalist of crystalline transparency, who finds herself at a loss to answer her son's guileless yet pertinent questions. Johnny, who on account of the red, white and blue rosette he has been 'flauntin' ' has known nothing but war between him and his Catholic comrades for the past few days, has been booed, stoned and called a 'swadler', is surprised by the kindness of the conductor, who manifestly disapproves of the festivities. Mrs Casside explains that although people can think wrong things, that does not stop them doing good ones. 'Kind people are to be met everywhere,' she declares with conviction:

> 'Even among the Catholic Fenians, Ma?'
> 'Specially among the Fenians. Your poor father often said that [they] were all honest, outspoken men. . Besides, some of [them] were Protestants, too.'

Johnny, however, has another burning question on the tip of his tongue:

> 'But we're not really Irish, Ma: not really, you know, are we?'
> 'Not Irish . . . Of course we're Irish. What on earth put it into your head that we weren't Irish?'
> 'One day, an' us playin', Kelly told me that only Catholics were really Irish; an' as we were Protestants, we couldn't be anyway near to the Irish.'

His mother's face reddens and she retorts venomously:

'Th' ignorant cheeky little Roman Catholic scut! . . . I could
tell the whole seed, breed and generation of the Kellys that
the O'Casside clan couldn't be more Irish than they are . . .
And Protestants are Catholics, too; not Roman Catholics, but
Catholics pure and simple; real Irish, without a foreign title
like Roman stuck on to it.'

These comments, despite a certain deliberate illogicalness, are
obviously of more than purely personal significance, for they
lay bare not only the susceptibilities of a minority, but also the
religious and national conflicts of Ireland.

Johnny, conscious now that 'The Cassides stretched back
farther than the year of one', will, moreover, never cease trying
to reconcile the irreconcilable. This is particularly apparent in
the chapter entitled 'Royal Risidence' (*Pictures in the Hallway*)
where on their way to visit Kilmainham jail, Johnny's Uncle
Tom, a tender-hearted colossus, who had so disliked arresting
miscreants that he had been obliged to resign from the police,
becomes the victim of his nephew's curiosity and reasoning.
Here, as in the tram, the dialogue is subtly focused on another
national hero, Robert Emmet. Johnny — the memory of Wolfe
Tone still fresh in his memory — is surprised to learn that Emmet
had been a Protestant, too. He asks why Emmet had also been a
rebel. Because he didn't like to have the English here? What
English? Johnny had never seen any 'knockin about'. Ah! *Soldiers?*
English soldiers like his brothers Tom and Mick? Wrong again?
True, Tom and Mick were *Irish*: Irish soldiers, then, as they
were both Irish *and* soldiers? Uncle Tom didn't agree? *English*
soldiers, did he say? Then Emmet must have wanted to get
them out of the country as well as the others . . . Oh! Mick and
Tom were *Irish* who joined the army to fight for England? What
an odd idea! . . . Why on earth fight for England? Because England
was their country? No, no, Uncle Tom was wrong there. Johnny's
Ma said his Da said *Ireland* was their country. So it was, but
they *had* to fight for England? Who made them? The Bible,
which said: 'Fear God and honour the King'? Then anyone who
didn't was wicked and bound to go to Hell, wasn't he? But Parnell

was anything but wicked and *he* refused to fight for England. He'd even said he'd rather rot in jail than obey any law made by the Queen, for English law was robbery. And Georgie Middleton had had a terrible row with his father because Georgie stood up for Parnell . . . He shouldn't have? Why not, if Parnell wasn't a wicked man and Georgie Middleton was a Protestant, too? Why *shouldn't* one Protestant defend another? Johnny would understand everything when he was older, when he was grown up like Uncle Tom? He'd know what was right and what was wrong, and these things wouldn't bother him any more? But Parnell, the Queen and their partisans were all grown-up and they never agreed about anything . . .

It is hardly surprising that under the cross-fire of his nephew's questions Uncle Tom should have been puzzled, and a little cross because he was puzzled, and that he should suddenly have seen fit to change the conversation. In spite of the comic aspect of this dialogue and its apparent naivety, it is obvious that O'Casey, by making use of a quasi-Socratic manner of questioning, raises a host of problems regarding the ambiguous identity of Ireland and reveals as much of the complexities and contradictions of her history as any scholarly analysis could have done. But then this is an integral part of his method: re-creating (or re-inventing) by a process of selection and elimination — with a mixture of instinct and experience — some incident in his past, which in itself could be quite banal, and making it either of national consequence or of universal appeal. This does not mean to say that he did not delight in story-telling or in the quirkiness, the raciness of dialogue for its own sake; it does imply, however, that O'Casey's mirror was not primarily that of a naturalist, nor of a narcissist, as certain critics, George Orwell foremost among them, would have us believe.

'Ireland', as O'Casey remarked, 'was rather more of a kaleidoscope than a shadow-show: always reshaping itself into a different pattern.'[5] Now, obviously, in order to render all the complexity of the socio-political panorama of an epoch, he painted vast frescoes with the fury of a Goya, where movement and colour gave vigour to his *tableaux vivants*, which he peopled with innumerable characters. It is with broad sweeps of his brush that he depicts major national events such as the Easter Rising, which I have analysed in detail elsewhere.[6] He also communicates the climate of his politically torn country through his own mercurial soul-states, as in the chapter dealing with the death of Parnell.[7] But there is another (though by no means separate) method which the dramatist uses to convey the changing colours and forms of the kaleidoscopic aspect of Ireland and which is closely allied to his conception of art:

> It is more than a mirror, for if what be conceived there be conceived with fierceness, joy, grace and exultation it will split the mirror from top to bottom as reality cracked the glass and scattered the threads by which the Lady of Shallot wove her pretty patterns from the coloured shadows that passed her window by. It is a big, wide, wonderful world of treasures . . . from which to pull beads of glittering glass or gems of the first water from its drab or colourful and intense tapestry of life.[8]

And it is by this juxtaposition of violence, joy and exultation that the countless pieces of this split mirror, shaken and ordered by the artist's imagination, assume coherent and swiftly changing patterns. Lyric and burlesque, the heroic and the anti-heroic, reality and myth jostle one another incessantly and are not always clearly distinguishable one from the other.

Myths, in the widest sense of the term, preponderate in the *Autobiographies*: popular beliefs, folklore, legends, the history of the gods and demi-gods of Ireland. As Eleanor Knott has pointed out in *Early Irish Literature*,[9] there existed in pre-Christian Ireland (as in all primitive societies) religious myths woven around gods who sanctioned the customs of the community and who later, with many modifications, were presented as legendary or historical figures. O'Casey, like many of his compatriots, dug deep into his national patrimony. Yeats, haunted by the esoteric and the supernatural (which Sean was not) had done so before him; so had Synge in *Deidre of the Sorrows* and in *The Well of Saints*, and it is plausible enough that

Swift modelled his Lilliputians on ancient Celtic beliefs. O'Casey's attitude is ambiguous. As he makes De Valera observe to Lloyd George in the satirical chapter entitled 'Pax' (*Inishfallen, Fare Thee Well*), 'A myth, sir, remember, is a thing that may, or may not, be true'. In the sections dealing with his childhood and adolescence, where there is still place for dream and illusion, myths interwoven with snatches of history are used with semi-seriousness, and heighten the epic quality of the *Autobiographies* as Celtic gods and demi-gods stride jauntily through the panoramic field alongside national heroes. The dramatist, admittedly, often uses the myth to point a moral, to evoke the past, to throw a searching light on the present or (as in 'The Hawthorn Tree' in *Pictures in the Hallway*), to contrast the glamour of legend – or superstitious belief – with the sordidness of the tenements. In that particular chapter, moreover, the hawthorn, 'the spice of Ireland . . . sacred to the good people' is the symbol of a better life. This 'grand tree' belonged to the slum dwellers, 'it was theirs and the first flowers would send them into the centre of a new hope'. But there were other smells, too: those emanating from another 'Big Tree' at the corner of the North Circular Road that had 'a scent of whiskey an' beer flowin' out of it'; the stench left by the dirt-hawks who came to empty out the petties and ashpits in the back yards, leaving such a trail of muck and mire in the houses that the women were forced to spend the whole day on their hands and knees, scrubbing and scouring after them, washing away the venom, 'persuaded that this was all in the day's work'.

In the 'Sword of Light' (*Pictures in the Hallway*) O'Casey again juxtaposes myth with the hard realities of poverty. In that chapter, however, which could almost be termed a symphony in black and white, the myth of the Sword, forged out of lightning and wielded by Celtic heroes (the symbol of the Gaelic Movement) is taken seriously in the sense that it represents the adolescent's quest for knowledge and his awakening national consciousness. As his friend Ayamonn – the tram conductor of 'The Red Above the Green' – hurries out of the house, leaving him the symbolic shilling which plays such an important part in *Red Roses for Me*, Sean thinks:

The Sword of Light! An Claidheamh Solis: the Christian Faith; the sword of the spirit; the freedom of Ireland; the good of the common people; the flaming sword which turned every way, to keep the way of the tree of life — which was it? where would he find it?

Looking at the smoky little lamp in the darkened room, he fancies that it has changed into a candle, 'its flame taking the shape of a sword; and in its flaming point, the lovely face of Cathleen, the daughter of Houlihan'.

Cathleen ni Houlihan is yet another aspect of the O'Caseyan myth and constitutes a transition between the myth taken seriously and that used to satirical ends in a mock-heroic manner. One of the outstanding figures to have immortalised this legendary 'heroine' had been Yeats. Although he disapproved of 'The Davisisation of poetry'[10] and literature of a purely political nature, his play *Cathleen ni Houlihan* had become a trumpet call to the Irish Republicans in the struggle for National Independence. Since the Tudor invasions and the subsequent persecutions, Irish patriots had, it is true, personified their country as a woman who was to a certain extent 'the wish-fulfilment form of the overthrow of Ireland's foes, and her own rise to wealth, comfort, security and jubilation',[11] and whether she went by the name of Cathleen, Dark Rosaleen or The Woman in the Shawl, she had become, under English rule, the symbol of the resistance movement, which could be referred to in veiled terms. (For example, in 'I Strike a Blow for You Dear Land' (*Pictures in the Hallway*), when Sean and Ayamonn dive into a pub after having got caught up in a tussle with the police, the barman whispers in their ear: 'Th' dhrinks are on me, see? I guess what you've been doin' — standin' be the' Poor Oul Woman, wha'?').

O'Casey, like many of his compatriots, fell under the spell of Cathleen at an early age, but though as the embodiment of Ireland she is undoubtedly the major feminine 'figure' of the epic, she is as much the anti-heroine as the heroine of the *Autobiographies*, for the dramatist's relationship with her was not devoid of bitterness and mockery. She began by being 'a tall white

candle before the Holy Rood',[12] the inspirer of the new songs
of Ireland 'forging fresh thought out of bygone history',[13] but
little by little, Sean was to find her somewhat pathetic, though
heroic still: 'busy in the woods . . . searching for leaves to weave
a garland, but finding naught but bramble . . . thistledown and
thorns, jagging her bare feet, but searching still'.[14] Perhaps he
already foresaw the day when the Gaelic League (of which he
was at one time a keen member) would care more for the 'fight
for collars and ties'[15] than for the well-being of Ireland. Moreover, O'Casey soon became wary of what he considered to be
the dangerously romantic attitude of certain of his compatriots
towards his 'heroine': that of Griffith, for example, in spite of
his undeniable patriotism; that of Connolly, who during the
Easter Rising would try to storm Dublin Castle as though he
saw 'the beautiful Cathleen ni Houlihan immured within, pining
away, chained hand and foot with ring-papers'.[16] O'Casey even
found Yeat's attitude equivocal: Cathleen was no queen of
an ivory tower, not just the symbol of a privileged woman intelligentsia, but that of the whole of Ireland and of the Irish working woman in particular. He even compares her to Mild Millie,
a Juno of the tenements, who in order to bear up against mis-
fortune 'goes wild with red biddy' (methylated spirits) but who
is full of fire, courage and quirky patriotism. As he contemplates
her dead drunk on the pavement after her mad dance — always
a manifestation of the Life Force for the dramatist — he observes
with bitterness and rage:

> She loves Cathleen ni Houlihan, in her own reckless way. In
> a way she is Cathleen ni Houlihan — a Cathleen with the flame
> out of her eyes turned downwards . . . [but] the pure tall
> candle that may have stood before the Holy Rood was sadly
> huddled now, and melting down in the mire of the street be-
> neath the British lion and unicorn.[17]

For O'Casey there were now two ni Houlihans running round
Dublin: the one coarsely dressed, brave and brawny 'at ease in
the smell of sweat . . vital, and asurge with immortality'[18] like
Millie herself; the other, traditional, 'respectable', the darling of

the employers, chanting: 'They who fight for me shall be settled for ever in good jobs . . . shall be rulers in the land'.[19]

The dramatist was to remain loyal to the first Cathleen his whole life, but he found the Cathleen of the Insurrection disquieting not to say alarming. Although she was busy shaking the ashes from her hair, she seemed to take delight in the fact that this was 'a rare time for death in Ireland',[20] to be prouder of her rich and powerful lovers than of those of the common run, walking firmly, 'a flush on her haughty cheek'.[21] She was, nevertheless, heroic if ferocious during Easter week (much in the manner of a goddess of antiquity), he admits, but at the outbreak of Civil War 'her chaplet of crêpe, worn for the dead . . . was going askew',[22] and though she ran distracted from Jack to Billy or from Billy to Jack, stamping her little foot on the floor for silence, unity, order, discipline, her voice went unheeded, till 'she sank, tired and wordless, on to the floor, anointed with the spits dribbling from the angry, twisted mouths of her own devoted children'.[23] It is not surprising, therefore that the Terrible Beauty was beginning to lose her good looks. Yet here we still find a note of compassion creeping in. Later, with the birth of the Irish Free State, there would be nothing but the scorn of lost faith: 'Turn your back on the old hag that once had the walk of a queen! What's ni Houlihan to you, or you to ni Houlihan? Nothing now . . . the weeds, the weeds, for her for ever!'[24] Then again, the riots sparked off by *The Plough and the Stars* did nothing to arrange matters. As the dramatist tells us in violent terms:

> For the first time in his life, [he] felt a surge of hatred for Cathleen ni Houlihan sweeping over him . . . She galled the heart of her children who dared to be above the ordinary, and she often slew her best ones. She had hounded Parnell to death, she had yelled and torn at Yeats, at Synge, and now she was doing the same to him. What an old snarly gob she could be at times; an ignorant one too.[25]

O'Casey had found a change for the worse in his 'heroine' during the Insurrection, but after the Civil War he was to find her hypocrisy, her pettiness, lamentable. It was she who was the mouthpiece of Irish womanhood, outraged to find a prostitute mixing with the heroes of Easter Week in his play, she who egged them on to scream that there wasn't a single 'pavement princess' from north to south, or east to west in the country. Cathleen, flouncing in her patched skirts, 'was talking big'.[26] The dramatist, exacerbated by the critics, disappointed by the politicians, indignant at the treatment meted out to such men as Dr Walter McDonald, professor of theology at Maynooth University and 'martyred' by the prelates, came to the conclusion that 'There was no making love to Cathleen, daughter of Houlihan, now untidy termagent brawling our her prayers'.[27]

The 'heroine' of the epic, just before and after the dramatist's self-imposed exile, had become an anti-heroine with a vengeance, but one must not forget that his love-hate relationship with her was a way of resolving inner conflict — that of the alienated Irishman — and that this mockery of the incarnation of Ireland was O'Casey's way of chastising (hence, in his eyes, of reforming) his country both socially and politically. During the English years of the *Autobiographies* he barely refers to her. It is only in the last volume, *Sunset and Evening Star*, that she makes a dramatic and unexpected entrance, somewhat in the guise of a sophisticated Mild Millie. A semi-comic complicity sets in between them in the pub called, significantly enough, the 'Rose and Crown'[28] in order to get the better of George Orwell, who declared that 'England was the object of O'Casey's hatred' and who saw fit to make some scathing comments about Cathleen.

Donal, at times Sean's mouthpiece, at times mocked as 'a zealous Irish Irelander', also puts in an appearance in this same passage after a long absence, his presence, as always, adding to the kaleidoscopic time-game: a kind of *chassé-croisé* between the past and the present, where O'Casey's opinions, acquired subsequently, are juxtaposed to those he held at a given moment. Donal is dazzled by ni Houlihan in her gold-threaded ensemble of steel-blue faille, though he is somewhat shocked by her varnished nails and heavy make-up. For Cathleen has changed: she has become a Modern Miss, has rebelled, tired of the volleys of prayers of her lovers, of the dramatists and storytellers lying 'flat

on their bellies' hoping to be admitted into 'a new dispunsen-
sation' (*sic*) by prostrating themselves before God and admitting
their 'dire disthress'. Cathleen speaks too loudly, her language is
racy; she prefers a stiff gin to the lemonade Donal offers her
and admits she is tired of being a Tall White Candle before the
Holy Rood. O'Casey no longer describes her with hate, adoration
or scorn. It is as though he has just come across a former mis-
tress, who is half prepared to admit, with Joyce, that 'Christ
and Caesar are hand in glove'. He regards her with a clinical eye
(the years have passed and she has become somewhat blowsy),
but for the first time a new sentiment exists: comradeship. It is
obvious that the dramatist savours the comic aspect of the situation, but, momentarily at least, he accepts Cathleen for what
she is: less liberated than she makes herself out to be, less frank
than the Mild Millies in whom O'Casey never ceased to place his
trust, yet, he seems to insinuate, capable of changing, of evol-
ving socially and psychologically. It is as though towards the
end of a long life he has become reconciled to a certain Ireland.

At all events, it is this last apparition of the nefarious, tragic
or burlesque 'heroine' of the O'Caseyan epic which, reminiscent
of the fantasy and humour of the first four books, redeems an
otherwise tasteless and vituperative chapter artistically speaking.
Considering the dramatist's temperament, it would, of course,
have been impossible that this mythical figure should have remained sacrosanct. On the one hand, she embodied a country
which in O'Casey's opinion could only come to terms with itself
thanks to incessant self-criticism; on the other, anti-heroics were
an integral part of Sean's psychological make-up (he himself is
as much the anti-hero as the hero of his own saga). Moreover,
the 'giants' of this epic are few and far between: apart from Jim
Larkin, Parnell, Bernard Shaw, Dr Walter McDonald, the Reverend
E. M. Griffith, Paudrig Pearse, Lady Gregory and Susan Casside
(the Mother Courage of the tenements), there are few others.
And even Pearse, 'while filled with a vision of a romantic Ireland,
a doer of things noble and a 'lover of things beautiful',[29] though
not held up to ridicule, is at least plunged into burlesque, not to
say grotesque, situations. Jim Larkin (and for O'Casey, Larkin
was, indeed, the Fire-Giver) appears in wild scenes of fantasy

and farce, whereas Shaw stalks sardonically in and out of 'Green Fire on the Hearth' (*Drums under the Windows*) in a chapter which denounces the 'mistory' of the garden of Eden and where a journalist describes the 'romance' of Adam and Eve in terms of the yellow press: 'Innocent boy meets innocent girl . . . Glamour! oh boys, glamour!' Where Jeecaysee (Gilbert Keith Chesterton) and Daabruin ("G.K.C.'s" detective Father Brown) are flung in for good measure as a foil to Shaw's rebellious and affirmative personality. (It is here, incidentally that O'Casey, a feminist in the true Shavian tradition, makes Eve overtly state the fundamental conviction underlying all his work: 'On we go, too human to be unafraid, but too human to let fear put an end to us.')

O'Casey, in point of fact, uses the myth in burlesque (or in serious) strain to several ends: as a kind of backcloth to enhance the stature of his heroes, to underline his own humanistic philosophy and to evoke the past grandeur of his country. For, however mocking his approach, he desired to see a new Ireland living her own life not through the distorting mirrors of Westminster, but with determination and realism, respecting as he did 'the life, the soul, the dream; the unending change, the temerity, the eternal jubilate . . . three in one and one in three, that are known as Ireland',[30] and which Shaw, great-grandson of an Orangeman, nephew of a hanged rebel and brother of an abbess, also embodied in his eyes. Therefore, in spite of what O'Casey considered to be the exaggeratedly romantic attitude of the Gaelic League, he paid homage to its efforts to encourage a national consciousness based on concrete and ancient values. What he fought mercilessly, however, was the neo-Celtic movement, or that of the Celtic Twilight championed by A.E. (George Russell), whom he nicknamed 'Dublin's Glittering Guy' and held up to ridicule along with Griffith, in 'House of the Dead' (*Drums under the Windows*), a ferocious, burlesque and macabre chapter where Portrane madhouse is synonymous with the 'Purple Land full of Druid moons' — that of the Celtic Twilight — and where the myth is used to mock the myth itself.

O'Casey used this incessant juxtaposition of reality and irreality in the above-mentioned passages (and elsewhere) much as he did in his expressionistic plays. Moreover — and not surprisingly — he intermingled narrative and dramatic methods all through the six volumes. Certain chapters (notably 'The Raid' and 'Comrades', in *Inishfallen, Fare Thee Well*) even constitute one-act or 'aborted' plays in order to stress the national significance of an isolated event and thus heighten the epic quality of the *Autobiographies*. As in *The Plough and the Stars* and in *Juno and the Paycock*, he uses inner and outer action in true Chekhovian manner. The outer action of the first four books is, of course, that of the English occupation, the Easter Rising, guerrilla warfare between the Irish Republican army and the British forces (with subsequent counter terrorism by the Black and Tans), the struggle for social rights, and the Civil War over the Peace Treaty. The inner action is that of Johnny, child and adolescent, awakening to life; the way in which the man, Sean, and the other characters in his saga face up to reality. (In the last two volumes, however, this double action is less evident, in spite of the Second World War, and consequently they lose in dramatic impact.)

'The Raid' powerfully evokes the unequalness of the fight between the 'ragged tits' of the tenements and a strong, organised army backed by 'mighty-moneyed banks', the outer action being that of 'The Dublin slums at war with the British Empire'. The introductory passage, though narrative in form, is reminiscent of the detailed stage directions in O'Casey's plays. It consists, moreover, of two distinct parts: the first dealing with the sordidness and poverty of the tenements, the second with the 'war' raging between the occupying forces and the guerrillas. The initial sentence is purposefully neutral in tone: 'The cold beauty of the frost glittered everywhere outside, unseen, unfelt, for the slum was asleep'. At the end of the chapter, however, the frost will be symbolically smirched with blood, that of the rebel 'dripping on to the white frost on the path, leaving little spots behind like crimson berries that had fallen on to the snow', contrasting with 'the dirty yellow-clad figures moving into the whiteness from one dark doorway, to move out of it again into another blacker still', with the brown slug-like tank creeping up and down the road, charring the dainty rime with its grinding treads'.

In the second sentence, we read of the uneasy silence echoing over the house, where everyone, sleeping or waking, knew that death lurked in the dark streets where filth and illness were 'sacraments', exterior signs of spiritual degradation, where 'this riddled horridness had given root to the passion flower'. Little by little, O'Casey builds up an atmosphere of uneasiness and tenseness: 'Lazy sleep had crawled in the dark hallway . . . a lousy sleep, dreary-eyed . . . All the cheap crockery stood quiet on the shelves'. Sean's eyes started to close, then, insidiously,

> Dimming thoughts swooned faintly from his mind into the humming whine of motor-engines coming quick along the road outside. Up on his elbow he shot as he heard the sound of braking, telling him that the lorries were outside of his house, or of those on either side. Then he shot down again to hide as a blinding beam from a searchlight poured through the window, skimming the cream of darkness in the room. There was a volley of battering blows on the obstinate wooden door, mingled with the crash of falling glass . . . A raid! All the winsome dreams of the house had vanished; sleep had gone; and the children dug arms and legs into the tensing bodies of their mothers.

The contrast between *swooned* and *shot, blinding beam* and *darkness* translate psychological shock; *dug* and *tensing* underline the intensity of fear; 'lorries outside of his house *or of those on either side*' conjure up the image of an ineluctable trap. There is mounting tension. Would it be the Tommies or the Tans? The latter, undoubtedly, for the Tommies would not smash in windows gratuitously. The Tans, though, were not above torturing and at any moment might sneak into his room, their faces blackened, and blind their victim with the flash of a torch, guns at the ready. Sean, who self-avowedly was no hero, wondered what it would feel like to have a bullet burning its way into his guts. He preferred not to think about it, for here, the angel of death was a rabid bitch. Then after the battering on the door, silence: 'The sad silence of a sleeping slum, alive with crawling men'. The dazzle of searchlights and pitch darkness follow one after the other intermittently, then when fear has reached its climax, is at its paroxysm, making him sweat and shiver, Sean hears the handle of the door 'give a faint brassy murmur'. It is not death that is at his door, however, but his voluptuous land-lady, Nellie Ballynoy, who enters and whispers in the darkness: 'Are you there, or did they take you? Are you gone or are you asleep or wha' ?'

The anti-climax is as unexpected as comic, reminiscent of *The Plough and The Stars* and it is here that the 'play proper' begins. This stage entrance, moreover, has been manoevered with careful craftsmanship, for Nellie has been alluded to previously as is generally the case with the principal characters. The same is true of the dramatic entrance of her husband, Charlie, the unlikely hero of this tragi-comedy, for at the same time as Sean, terrified, listens to the hammering on the door he hears 'the quick pit-put, pit-put of stockinged feet . . . hurrying along the hall to the back-yard', and concludes it must be one of the men of the house carrying ammunition to those who take part in ambushes, anyone except thin, delicate Charlie Ballynoy who cares for no manner of politics. Nellie, herself, doggedly trying to seduce Sean, tells him that her husband would be of no good in an emergency, incapable of standing up to the Tans as he was born timid 'with a daisy in his mouth'. Moreover she confides that 'One night when he was – you know – I jerked him clean outa the bed onto th' floor – th' bump shook th' house! . . . Ever after . . . I've had to handle him like a delicate piece of china! No: poor Charlie's style's too shy for me.'

These comments, of course, heighten the dramatic intensity of the dénouement, for the captured prisoner, who hid an arsenal in his shed, is none other than this outwardly pathetic and insignificant figure, the resister Sean heard jumping over the wall, with fear, but without fuss'. He is still a little pitiful, 'a thin, forlorn figure . . . amid a group of soldiers with rifles at the ready', but there is heroism in 'the lips in the pale face . . . tight together . . . and the small head held high' who lifts his iron-locked hands dripping with blood to shout: 'Up th' Republic!', while Nellie herself, a typically ambivalent character, yells: 'That's me husband! . . . a good man an' a brave one. Yous'll never shoot the life outa Ireland, yous gang o' armed ruffians! Here, take me too, if yous aren't afraid'.

This aborted tragi-comedy is typical of O'Casey's epic for more than one reason. The contradictions of the three-dimensional figures reflect the complexities of the Troubled Years and of the country as a whole: Nellie, with her mysticism, guile, courage and cowardice who asks why a land 'overflowin' with prayer and devotion should so often be plunged into dhread in the dead o' night for nothin'?' reflects them. The same is true of Charlie Ballynoy, the slum-dweller, who with all his timidity dares to defy the British Empire, and who does not merely play at heroics as do so many of O'Casey's characters, whom the dramatist mocks mercilessly. Then again, there is the contrast between the two occupying forces: the Tans who tortured, riddled young heads under old buckets and the Tommies, 'warm, always hesitant about knocking a woman's room about . . . encouraging . . . even the children to grumble at being taken away from their proper sleep'. 'The Raid', moreover, translates O'Casey's horror of war which is so apparent in his plays (particularly in the *Trilogy*[31] and in *The Silver Tassie*); that of social degradation, too, made visible in the rottenness and ruin of the tenements. Yet the chapter is not devoid of hope: the fight was unequal, but in the end 'the slums would win'. Most important of all, his faith in the Life Force (which Nellie incarnates) remains unshaken; as he himself puts it: 'In the midst of death we are in life.'

This theme is also to be found in 'Comrades', which, however, is far more virulent and pessimistic in tone, a diatribe against the Civil War O'Casey condemned unconditionally. In the chapter preceding this one, he had already made scathing comments about Griffith followed by the coming middle class; about De Valera and the clergy standing 'quiet on the left', only to come to the conclusion that: 'Not a leader had the power or personality . . . to check the drift to an armed fight for dominance'. Now that the Black and Tans had been withdrawn with the British cavalry, the Irish were out to 'bite' one another: the Free State army on the one hand, the Republicans on the other. Soon 'Kelt was killing Kelt as expertly and as often as he could';

Cathal Brugha and Rory O'Connor, the Republicans, and Michael Collins, the Free Stater, would, along with Griffith, all escape into the grave. No one cared a whit for Document No. 2,[32] nor about abolishing poverty. 'It was all just a spate of words that Alice in Wonderland wouldn't understand'. Yeats was climbing the winding stair of Thoor Ballylee wondering what it all meant, while 'the whole of Ireland was following a hearse and Ireland herself was driving the horses'. Yesterday, Ireland's terrible beauty 'had the green freshness of spring . . . today it was withered and well in the fire'.

'Comrades' is what might be called an artistic crystallisation of the sentiments expressed in the more discursive and polemical chapter which precedes it. The form again is rather like that of a one-act play and is even cinematographic in nature. The plot is relatively simple. Sean meets Mick Clonervy, a farmer's son who has been made a colonel. While they are chatting, a cyclist passes by nonchalently singing 'Home to our Mountains' from *Il Trovatore*, his head moving to the lilt of the tune. Their eyes follow him as he goes along the Green where the Free State troops are quartered and suddenly they see him swing a bomb through a pane of glass. Sean, half-deafened by the explosions and by the screams of the wounded, watches Clonervy snatch a gun from a holster, and two plain-clothes men jump on to their bicycles and tear after the terrorist, while he himself hurries into Stephen's Green among the indifferent ducks and drakes. The bomb-thrower pedals furiously through the Dublin streets; passers-by dive into doorways for shelter. Fast, faster, the pursued Republican, Lanehin, sweat pouring into his eyes, heads for the hills, murmuring 'as life rolled off behind him like thread unwinding from a turning spool: "They'll get me yet"'! As the road grows rougher, uphill all the time, he lets fall his bicycle, dashes through the thorn and gorse which tear his legs, staggers towards an old stone wall, spreads his arms along the top of it and waits, unarmed, for Clonervy, the Free Stater, his former comrade who had served under him when they were both fighting the Tans, to catch up with him. Eventually he turns round to see the three men sitting in a semi-circle thirty feet away, guns cocked in their hands. They eat, drink, smoke. The colonel breaks off a sprig of heather and fixes it in his cap, then he advances towards Lanehin without a word. After a long silence the latter, half dead already, whimpers: 'I surrendher . . . Jesus! Yous wouldn't shoot an old comrade, Mick!' Clonervy's arm whips forward, he crashes the muzzle of his gun through Lanehin's chattering teeth and pulls the trigger.

In this particular, yet typical incident, O'Casey lays bare the atrocities of the Civil War, with all its gratuitousness. The situation itself is full of dramatic irony: two Irishmen, who together, had fought a common enemy for the freedom of their country, are now at each other's throats; Lanehin, the Republican, barely more than a boy, throwing bombs with a song on his lips like a child playing with a toy; Clonervy killing for the pleasure of the thing and asserting his sense of superiority as a newly made colonel who had formerly been a sergeant in the 'crush' where Lanehin had been a captain, his superior.

The psychological analysis of the two men is subtle and reveals the flaws of the situation. Clonervy is a fraud:

> The soft, swelling, childish cheeks . . . the unsteady mouth, circled by thick, leechy lips, told Sean that here was a young man without a chance of ever being other than he had been years ago . . . prodding hundreds of frightened cattle on to the boats for the English market . . . heedless of the sickening steam from their distended nostrils.

There is, in fact, an element of butchery about him and though 'the smart, elegant uniform fitted the body [it] failed to fit the spirit of the man', which made Sean think: 'This new corps of officers will never do. Utterly unaware of the elements of military life, and has no desire to learn them.' Clonervy therefore symbolises not only sadism and social pushing, but inefficiency to boot. Lanehin, on the other hand, is 'lilting', 'graceful', insouciant. His comment on the bomb-throwing is: 'After all . . . there wasn't a lot of damage done'; to which the colonel replies: 'Oh, not a lot . . . only one of us had an eye knocked into a jelly, and another got his chest rieved asundher.' Lanehin, though pathetic, is consequently made to represent the total irresponsibility O'Casey never ceased to criticise in his plays. Moreover, in this chapter the dramatist systematically pulls to pieces what, for him, was the sham romanticism of the Civil War. With typical malice, it is Clonervy who is chosen to tell Sean about Yeats's views concerning the nobility of the cause:

> Yez are heirs to a great thradition; the famous Fenians . . . McCool, Oisin, Oscar; thruth on their lips, sthrength in their arms, an' purity in their hearts, says he. Your're tellin' me! I says to him. Them was th' days, sir. An' listen, Misther Yeats, I says, we have as much today; for we have to demonstrate a good example now to th' whole o' th' livin' world!

The 'example' Clonervy gives, and which for O'Casey was typical of many, speaks for itself in this ironically titled chapter. It is not that the dramatist denied the heroism of certain of the fighters: he paid equal homage to Cathal Brugha, the Republican 'too honest to find comfortable companionship in the lesser men around [him]' and who honoured the Irish tricolour, and to Michael Collins, the Free Stater 'who was the makings of a great man', both of whom paid with their lives for 'the holding high of an abstraction'.[33] What he abominated, however, was this fratricidal waste, which in 'Comrades' he contrasts at the most dramatic and sordid moment with the affirmation of the Life Force: the instant Clonervy shoots his former friend, the duck and the drake in Stephen's Green, he 'brilliant as a courtier in a gay king's garden . . . fulfil God's commandment to multiply and replenish the earth'.

This rage for life also explains why his attitude towards the violence that reigned during the Troubled Years was deliberately anti-heroic whatever his admiration may have been of the revolutionary leaders such as Paudrig Pearse, who, dead, 'still [held] Ireland by her rough and graceful hand'.[34] It explains, too, why he found Christian Protestants and Christian Catholics 'busy bestowing the chrism of death upon each other'[35] particularly aberrant. O'Casey, of course, was too profoundly Irish to have been indifferent to the cause of the nationalists, and though his loyalties belonged first and foremost to the cause of labour, he realised that each group could learn from the other. It is natural enough, therefore, obsessed as he was by his country's welfare, that major political and social events should preponderate in O'Casey's saga, whether they are described with lyricism, or expressed as irony, fantasy or farce; the Great Lockout of 1913 in the chapter entitled 'Prometheus Hibernica' (*Drums under the Windows*) is one example where — and this is often the case in the *Autobiographies* — hard facts are not always easy to disentangle. But this is part of the dramatist's kaleidoscopic method; he did not set out to write a history of Ireland, but, reliving 'the savage and wild joy he would never know again',[36] to reveal 'a deeper life than the life we see and hear with the open ear and the open eye'. This, for him, was 'the life important and the life everlasting [which] . . . can be caught from the group rather than from the individual'.[37] That is why O'Casey does not content himself with the mere telling of his own tale, nor does his mirror reflect exclusively the happenings in his own House, Ireland. It is not surprising, therefore, that the central theme of his epic should be 'The showing forth of man to man'.[38]

NOTES

I Knock at the Door (1939), covers the years 1880–90; *Pictures in the Hallway* (1942), 1891–1904; *Drums under the Windows* (1946), 1905–16; *Inishfallen, Fare Thee Well* (1949), 1916–26; *Rose and Crown* (1952), 1926–34; and *Sunset and Evening Star* (1954), 1934–53. The six books have been collected in a second two-volume edition under the generic title *Autobiographies* (London, Macmillan, 1963), and it is this edition which is quoted in the text.

1. Desmond Ryan, *Remembering Sion* (London: Baker, 1934), quoted by Robert Hogan in *Feathers From the Green Crow* (London: Macmillan, 1963), p. xi
2. Notably by F. S. Lyons, *Ireland Since the Famine* (Glasgow: Fontana, 1973), and by David Krause, *Sean O'Casey: The Man and His Work* (London: Macgibbon & Kee, 1967)
3. Ibid., p. 7.
4. *Autobiographies, II* (London: Macmillan, 1963) p. 137.
5. *Autobiographies, I*, p. 602.
6. Cf. my article in *Sean O'Casey Review,* vol. 2. no. 2. (1976), pp. 141–54.

7. Cf. my article in *Etudes Irlandaises*, no. 4 (Université de Lille, France, 1975) pp. 53–77.
8. Sean O'Casey,*Blasts and Benedictions*(London: Macmillan,1967)p.10 .
9. (London: Routledge & Kegan Paul, 1966) p. 14.
10. O'Casey, *Blasts and Benedictions*, p. 177.
11. Ibid., p. 173.
12. *Autobiographies, II*, p. 549.
13. *Autobiographies, I*, p. 409.
14. Ibid., p. 411.
15. Ibid., p. 460.
16. *Autobiographies, I*, p. 650.
17. Ibid., p. 475.
18. Ibid., p. 609.
19. Idem.
20. Ibid., p. 661.
21. Ibid., pp. 665–6.
22. *Autobiographies, II*, p. 72.
23. Ibid., p. 72.
24. Ibid., p. 125.
25. Ibid., p. 150.
26. Idem.
27. Ibid., p. 245.
28. Ibid., This scene takes place in the chapter entitled 'Rebel Orwell' (*Sunset and Evening Star*).
29. *Autobiographies, I*, p. 617.
30. Ibid., p. 560.
31. I.e. *The Shadow of a Gunman*, (1925), *Juno and the Paycock* (1925) and *The Plough and the Stars* (1926).
32. For a detailed explanation cf. Lyons, op. cit., pp. 442, etc.
33. *Autobiographies, II*, pp. 77 and 79 respectively.
34. *Autobiographies, I*, p. 665.
35. *Autobiographies, II*, p. 34.
36. Robert Hogan quoting Desmond Ryan in *Feathers from the Green Crow*, op. cit., p. xi.
37. O'Casey, *Blasts and Benedictions*, pp. 113 and 114 respectively.
38. *Autobiographies, II*, p. 623.

10 Sean O'Casey as Wordsmith

BERNARD BENSTOCK

In many ways Sean O'Casey's six volumes of autobiography, collected under the cumulative title *Mirror in My House* in America and succinctly as *Autobiographies* in Britain, are far from conventional essays in the memoirs genre. Consistently presented in the third person, with a central figure that modulates from Johnny Casside to Sean Casside (and an occasional O'Casside), they are quasi-narrative in guise for most of the first three or four volumes, but increasingly more expository and discursive thereafter, developing into platforms for literary criticism and general commentary. Since autobiography has historically proven itself to be as varied in style and individual in the handling of language as the novel, it should not be surprising that O'Casey's techniques prove to be somewhat unusual and highly personal, yet they have met with some odd pockets of resistance. Perhaps the tendency toward greater vernacular style and rather direct approach marks the twentieth-century product of personal relevations, and O'Casey's may suggest a previous century to some. Or it may merely have been the shock of hearing a dramatist's personal voice, for although he had published some critical essays prior to the first book of autobiography, O'Casey was best known for the voices of his dramatic personae. That he should have chosen to express himself in tones of self-conscious eloquence may have seemed inappropriate for a playwright of the urban proletariat who admitted to being self-taught.

The six volumes weave their way like a snake through the fifteen years of their writing, through some seventy-odd years of

O'Casey's life, from past into present, shedding its skins as it goes, until it rewinds into itself: the last book, *Sunset and Evening Star,* comments on the reviews written about the preceding five, from Oliver St John Gogarty on *I Knock at the Door* to Louis MacNeice on *Rose and Crown.* Reviewing the reviews gives O'Casey an opportunity to comment in his own voice on what sort of hybrid the accumulated autobiography actually looks like, and to lay the ghost of a major accusation, that its language is dependent upon the experimental sense of word-play fashioned and copyrighted by James Joyce. George Orwell had asserted that *Drums under the Windows* 'is written in a sort of basic Joyce, sometimes effective in a humorous aside, but it is hopeless for narrative purposes', at which O'Casey fumes, 'Basic Joyce! Bad or good; right or wrong, O'Casey's always himself.'[1] His antipathy to the 'low note about cogging from Joyce' is hardly surprising since, like many another writer in Joyce's wake, he had been accused of indebtedness, and his avowed admiration for Joyce's cosmic laughter makes him one of those who has not denied Joyce even once before the cock crowed.

Whereas many a new writer attempting to digest Joyce finds himself like the boa constrictor that swallowed an elephant, O'Casey managed to assimilate the Joycean impact particularly well in the autobiographies, primarily because he recognised a natural affinity for certain Joycean tendencies and because he was sufficiently advanced as a creative writer, with over a dozen plays to his credit. Although *Ulysses* – and later *Finnegans Wake* – contribute various possibilities, it is in *Juno and The Plough,* in *Within the Gates* and *The Star Turns Red,* that the autobiographies have their genesis. The dizzying blends of playfulness and polemic, of caustic commentary and unashamed sentiment, are already established, and the tendencies toward fanciful language, puns and word play, malapropisms and neologisms, are already there. Their deployment in what has usually been considered so prosaic a genre as autobiography contributes to the uniqueness of *Mirror in My House.* The range of prose styles in O'Casey's *Mirror* reflects the variety of subject matters, from the life story that is being told to the events in Ireland and the world that are being chronicled, from the development of a young man to the opinions of a mature artist, and from the 'backward glance at things that made me' to the evening star that outlives O'Casey's own sunset. Despite the necessary modulation from the active life of a young man growing up to the sedate world of an old man thinking his thoughts, the autobiography remains a consistent and coherent whole.

Rarely has anyone attempted autobiography as mock-epic in comic prose, and it is this characteristic generally that allies O'Casey's volumes with Joyce's later work. From the first alliterative catalogue in the opening chapter of *I Knock at the Door* O'Casey establishes a technique that will continue throughout all six books, as he pictures the life of Dublin into which his Johnny Casside is born:

> bustles, Bibles, and bassinets; preaching, prisons, and puseyism; valentines, victoria crosses, and vaccination; tea fights, tennis, and transubstantiation; magic lanterns, minstrel shows, and mioramas; music-halls, melodramas, and melodeons; antimacassars, moon lighting, and midwives; fashions, fenians, and fancy-fairs; musk, money, and monarchy.[2]

The precision of detail, the accuracy of observation, the sustained handling of the syllables and the care with which the items are enumerated and balanced belie the casualness with which they seem to have been tossed together. Later efforts at epic cataloguing may show O'Casey to be wilder and freer with the comic effects, but this initial presentation indicates the skill of a joco-serious master of heightened language. If O'Casey was encouraged in this experiment by the eight British beatitudes in *Ulysses,* he immediately proved himself more than comfortable with the challenge.

Where alliteration was coupled with cataloguing in the first chapter of *I Knock at the Door,* punning provides the second ingredient in the last chapter of *Pictures in the Hallway* for 'The Buttle of the Boyne' ('King Billy, Brandyburgers, French Hueforgetmenots, Swiss Swingillians, Dutch Blue Guards, Scandalnavians, the Dublin Quay Police') and for a battle of the books in *Drums under the Windows* ('Layo-tsetze, Spangler

Sbungler, Confusian, Cant, and Emer's Son, the pure-souled One, Spunooza').[3] There is a greater sense of audacity in the last list, as O'Casey mocks idealist philosophers, and an inspired snipe at the specifically Irish in his version of Emerson. Audacity is the operative factor in many other catalogues, particularly at the end of that volume, in a list of the twelve 'Blessed Saints' of O'Casey's Ireland —

Cing Bully of the Boyne of Contention, Carzen of the Papes, Mishe Lemass More, a Talbot a Talbot, Lily Bullero, Shantee Ohkay, Roody the Shrover with his Pendraggin Piety, the Irish Sweep who Beat Miraculous Melody from a Drum. Elfie Byrne of Ballyblandus, Guffer Gaffney, Prayboy of the Festerin World, Billora et Labora O'Brien, and Gee Kiaora Jesterton the Laughing Diwine[4]

Yet there are few if any 'accidentals' in the puns. North Irish Protestant politicians and pious Roman Catholics give the grouping its common denominator, with each element offering a different pun technique. Dialect transliteration informs 'Cing Bully': the hard C mocks the tension between the Englishman saying Seltic and the Irishmen saying Keltic (spellings used often by O'Casey in the autobiographies to distinguish the nationalities of his speakers), while the ubiquitous 'u' for almost every vowel identifies O'Casey's Ulsterman throughout. That Sir Edward Carson could be mistaken for a papist is as hilarous as his role as Tarzan of the Apes, while Sean T. O'Kelly and G. K. Chesterton suffer by having their initials mishandled. Perhaps the best piece of mockery is towards labour leader William O'Brien, whose name is feminised, Latinised, dualised, and made into a mock motto.

What might on occasion begin as sheer playfulness (punning for its own sake or as a mere *tour de force*) can develop a decided punch in its final factor. An innocuous group of patron saints for Ireland's industries eventually arrives at a religiast who typifies theocratic narrow-mindedness, and the ultimate source of O'Casey's catalogue technique is identified and credited:

Textiles under St. Clotherius, Building under Saints Bricin and Cementino, Brewing and Distilling under St. Scinful, Agriculture under St. Spudadoremus, Metal Work under St. Ironicomus, Pottery under St. Teepotolo, Fishing under St. Codoleus, Book-making under St. Banaway, the whole of them presided over by the Prayerman, St. Preservius, a most holy man of great spiritual prepotensity, who was a young man in the reign of Brian Boru, and who passed to his rest through a purelytic seizure the day he tried to read the first few lines of Joyce's damnable *Ulysses*.[5]

It is primarily in the Cyclops chapter of *Ulysses,* the chapter that is the most Irish and one of the most comic, that such parades of saints pass by, and of the odd score of such punned lists in *Mirror in My House,* almost half of them have important analogues in the Cyclops chapter.

Like Joyce, O'Casey insisted upon variety: no two catalogues are the same in principle, and a wide variation of techniques governs their developments. The closest O'Casey comes to imitation is in the gathering of the clans in *Drums under the Windows* where he parallels Joyce's twelve tribes of Iar almost exactly for ten of the dozen,[6] only to add a string of Irish heroes and martyrs (echoing Joyce's 'heroes and heroines of antiquity), followed by the products of Irish industries, down to Guinness's stout. The shift from ancient to recent (including the Manchester Martyrs) and the modification from men to manufactured goods adopts another Joycean principle, the sudden and often jarring change of pace. Incongruity itself becomes a catalogue device, both in *Ulysses* and in *Drums,* and the listing of strange bedfellows makes for greater hilarity as the Irish pour out of their warrens to protest the slur against the nation in Synge's *Playboy:* for O'Casey the odd amalgam of protestors involves

Shamus O'Brien, Kelly and Burke and Shea, Clare's dragoons, Lesbia with her beaming eye, the Exile of Erin, the Rose of Tralee, the Athlone landlady, Eileen Allanna with Eileen Aroon, the man who struck O'Hara, Nell Flaherty's drake, Daisy Bell arm in arm with Thora, the man who broke the bank at Monte Carlo, Kitty of Coleraine with the two little girls in blue.[7]

Like the 'Irish heroes and heroines of antiquity', many of these aren't Irish at all, and most of them derive from songs (a favourite O'Casey source) and some directly from the *Ulysses* list. Particularly O'Caseyan, however, is the Man Who Struck O'Hara, used at various instances in the autobiographies for comic purposes, and the Kelly-Burke-Shea trio from the Irish song, a trinity that O'Casey employs often as personifications of Irish 'traits'.

Essentially the temptation to reel off a grocer's list of items or names is a comic one, and O'Casey uses any excuse to catalogue, from characters in his own plays to those in Dion Boucicault's, from ridiculous religious orders ('Laurestinians, Holy Hards of Eireann, Vigilantians of the Clean Mind',[8] etc.) to real religiasts of Ireland followed by parodic by-products ('Columbus, Bridget, Kieran of Kilkenny, Finbarr of Cork, Codalot of Queery Isle',[9] etc.), and holy Irish books, not excluding Joyce's ('Book of Kills; the Book of O'Money; the Book of Ripe and Edifying Thoughts in the Head of Kinsale; the Book of the Old Done Cow; the Book of the Curious Chronicles of Finnegan's Wake (That's over his head); or the Book of the Revised Version of Cathleen's Thorny Way?')[10] – all of these from *Drums under the Windows* alone. Even those that begin as a straightforward compilation soon go askew, while others blend from one technique into another: 'bells of St. John Lateran, of St. Jim Clatterin, of St. Simon Slatterin, of St. Finian Flatterin, of St. Nicholas Natterin: bells of St. Mary's, bells of St. Clement's, and bells of Old Bailey; bells of St. Martin's and the big bells of Bow'.[11] Yet even this pre-eminently jocular vein can be worked for serious intent, as O'Casey proves at the end of *Drums,* where the Fenian dream is remembered (like the Citizen in *Ulysses* allowed to voice his legitimate complaint against the destruction of Irish overseas trade):

our potteries and textiles; Huguenot poplins woven since Jacquard de Lion first sang *The Palatine's Daughter*; crowded bales of supreme cloth, red, green, green russet, and yellow to

Cologne, Naples, Catalonia, Ypres, and the Rhine. To send out fine marbles, green, red, jet, and dove grey, fine and smooth, as Spenser vouches for in his *Faerie Queen,* to Bologna, Brabant, making palaces for princes of Lithuania; to give to the civilised world again beef, lard, tallow, bacon, butter, wax, wool, tanned leather, well embroidered; hawks and horses, gold from Wicklow, and silver from Tipperary, coined and uncoined; to send the whitest linen to the Netherlands, Italy, and the city of Chester. To make the land a centre of prime books, well tooled and illuminated, like them of old, the book of Fenagh, of Monasterboice, the psalter of Cashel, and the Red Book of the Earls of Kildare.[12]

The same skills that were so often used for the comic and the absurd, the literary craftsman here employs for poetic effect, a moving crescendo to his view of the Easter Rising aftermath.

Of the various means of expanding language utilised by the epic-chronicler-autobiographer none is more derided than the pun, the commonest and yet most controversial way to derive extended and ambiguous meaning from the single word. At once the simplest form of wit and the most concentrated, its effect varies greatly and its detractors groan in agony. Joyce admitted that some of his puns were trivial, but contended that others were quadrivial, immediately turning the figure of speech to advantage, bifurcating the meaning of a word and improving upon the construction. Even more than Joyce, Sean O'Casey can be accused of savouring many slight and silly wordplays, but it remains a vital aspect of his handling of language. A primary use depends upon dialect, that interplay of the various tongues speaking English in the British Isles, and his dramatist's ear accounts of many of these. Another important consideration was in name-change, as he determined immediately by altering himself into a Casside; changing names to protect the 'innocent' is this fictionalised form of autobiography allowed for many variables. Of the two teacher-tyrants who plagued the young Johnny, one already had a name that couldn't be improved upon, Hunter; the other required only a one-letter extension, from Logan to Slogan to transform him into more than just another

Irishman. Changing the firm name of Eason's into Jason's did little to either disguise the original or to gain much in the translation, but altering the Dublin concern of Leedom, Hampton & Co. into Hymdim & Leadem produces wonderful reverberations on characters O'Casey describes as religious and bigoted. With hundreds of proper names paraded through the six books, there are numerous possibilities (when the temptation proves too great) for such wild violations.

One of the more sedate tricks is merely to *expand* the name, making it sound pompous and pretentious: Arthur Griffith becomes Art Up Griffith; Douglas Hyde becomes Dr Douglas de Hyde (Gaelic version: 'An Hideach abu!'); Thomas Davis becomes Thomas a Davis; Padraig Pearse becomes Padruig Mac Pirais; and Benjamin Guinness becomes Benjamin McGuinness (would he and his brother, Lords Iveagh and Ardilaun, recognise themselves any better as 'Hillolureus and Ardalaunus, brother patrons of free-drinkers'?).[13] Between McGuinness and Ardalaunus the wide range of the name-change game becomes apparent, and most of O'Casey's punned perversions are far more caustic than either. Those he was particularly contemptuous of are transformed unkindly: Cardinal Logue (Log), Eamonn de Valera (De Valuera), Matthew Talbot (Mutt Talbot); somewhat less severe are the designations for the Midland Railway and Adelaide Hospital (Meddleland and Addlelaid), for the churches of St Barnabas and St Damian (Burnupus and Damaman – elsewhere Damnaman). Edward Martyn (Myrrhtyn) is only one member of the Abbey Theatre hierarchy to be toyed with; in a scene of public outrage against Synge's *Playboy,* the misnomers are in the mouths of the protestors: 'Singe or Sinje . . . Yeats or Bates . . . some oul' one or another named Beggory or something.'[14] At times the puns are so obvious as to be commonplace (calling Hitler the Furor), but at others they are internally functional: Jacobs Biscuits as 'Bakecob's' and Graham Lemon's confectionary as 'Lemon's of Suckville Street'. The punning becomes so expected with certain names ('Bishop O'Dawn O'Day') that the reader may come to assume that an unfamiliar name like Father Furniss has already suffered from O'Caseyan distortion (after all, he is credited with having written *The Sight of Hell*) until O'Casey turns around and renames him Father Furnace. It's often touch-and-go in the autobiographies attempting to determine whether a cleric's name is an O'Casey invention or the real M'Coy.

Punning in English alone provides a treasure of small gems through the autobiographic volumes. The naming of a pair of cherubs Asseguy and Bellboomerang has its deadly aspect, as does the Knight of the Burning Apestle. Religion throughout provides a favourite O'Casey hunting ground for pomposity and hypocrisy, but at times it also offers a poignant moment, as when the frightened sick murmur their prayers, 'Holmarmotherogodprayfrusmisrablesinnrs nowana thourofhoudeath'. The portmanteau word collapsing Hallelujah and ballyhoo into 'Ballyhoojah' nicely balances real exultation with meaningless noisemaking. But the Church has no monolopoly on the pompous and the hypocritical, and O'Casey delights in needling these sins wherever he finds them: among the aristocracy ('gay in medievil funcy dross'), among the leadership of the Irish Volunteers ('God's gillie, Eoin Mac Neill, Chief of Stuff, and Bulmer Hobson, God's gillie's gillie, the Volunteer Sacredary'),[15] among the Irish intelligentsia (calling AE 'Da Russell' and 'Mr. Talkinghorn'), in British pomp and circumstance ('Ulster's king of harms'), in bourgeois pretensions ('the business lordeen of the place' — the cunning use of the Gaelic diminutive echoes Joyce's reference to Father Dinneen, compiler of the Gaelic-English dictionary, as a 'priesteen'). Having turned down the offer of participating in an Irish Academy — as did Joyce — O'Casey could well dismiss it as 'the Acodemy of Blethers'. With well-sharpened pin in hand he lets no balloon pass by unmolested; in *Pictures in the Hallway* James II is pictured going into battle with green ribbons labelled 'Erin Go Brag'.

Punning in Gaelic is not greatly prevalent in the autobiographies, although the previously cited *An Hideach abu!* is one of the best bilingual efforts. Latin, however, provides O'Casey with dozens of opportunities, and although he was at best an indifferent scholar of the tongue, he was a storehouse of mottoes and shibboleths and the odd quotation. Again, his favoured technique is the deflation of the self-exalted, and Prime Minister

Ramsay MacDonald is hailed as *Lux Britannica* by waspish O'Casey. Griffith's pamphlet, with the English title of *The Resurrection of Hungary,* is maliciously latinised into *Resurgamise Upsadaiseum Hungarius,* a construction that evolves into a typical O'Casey paragraph of mock-epic cataloguing, odd juxtaposition of characters, and a final song title that deflates the entire overblown occasion down to a simple absurdity:

It was all written in the book of *Resurgamise Upsadaiseum Hungarius,* a huge tome five feet long, three feet wide, and two feet deep, containing in itself all the lore that is or ever was, all laws, licences, customs, pardons, punishments, perquisites, genealogies, constitutions, magna chartas, social contracts, books of rights, das kapitals, origins of species, tallboy talmuds, speeches from the dock, carried about everywhere on the back of Up Griffith Up Davis, as a pedlar carries his pack, compiled from the original sources by the sage himself, deep in a corner under a secret rowan-tree, in the dim cloisters of the old Abbey of St. Fownes, the Soggart Aroon acting as secretary, assisted by Kelly and Burke and Shea all in their jackets green, with the Bard of Armagh stringing the harp to *He's the Man You Don't See Every Day* to give their minds a lift.[16]

The titles of songs in the autobiographies range from this innocuously Irish ditty to the fairly obvious ('the sacred choir of Micuirmick, chanting the palacestraina of *Rome, Sweet Rome*') to the quietly subtle ('the Gulled of Dreamy Jerontius, chanting in slow time, *Oh for the wings of Above*').

The Latin neologisms strung together by Sean O'Casey are usually flagrantly outrageous, although occasionally the reader encounters a wild touch of whimsy, as in the chant *Deo dublin-laddi.* More often an old chestnut takes on a novel ending, *In hoc signum pinchit,* or a novel construction ends with an obvious leg-pull — *Trio Juncta in lacunae, per amica violentio lunee.* In these cases O'Casey saves the punch for the end, but elsewhere (as in the hilarious *Upsadaiseum* version of a resurrection) it is impregnated into the middle: *nullo tremulato antea profundi craniumalis omnibusiboss epsiscopalitis*. In some O'Casey lets himself be carried away unabashedly (*Hibernia salubrio, este pesta quaesta essentia terrfica tornadocum!*), while in others he is merely merry if somewhat ominous (*in signia somnia, dimnia, domnia*). A select target, however, was the papal pronouncement on social conditions, where O'Casey felt that the Church failed to see the real situation but merely winked a blind eye. The *Rerum Novarum* rankles often, in the plays and in the autobiographies: in *Drums under the Windows* it provides a mock-slogan for the working classes, 'Rear Up the Workers' Chiselurs in the Rearum Novarum Way';[17] in *Rose and Crown* O'Casey pits Karl Marx against the Pope, ' — Well, said Sean laughing, the Roman Church builds her social contract on the Rearum Noharmum Harum Scarum Rerum Novarum, but we build ours on the Communist Manifesto';[18] and in *Sunset and Evening Star* it is Shaw, Joyce, and Yeats:

> Stop them! Rerum novarum oram pro noram. Maanooth is in an upsoar. Oh, catholic herald, come blow your horn, before a wild oak comes from the little acorn. St. Patrick's coming down on a winged horse. Was there ever such a one as the Bull from Shaw; was there ever such a one as the pastoral from Yeats; was there ever such another as the encyclical from Joyce![19]

O'Casey pretends to no great reverence for the dead language, as his reply to Louis MacNeice in *Sunset* clearly indicates,[20] but he employs it like the devil quoting scripture, even inventing his own Latin motto: 'Poverty Must Go — *Declenda est pauperium*, or whatever the hell the Latin was'.

His reverence for the English language stopped short of idolatry as well, and although he may not have run it through the ringer as Joyce did in *Finnegans Wake*, he none the less wrinkled it and roughed it up a bit at will. His prime motive was to make it sing and laugh, to express its own melodic and satiric mood, even when he himself was deadly in earnest. Although an indifferent poet O'Casey was still a persistent singer of his own songs, from snatches of verse interwoven into the fabric of his narrative to patches of doggerel broadly sewn into his dialogues and diatribes. The tendency to versify as the whim takes him is prevalent through all the volumes, from the Castle Ball of *I Knock at the Door* to the ode to Walt Whitman towards the end of *Sunset and Evening Star,* but two of the most delightful instances occur in *Rose and Crown,* instigated apparently by a fireside chat with a friar. The blend of bishops-and-business results in a parody of 'Silent Night' ('Holy nickel, sanctified cent,/Bless each proper lady and gent', etc.),[21] while the assumed infallibility of the Catholic Church engenders a threnody in the style of Vachel Lindsay:

> Fat bucks of bishops in a barrel-roofed room,
> Yell'd out, roar'd out threats of doom —
> Bell, book, and candlelight standing on a table —
> Pounded with their croziers in a frenzy of fume,
> Hard as they were able,
> Boom boom boom.
> Excommunicamus, if you dare presume,
> Bell, book, and candlelight will bring you what is due,
> Bring you what is due and hoodoo you,
> If you dare presume,
> Doomday doomday doomday doom![22]

What is most infectious in O'Casey's handling of language is his inability to resist the temptation to lilt. Lilting persists as the O'Caseyan antidote to all that is lugubriously sombre — especially that which is unnecessarily so. He respects the serious and stands in awe of the tragic, but has little patience with gratuitous gloom, either in Graham Greene's novels or in medieval drama. He scoffs at MacNeice's claim that there was gaiety in the Miracle Plays: 'To call such entertainments gay would seem to say that Mr. MacNeice has turned humour all tapsalteerie O.'[23] The culminating phrase itself is a sample of the O'Casey lilt, letting MacNeice know what real gaiety sounds like — all tapsalteerie O! To Yeats' stark versions of Japanese Noh plays O'Casey says a resounding No, and offers his formula for worthwhile drama: 'A play poetical to be worthy of the theatre must be able to withstand the terror of Ta Ra Ra Boom Dee Ay, as a blue sky, or an apple tree in bloom, withstand any ugliness around or beneath them.'[24] What applies to glum drama can hardly be expected to be effective against so potent a force as Fascism, yet O'Casey employs his comic incantations in exorcising even the Black Shirts, scoffing at those Communists who found themselves in a funk when the Mosleyites surfaced in England. Describing a British Union of Fascists meeting in the Albert Hall, O'Casey derides its real power, laughs it into perspective, mockingly compares its furor to the *Playboy* riots, teases his terrified comrades, and wanders off, lilting to himself:

> Bands playing and audience chanting Mosley's the Only Boy in the World, and England's his Only Girl. England's Pick-me-up. The Duce Anglicanem. The living Song of the Shirt. Shirts were in demand everywhere. Men on the make were everywhere seeking fresh gods and pastures new, and the symbol was a shirt. Even Ireland started to wear them; but to give her her due, those who bought them soon sold them to be used as football jerseys. It was a Shift that caused the great commotion in Ireland; a Shirt everywhere else: Song of a Shift in Eirinn, song of a Shirt in Sasana. Mosley led the stuffed shirts in England. He caused quite a sensation of fear among some of our Communists, who didn't know a bumbell from a Jo Anderson, me Jo John. The Black Shirts couldn't get going. They were heard in silence, and, after a meeting, seemed to slink away, rather than to depart; fold their taunts like the Scarabs, and silently steal away.[25]

O'Casey's talent for lyrically reducing the inflated to things of shreds and patches is complemented by his skill is augmenting the blue sky and the apple tree into a jazz number. Listening to a radio sermon in America produces a parody which begins, "By the courtesy of the Louisiana loo loo Motor Corporation, you are about to listen to the Voice of God"; and then some pipsqueak of a cleric would minimise God to his own conceit of himself',[26] and ends with his own locating of the voice of God in the music of Mozart and Beethoven. His parodic sense is often over-exuberant, but at times delicate and subtle, as when he almost imperceptibly takes Eliot's 'Ash Wednesday' apart, an exercise in criticism by parody that might even have delighted Ezra Pound:

> the time T. S. Eliot was passing through his *Ash Wednesday* in prayer and meditation within the desert in the garden and the garden in the desert, in and out between the blue rocks, going in white and blue, colours of Mary's mantle and Mary's frock, hoping to hear and hear not, to care and care not, to be still among a thousand whispers from a yew tree.[27]

The strokes are deft, the touch is light, and the tone is perfect, especially for a caustic satirist who has been accused of using a hammer to kill a flea.

Not that he disdains to take up whatever weapon comes most easily to hand, and language provides him with some powerful hammers as well as sharp scalpels. Easily dismayed at the sight of clay feet, O'Casey at times forgets that they do not always belong to idols. That Lady Gregory should read *Peg O' My Heart,* or that Yeats should read Zane Grey and Dorothy Sayers (not having read the latter, O'Casey must have been unaware that she anticipated the puns he makes on Wimsey's name and had worked it into a coat of arms) proved traumatically disappointing, but it seems hardly commensurate with the 'business lordeen' who talks of Edgar Wallace 'but went silent when the name of Milton smote his ears'.[28] Levelling so Miltonic a word as 'smote' at poor Mr Nash may not be cricket, but what a lordly word it is — and, after all, it is only a single word, but with the potency of the trivial jawbone of an ass. Finding and marshalling that powerful word is often O'Casey's strong point, no matter how disingenuous he may make it sound. The *mot juste* applied with justice and the apt phrase discretely deployed are O'Casey's linguistic weapons, in conjuction with his scoffing laughter and mocking guffaw, as when he brushes off the reviews of *Drums under the Windows* by neatly summarising that 'all the bum critics of Ireland filled the Irish air with hums, hems, and hail Marys. Hugh Walpole once wrote that "O'Casey is an uncomfortable writer", and the Irish critics gave the amen of He is So.[29] With a 'hem' and a 'haw' and an added 'amen', Sean O'Casey plays his diminuendo as a weaver of magical words, ascending often to a crescendo of tapsalteerie O and Ta Ra Ra Boom Dee Ay.

NOTES

1. Sean O'Casey, *Sunset and Evening Star* (New York: Macmillan, 1954) p. 144.
2. Sean O'Casey, *I Knock at the Door* (New York: Macmillan, 1939) p. 3.
3. Sean O'Casey, *Drums under the Windows* (New York: Macmillan, 1946) p. 82.
4. Ibid., pp. 428–9.
5. *Sunset and Evening Star*, pp. 294–5.
6. *Drums under the Windows*, p. 147.
7. Ibid., pp. 172–3.
8. Ibid., p. 224.
9. Ibid., p. 233.
10. Ibid., p. 297.
11. *Sunset and Evening Star*, p. 271.
12. *Drums under the Windows*, p. 427.
13. Ibid., p. 233–4.
14. Ibid., p. 175.
15. Ibid., p. 407.
16. Ibid., p. 14.
17. Ibid., p. 326.
18. Sean O'Casey, *Rose and Crown* (New York: Macmillan, 1952) p. 151.
19. *Sunset and Evening Star*, p. 251.
20. Ibid., pp. 279–80, 290–2.
21. *Rose and Crown*, p. 198.
22. Ibid., pp. 205–6.
23. *Sunset and Evening Star*, p. 279.
24. Sean O'Casey, *Inishfallen, Fare Thee Well* (New York: Macmillan, 1949) p. 374.
25. *Sunset and Evening Star*, p. 159.
26. *Rose and Crown*, p. 253.
27. *Sunset and Evening Star*, p. 50.
28. *Rose and Crown*, p. 182.
29. *Sunset and Evening Star*, p. 135.

Index